FROM
CAIRO
TO
CAIRO

To J.D. and Deanna,

thanks so much for
an amazing weekend in
Calgary. I'll have to try
to visit more often. I hope
you enjoy this read!

— Kieran
April 3, 2011

FROM
CAIRO
TO
CAIRO

Kieran Nelson

BAYEUX

FROM CAIRO TO CAIRO
© Copyright 2010 Bayeux Arts
119 Stratton Crescent SW,
Calgary, Canada T3H 1T7

www.bayeux.com

Cover and Book design: PreMediaGlobal

Library and Archives Canada Cataloguing in Publication

Nelson, Kieran, 1983–
    From Cairo to Cairo / Kieran Nelson.

ISBN 978-1-897411-24-7

    1. Nelson, Kieran, 1983—Travel—Middle East. 2. Middle East—
Description and travel. I. Title.

DS49.7.N45 2010   915.604'54   C2010-907150-6

Printed in Canada

Books published by Bayeux Arts are available at special quantity
discounts to use premiums and sales promotions, or for use in corporate
training programs. For more information, please write to Sperial Sales,
Bayeux Arts, Inc., 119 Stratton Crescent SW, Calgary, Canada T3H 1T7.

The ongoing publishing activities of Bayeux Arts, under its "Bayeus" and
"Gondolier" imprints, are supported by the Canada Council for the Arts,
the Alberta Foundation for the Arts, and the Government of Canada
through the Book Publishing Industry Development Program.

FROM CAIRO TO CAIRO

1

INNOCENTS ABROAD

It looked like nothing more than a misshapen mound of gravel in a cityscape. It rose before us within the archaeological compound, without even a breeze to disturb its dry white dust. The sun above us was an overpowering brilliance in a vacant sky. Atop the mound was a lone Roman triumphal column of red stone. Near it sat a small sphinx which I almost suspected might have been dragged here by the Egyptian government to spice up this tourist attraction. Just a mound of dust, and two unrelated monuments. . .that was all.

It wasn't much to look at. But all the same, I was quivering.

"What's it been Kieran? Seven years?" Sean asked me.

"Seven years."

We kicked about the site a bit and took some photos. I wanted to explore every inch of the place, from the base of the column to the trash-littered corners of the compound. I felt that thrill of the blood unique to moments when, at long last, I finally found myself standing before one of the monuments which in my childhood I had only dreamed about. Here it was. Even though it was nothing but a mound of gravel.

We had made it to the last remaining ruins of the Library of Alexandria. The central Library had long since passed away without a trace; its foundations no doubt lay deep beneath the dozens of concrete high rises the Egyptians had since erected. We were staring instead at the ruins of the second, lesser library, a temple called the Serapeum. This was the Library's embassy to the world—a place where a smaller collection of scrolls was once available to wandering scholars. Yet even a visit to the ruins of the daughter library was enough to pay reverence to its once-glorious Mother.

It was a symbol that had once meant everything to our personal mythology. Seven years had passed; the waves of fortune had washed away the sandcastle ideals of early youth that I was so sure were made of stone. And now, at the end of things, here we stood.

The trip of a lifetime was over. We had set out as children; we returned sober adults. I had not foreseen an ending such as this. The trip had strained our friendship, put our lives at risk as well as our freedom, and had produced a lot less footage that we may have liked. Now, in Alexandria, we were parting ways. For how long, we could not know.

"I think I'll go west, to Siwa" Sean told me. "I really want to see an oasis before I leave."

Five months. It was a long time to spend traveling together. Too long, for us, by about four months. We had parted in Jerusalem—my path led to Egypt, his to the highlands of Israel and the West Bank. Months later, we reunited to climb Mount Sinai with my friend Sarah, and relax to the sound of waves and a beach fire in a hippie resort in Dahab.

Five months. It was enough time to change one's life. It was enough time for dreams to come into focus; for wretched uncertainty to give way to utter clarity. Sean was in that tormented period just out of university, when limitless opportunities make decisive action all but impossible. After five months in the Middle East, he was headed home to work for the man and apply for grad school. I was headed north to Europe, to see a girlfriend I had never met, take the trans-Siberian east, and circle the earth.

The Library was all we had left to see. It was the last salute to the old days. We owed it to ourselves. Now, we were standing there, before its skeleton.

The only thing left of the great temple was a collection of underground tunnels, which we explored avidly. It was a cream-coloured labyrinth, lit by the occasional hole to the surface, which held no evidence that any books had ever existed there. The only notable bits of stonework were square compartments in the walls, at about waist height, which were too small to have held scrolls. And there was no space anywhere in those passages where a scholar might have sat down to work.

Before leaving, we scratched our initials into the wall. Around it, with a knife-sharp piece of sharp stone, I scratched the outline of a serpent biting its tail. This was Ouroboros—a symbol we had chosen for its inexplicable appearance in dozens of unconnected human cultures. Inside of it, we scratched two more sets of initials. Sean's friend Nick. And my cousin Ryan.

I cannot say what fatal principle animated our hands to scratch this symbol on the walls of the ancient library. Honour, perhaps. Or reverence. But whatever it was, my usual squeamishness about graffiti on the world's heritage sites went to the wind. At that moment, I didn't care how many thousands of years old these walls were. I was here, with breath in my lungs and blood in my veins, standing upon ground that I once considered holy. That I still considered holy.

We finished our carving, looked at it, and departed.

"Kuuntu fayn? Kuuntu fayn?"

An Egyptian guard waved his arms about, haranguing us for being late. It was past closing time. We wandered toward the exit, looking around for a cabbie to cheat.

"Well, I'll be here for at least ten days more," I said. "I want to spend some more time with Nermine. You know, she invited us out with her friends again."

Sean said nothing. He hadn't really done a lot of talking when we met the four young Egyptians in that cafe that looked like a rainforest. I think he kind of resented being there.

I left him at an internet cafe. There was no particular fondness in the way we said goodbye. It was a parting of ways—an acknowledgment that a friendship's energy had been naturally exhausted, and that both parties had to go off to seek their fortunes.

Bye, we said. Keep in touch.

Traveling is distinct from every other activity in that it can make or break friendships or relationships. I could already recall a list of people with whom I was either best friends or barely on speaking terms as a result of a journey. Fortunately, the second list was rather small.

I began to travel before I even really grew up. My first trip out of North America was to

Scandinavia at age ten. My next was to Australia at age fifteen. In my parents' care, I had seen enough of the world to spur my hunger for more. Canada bored me; it was far too normal. At age eighteen, I made a personal vow to learn to speak six languages before I died. Already I had added Spanish and French to my native English. Arabic was next.

Travel. It was a brilliant way to postpone university, or to remove myself from the physical vicinity of parents pestering me to make something of my life. My mother had always doubted I would ever find the money to visit the places I claimed I would. But a windfall came my way: a job digging trenches and setting up tents in the Yukon wilderness. Year after year I had worked there during the summer months, built up a bankroll, and traveled like a destitute student for the time the Yukon was covered with snow.

But this summer was different. It was 2007, and an economic boom was raging. Last year I had asked for a raise and gotten it. And they paid me too much. Too much because, by my calculations, I could make this money last twelve whole months, from Egypt to Siberia. I wouldn't have to dig ditches next season.

Sean followed me to the Yukon that year, and got landed in one of the company's 'hero projects,' which tested the endurance of his wiry Chinese frame. He tramped through kilometres of swamp and muskeg, and breathed in hundreds of mosquitoes, while I spent most of the summer being bored to death in a hotel room.

By late September, we were almost ready.

The Middle East. For students of politics and history such as we, it was a mighty destination. It was a world we had too long seen misrepresented on television screens and preached about in academic texts. We had to investigate it for ourselves. We were in for the full experience; a bona fide adventure.

And that adventure may never have come about without a formidable, platinum-blonde friend of mine named Nickie. It was Nickie who taught us the words 'citizen journalism.'

Nickie had a giant camera, whom she had named 'Zelika' on a trip to Thailand. She had traveled there numerous times to film a documentary about an insurgency in the Muslim south. She had eaten dinner with the prince, met generals and military officials, interviewed masked insurgents deep in the jungle, and woken up to the sound of exploding bombs.

The tales she told made my hair stand on end. And I think I wanted some of my own.

Nickie had contacts with Current TV in America, the Real News in Canada, and a few other stations which indicated their interest in short films of personal stories we found along the way. It was citizen journalism: technology had developed to the point where four young people and a handheld camera could make the news, and we were out to try our hand at it. We were seeking the Middle East that we didn't always see on TV.

"No matter what comes of this film project," Nickie told us back in Vancouver, "at the very least, you will get to see what it is like to travel with a camera. It is a totally unique experience. You go places you would never normally go, and see things you would never, ever, normally get to see."

The fourth member of the journey was Kristen, my younger sister. She was halfway through a history degree, and like us, was fascinated by the Middle East. She hungered for her first true foray outside the West, and bristled violently at any suggestion that she was 'tagging along.'

Sean and I would go early and rent a flat in Cairo. Nickie and Kristen would come in late November; we would fly to Lebanon and travel overland through Syria, Jordan, Israel, and Palestine, before returning to Egypt. Though I planned to spend five whole months in Egypt and the Middle East, the centerpiece would be this five-week whirlwind, from Cairo to Cairo.

But during those first days in Egypt, all the tension, all the danger, all the wonder was in front of us. Sean and I busied ourselves by enrolling in

Arabic lessons, smoking sheesha until our eyes rolled back in our heads, and strolling the streets of Cairo until the wee hours of the morning.

On one such a night, we stumbled back from a local cafe, my head swimming from the unforgiving buzz of apple-flavoured tobacco. The sidewalks overflowed with people: slick-haired young men in Euro-style sweaters and faux designer jeans; rotund, middle-aged businessmen in pant suits gabbing into cell phones; gorgeous young women in veils of every colour, wearing clothing that covered all but showed their every curve. We passed sweet shops laden with mountains of pistachio candy, restaurants with friendly, pestering hosts, and clothing stores displaying negligees that would make Western women blush. The road twittered incessantly with car horns, and we occasionally dived off the crowded sidewalk to pick our way through the bumpers of the permanent traffic jam that was every Cairene street. That night, I collapsed exhausted into bed, listening to the unrelenting din of the cars in the road below.

One hundred and fifty years before me, another young traveler had attempted a similar journey. Mark Twain, in his early thirties, took a steamship from America to Europe and the Middle East with a group of tourists, a journey he described in his book, *The Innocents Abroad*. He visited a very different Middle East from the one we visited today:

a Middle East united under the Ottoman Empire; a Middle East without Israel, terrorism, or guerrilla war; a Middle East relaxing in the peace and traditional lifestyle it had known for centuries.

It was a world unknown to the average Westerner such as Twain. In the preface of his travelogue, he washed his hands of any attempt to make his journey seem like a momentous voyage of discovery, or indeed, anything more than a pleasure trip. The purpose, he wrote, was simply "to suggest to the reader how *he* would be likely to see Europe and the East if he looked at them with his own eyes instead of the eyes of those who traveled in those countries before him."[1]

As I counted the cracks in the uneven ceiling of that seedy Egyptian hotel, I reflected on just how much the viewpoints of those that go before you can obscure the true nature of a place. Despite, or perhaps because of the myriad media of the information age, to me, the Middle East was still a mystery—a nebula shrouded in prejudice. Little did I know at the time that I was one of hundreds of young travelers streaming in from the West, lured by a profound fascination with the Middle East: with the depth of its conflict, with the antiquity of its civilization, with the power and allure of its faith.

[1] Mark Twain, *The Innocents Abroad*, preface.

We had finally arrived. Finally, we could discover this unknown world for ourselves: meet its people, walk through its streets, gaze upon its monuments. Finally we, like Twain, could see the Middle East with our own eyes.

2

EGYPTIAN REAL ESTATE

Mustafa was half an hour late. Hassan and I sat bored on the couch of the spacious Egyptian apartment, barely communicating due to the language barrier. I pulled out my Arabic homework and Hassan looked over it, correcting every mistake of my shaky pencil as it made its attempted to write from right to left. Finally, a man appeared at the door, wearing khakis, a casual shirt, and a skullcap.

"*Salaam alaykum,*" said Mustafa, offering me his hand.

"*Wa alaykum as-salaam*" I replied.

Mustafa sat on the sofa across from us, peering at us through bifocals, looking distant and business-like. He opened a leather briefcase and pulled out some papers, and shuffled them intently, shaking the gold watch which was slightly too large for his wrist. His beard was flecked with grey.

"So you like the flat?" he asked me. His English was superb.

"Absolutely" I said.

It was a three bedroom flat with a clean kitchen, a large living room, and tacky, overstuffed furniture. The windows opened onto the back streets of Dokki, a quiet suburb neatly tucked away from Cairo's downtown madness. The bathroom was a cold, tiled affair with a pink bathtub; the shower was a long curled pipe which may have been tall enough for some Egyptians but wasn't tall enough for me.

The flat was. . .barely satisfactory. I wanted it right away.

"There is only one problem," I told Mustafa. "The hot water tap in the bathroom does not turn on. Do you think we could get that fixed?"

"Yes, that is no problem," he replied, looking mirthless and dignified through thick glasses. "The repairman to come tomorrow at two."

The Hotel Flypaper was getting old. Sean and I would return to our room each night with our eyes stinging from the emissions that haunted Cairo's streets, only to lie awake listening to car horns and growling motors until the wee hours of the morning. When the sun came up we would rise to greet a fresh crop of swollen insect bites, and then wander groggily down the hallway to the shower in nothing but a towel, scandalizing the Muslim maid on the way.

It was time to get a proper apartment.

"We have an agent who can help you find one," said Ahmed, the director of our Arabic school. "He will be in to meet you tomorrow after class. At one-thirty."

Sean and I sat waited restlessly, checking our emails for two full hours after the anointed time, checking our watches every ten minutes. We thought of the homework we had to get done, of the film plans we had to lay. . .of everything we could be doing with the time we were spending waiting for our lackadaisical agent. Eventually, too demoralized to be angry, we took to staring blankly at the wall.

Here, things ran on Egyptian time.

Eventually, a tall, dark-skinned Egyptian entered the room, grinning from ear to ear. He extended a long, skinny arm and clasped my hand with a traditionally limp Arab handshake. He introduced himself as Hassan.

"*Yallah?*" I said to him.

"*Yallah!*" he replied. Let's go.

Sean and I watched as this lanky Egyptian outpace us at barely a stroll. It was impossible to keep up with his towering, spider-like legs. We walked down the bustling market streets of Dokki, under the heavy October sun, periodically running to catch up with our guide. Hassan showed us apartment after apartment, and after hours of trying, we still couldn't find one we liked. Some had beaten-up mattresses or shoebox kitchens; others had black outlines of absent pieces of furniture etched into the carpet. Each time, Hassan would pull out his cell phone, and with an *'as-salaamu alaykum'* and a few words, we would set out towards the next place; him walking casually, us following at a jog. Eventually, we came to Mustafa's flat.

"Three bedrooms—you think Salman would like to stay with us?" Sean asked me.

"It's worth a shot," I replied. "Let's ask him tomorrow."

Salman was one of the two other students in our beginners' Arabic class. He was an Iranian who had spent half his life growing up in Holland. Like us, he was twenty-four. He could carve Arabic letters on the board from right to left with flowing ease. Farsi, his native tongue, was written in the same characters. He was spending at least a month in Egypt, and then going to Morocco.

Salman liked the idea of staying a bit closer to the school. We decided to get the place. Sean handed me a stack of Egyptian hundred-pound notes, and I went back that evening to close the deal.

"How long would you like to rent the flat?" Mustafa asked.

"Until April. We need it for six months."

Mustafa presented me with a contract, written entirely in Arabic. I could have been signing myself into chattel slavery and I never would have known it. My lawyer father would have cringed. But since this piece of paper was my only deliverance from nights of silverfish and car-horn lullabies, I scratched my signature at the bottom without thinking twice. I handed him the damage deposit, and there was much smiling and limp handshakes.

On his way out the door, Mustafa turned.

"Oh, I almost forgot. This is a Muslim neighbourhood. You cannot bring girls here."

I froze.

"What?"

"You can have male friends over, but no girls. It's very important. No girls allowed here."

"But—" I stammered, "after Salman leaves we will need another roommate. What if we have a girl roommate?"

"You can have male roommates, but no girl roommates. There are no girls allowed here at all. Ok?"

No girls??

I collapsed in a chair at a nearby sheesha shop, my limbs aching, my shirt rough and sticky from wearing it for two days without washing. It was a hot Egyptian night, and I was too exhausted to be angry. I sucked on a water pipe, and sipped a powerful Arabic coffee. The sheesha filled my lungs, and I waited for its stupefying buzz to waft upwards and paralyze my brain.

No girls??

A Muslim neighbourhood, he said.

Though I had barely been here a week, I had already noticed a great difference in the way that women and men interacted here. There were separate train cars on the metro for women. There was a separation in the mosque; women invariably occupied the smaller side. The myriad coffee shops I saw along Cairo's streets were filled exclusively with men—sitting, smoking, playing dominoes. Women didn't seem to have a place to publicly congregate. And there was no institution at all, it seemed, where women and men mingled together casually.

I sat heavily in my plastic chair as the coals on the top of the sheesha pipe slowly burnt themselves to ash. My head was singing and my mouth was dry. I ordered a lemon juice, and the happy waiter reappeared with a glass of it absolutely saturated with sugar.

No girls. So now Nickie and Kristen would not have a place to stay when they arrived, or we would have to creep into the place like thieves. Half a week spent searching for houses and neglecting our Arabic homework, and we were right back where we started.

"No girls?? Why did you accept?"

Sean was annoyed. So was Salman.

"I don't know why I accepted! I thought I'd tell you about it, and then we'd decide what to do. We can talk to Ahmed from the school tomorrow, and see if he thinks it's ridiculous or not. I mean, what if everyone in the neighbourhood tells us this? We've just spent four whole days looking for a house, and I'm exhausted. I just want to unpack my bags and start feeling like a person again."

Ahmed scowled when we told him the news.

"That's none of his business!" he snapped. "We'll call him and go over there tonight to get your money back. We'll get you a different flat." He called Hassan and told us that we would meet at Mustafa's flat at seven to get our money back.

Seven o'clock came. Seven-thirty came. My stomach was an empty cave; it threatened to fold in on itself. Eight o'clock came. I called Hassan. He said he'd be there at nine o'clock sharp. Now it was too late to get food—we had to be back in an hour. Nine o'clock came. I called him; he said he'd be there for sure at nine thirty. I swore in four languages and soccer-kicked a pair of sandals against the opposing wall. Salman stared at me from the couch; Sean chuckled from the next room. Welcome to real estate in Egypt.

At nine forty-five, the two men arrived, along with the plumber who was supposed to come at two.

"My friend, this is unfair!" Mustafa protested. "Why do you tell me 'yes' one day, and 'no' the next day?"

He demanded almost a hundred dollars for the day and a half we had spent there. I flatly refused. Calmly and patiently, Salman told him it was unreasonable that he sign the deal and only afterwards tell us about the 'no girls' provision.

"My friend, I am a Muslim, like you. It is insulting that you think I would bring women into the flat for sex."

We eventually agreed on forty dollars. Salman decided he would remain in the hotel he was living in for another month; Sean and I shuttled back to our central Cairo hotel. We arranged with Hassan to search for a different flat the next day—one with fewer cultural restrictions.

As I stood on the balcony of our hotel and watched the traffic swirl below me, I reflected on the whole experience. It was Salman's presence that had really saved the day, and made Mustafa relent. Certainly, he acted as a good mediator between two stubborn and angry people. But what was more, there was a dynamic that developed when the he and Mustafa were speaking that wasn't there when Mustafa and I were alone.

The landlord was more sympathetic towards him because he was a believer.

For this was Egypt—a deeply Islamic society—and I was an infidel. People would welcome me, drink tea with me, and be absolutely delighted to spend time with me. But at the end of the day, I was not a Muslim, and that really meant something here.

On a previous trip to Africa, I learned the true meaning of 'culture shock.' It was the uncomfortable feeling of not fitting in—that the people in society around you acted in ways that you just didn't understand. In Canada, we were taught political correctness: if we saw someone in exotic dress, praying in public, or eating strange food, we would simply say "that's their culture," and think nothing of it. Political correctness was a placeholder for genuine comprehension; a willful, blissful ignorance; an accepted alternative to thinking something racist.

But, faced with culture shock, political correctness collapses within days. It is one thing to live in a 'multicultural' society of mostly Westernized people; it is quite another to live in a place where another culture swallowed you whole. When you are surrounded, day and night, by people who think and act in a completely different way than you, blissful ignorance is no longer possible. You are forced, with all the discomfort that results, to question why.

And only one week into my sojourn in Egypt, I was already encountering on a daily basis a cultural trait that I could not wrap my head around. It was the sheer omnipresence of Islam.

What was it that was so incredible about Islam, that the Egyptians had to bathe in it? I went to the grocery store, and eight hours a day they played Qu'ranic chanting at ear-splitting volume. As I passed the local laundromat, the family elder was always seated with a scratchy radio on the table in front of him, blasting prayers. I heard it in the taxis. I heard it in the streets. I heard it booming in the metro stations. I heard it galloping out of the tinny loudspeakers of the mosques, five times a day.

"Are you a Muslim?"

I heard the question everywhere I went. I heard it at the barbers, at the coffee shop, at the corner store. I heard it from taxi drivers, from temple townies, from elderly ladies. When I told them no, I was a Christian, there was nervous laughter and an uncomfortable shifting of feet.

"It doesn't matter!" they would say. "There is only one God, one God!"

Well, it clearly does matter, I thought, or you wouldn't have asked.

I saw prayer mats in every taxi and in every shop. I saw people stopping their daily work and spreading out their mat on the side of the street to pray. I saw old crones with crooked backs bending over desks, since they could not perform the full body prayer. I saw prayer beads swinging from rear-view mirrors; I saw pocket copies of the Qu'ran whipped out in the metro and read aloud. I saw old men, waiting for the train doors to open, methodically whispering prayers to themselves. Everywhere I went, I saw skullcaps, beards, and prayer scars.

Egyptians, or at least the men, seemed to highly value the little blotch of black that formed over the years as they touched their foreheads to the prayer mat, five times a day. Some of them were as small as a fingerprint, others were the size of silver dollars. Some of them spidered across a man's face and down the top of his nose. I even heard that at beauty shops, there was a cosmetic powder men could buy to create a prayer scar for themselves, if they wanted to appear more fervent than they actually were.

And why, I wondered, was everybody called 'Mohammed?' People in the West didn't name their kids 'Jesus,' not even during the more religious ages of centuries past. I thought this was a good thing: it kept the name rare and sacred. But here, it was omnipresent. Two teachers at our Arabic school were named 'Mohammed.' They guy at the pizza shop was named 'Mohammed.' The man who worked the desk at the hotel was named 'Mohammed.' And if your average guy wasn't Mohammed, he was Ahmed, or Mahmoud, or Mehmet, or some other incarnation of the Prophet's name.

I rubbed my forehead. I had a headache, and it wasn't just the exhaustion or the fumes in the air. I could understand that my society was not religious, and that Egypt was a very different place. But I could not understand why the Egyptians filled their minds with Islam in every spare minute of their time; why they shaved their beards like the Prophet and always had his prayers on their tongues.

I lay awake in my bed and studied the ceiling cracks. One of the reasons I had come here was to understand Islam; to live in an Islamic culture for a while. I realized with chagrin that I was being prejudiced and Western, but I also realized that no amount of political correctness could wash those thoughts away. Where I was from, religion was a personal matter; here it was inescapable. In the West, religion was kept in the home; in Egypt, it ruled almost every aspect of public life.

And no matter how I tried, I could not for the life of me comprehend why.

"Hello, my name is Mohammed."

A chubby young man met us at the door with a wide smile, and led us inside to look around. He was a Palestinian living in Egypt, he explained, studying dentistry. We tiptoed around his father who was praying towards Mecca with his long robe tucked into his underwear, and went in to examine the place.

The kitchen had oil splatters all over the stove, and a dusty layer of grease that covered every surface. Rotting food inhabited the fridge. The living room was done up with brown furniture and curry drapes, looking like some botched upholstery experiment from the sixties. The bathroom had a shower hose but no shower head, but the water was wonderfully hot, and the cracked toilet seat worked just fine. The bed mattresses all had divots in the center, and the air conditioning would not turn off.

"We'll take it!" we said immediately. Mohammed brought out the contract out for us to sign.

"Now, my sister and my friend Nicole are coming in November. Is there any problem if we have women sleep here?"

"No problem at all. This is your place, you may do as you like."

We signed the contract, and shook Mohammed's hand. He grasped it in a strong, American grip. The next day, we moved in. And at long last I went into my room, unpacked my bags, and began to feel like a person again.

3

GARDENS AND FOUNTAINS

Friday is the day of prayer for Muslims, just as Saturday for Jews or Sunday for Christians. In Arabic, the word for Friday was *'yom al-joummah.'*

"The word *'joummah'* means 'gathering,'" said Somaia, our slender, black-veiled Arabic teacher. "'Friday' means 'day-of-gathering.'"

We sat in the white-walled classroom, graced with florescent lights and an air conditioner that alternated between too warm and too cold. When the class began to drag, I would wait patiently for the explosive holler of the orange vendor in the street, which marked half an hour before the class was over.

"It is also the root word for 'mosque,' and for 'university.' These things are very much connected in our culture."

Friday was not only a special day for Muslims; it was a special day for me. It was the day we got a break from Arabic class: the day we were released from the strict tutelage our humourless instructor who forbade us to transliterate pronunciation and who assigned vast tracts of homework that we didn't do.

And on this particular Friday, one of my first in Egypt, I decided to walk around and observe the day of prayer in the streets of Cairo.

Yesterday, on the same walk to the metro, the market street of Soliman Gohar was bustling with commerce. Pyramids of fruits and vegetables were piled on tables beside the road, while Egyptians in flowing dress inspected them critically before stuffing them into plastic bags. Women sat by baskets packed with ice and Nile-caught fish, while ocean sponges were stacked in coloured bins at their feet. Falafel balls sizzled in metal bowls of oil, waiting for corpulent chefs to serve them in flatbread with scoopfuls of multicoloured Egyptian pickles. Cars picked their way clumsily through crowds of pedestrians; cyclists passed with racks of flatbread the size of a door balanced on their heads.

But today, Friday, was completely different. Metal curtains were pulled down in front of the shops; doors were locked and windows were barred. Grey water pooled in the potholes of the half-paved road, the runoff from shop owners scrubbing the sidewalk. Along the whole street, there was barely a soul to be seen. Except, of course, at the mosque.

The mosque on Soliman Gohar street was a boring rectangle, with neither dome nor minaret. Green mats had been spread down the sidewalk, to accommodate a multitude that could never fit within the its modest walls. A sermon was flowing out of the loudspeaker, and as I flanked the seated crowd of men, I caught a glimpse of the imam within, robed in brown and white, preaching into a microphone. But as I lingered, I caught some deeply hostile stares from some watchers on the mats. Three older men with graying beards and furrowed frowns stared gravely at me and the bulky camera dangling from my wrist.

'Carry on' they seemed to say.

I reached the stairs and descended into the metro. On the platform, waiting for the train, incantations were pealing out of the station's speaker system at an unconscionable volume. The station was nearly deserted, a true rarity for Cairo—a lone passenger stared at me from across the tracks.

I was surprised the trains even ran today.

Unlike in Christianity, in Islam, it was permitted to do work on the day of prayer if one so wished. But nevertheless, on Friday in Egypt, society was manned by a skeleton crew. I had imagined that at least in the center of town, the influence of big-city commerce would have compelled at least a few shops to keep their doors open. But downtown Cairo was a ghost town. There were few shops un- shuttered, few cars in the road, and only a trickle of people. I was hoping at least that my favorite res- taurant was open. I was hungry for *kushari*, a cheap Egyptian dish of lentils and pasta.

As I passed Midan Tahrir, Cairo's largest square, the noonday prayer rang out from a minaret across the plaza.

"Allahu akbar!" it wailed. God is great.

Immediately, the pedestrians in the square formed together in a line. Taxis stopped and drivers as well as passengers got out, ripping prayer mats from the dashboards and positioning them on the ground before them. At least thirty men filed up, all standing with hands folded, and feet shoulder- width apart, all looking solemnly at their prayer mats, all facing Mecca.

There was a commotion at the end of the line: one man was without a prayer mat. He and the man beside him dashed to a flattened cardboard box that lay discarded nearby. They pulled it into position just in time.

"Allahu akbar!"

In one motion, the whole line bent forward at the waist and placed their hands on their knees. Af- ter a pause, there was another incantation, and the line stood back upright. The men stood with closed eyes and still faces, deep in meditation. Again the mosque incanted, and line fell forward onto its knees. At another word, the men bent forward and gently kissed their foreheads to the mats before them. They regained the kneeling position, whispered a prayer, and then touched their foreheads to the mats once more before returning to their feet, legs shoulder-width apart, preparing for the next prostration.

The ritual was moving even to watch. I had never seen such devotion. The Egyptians had a discipline of faith unmatched even in the small pockets of religion I had encountered in the West. I had not seen such faith in the grey-haired Catholics which filed into the thinning pews of my local church. I had not seen it in the prairie Christian tree planters with whom I had worked for a summer in the Canadian wilderness. I had not even seen it in Africa.

In Canada, religion was kept in the home, and shunned in public conversation. But in Egypt, religion was total. It governed the food people ate. It governed the way people dressed. It filled the air with prayers; it halted commerce in the streets; it dictated social codes and sex lives. Hundreds of years ago, in medieval times, the West was once like this. But I grew up in the modern age: in an ex-Christian society, where faith was a private matter, where relativism ruled the public sphere. And in the fervent society of Egypt, I marveled—half in discomfort, half in fascination—at the devotion practiced by one and all.

"You say, you are interested in Islam? You want to learn about Islam?"

My interlocuter's eyes were wide with religious-inspired joy. I regretted it as soon as I had said it. To me, it meant that I wanted to understand more about Egyptian culture. To him, it meant that I was a possible convert, a lost soul waiting to be saved.

"What is it that you want to learn?"

I smiled defensively. We were seated in the courtyard of Al-Azhar, one of Cairo's oldest mosques. This curious, bearded Egyptian had noticed me wandering about and struck up a conversation. As I sat with him outside on a brown mat, I didn't really know how to answer. I realized that it was probably too late to hide the St. Christopher medal swinging from my neck.

"We have many books inside. All free! Take whatever you want!"

He led me inside to a small table laden with publications. There were brochures called *Islam on Terrorism*, and *Women in Islam*. I picked up one that looked fairly holistic, entitled *An Illustrated Guide to Understanding Islam*.

"You have friends at your Arabic school?"

My wide-eyed, bearded friend was still hovering about me, giddy with excitement.

"Uh. . .yes."

"Here, take these for your friends!"

He shoved more pamphlets into my arms. "Take these for your Spanish-speaking friends. And these for your German-speaking friends. Here is one for your Italian-speaking friends."

This book, the *Illustrated Guide*, had been translated into almost every written language that existed. There were copies in Finnish. There were copies in Danish. There were copies in Hungarian, Greek, and Polish. They had not just chosen the widely-spoken languages, such as French or Russian. They had translated it, methodically, into all the languages they could. As I searched further, I found copies in Mandarin, Japanese, and Korean.

"Please tell me if you want more. And call me if you have any questions—anything you want to know. My name is Mohammed. Here is my number."

He entered his number into my cell phone, all without my will. And I was simply too polite to stop him.

Before my encounter with this proselytizing Egyptian, I had been marveling at one of the oldest and most famous mosques in Islamic Cairo. I entered in from the hot street, buzzing with the commotion of a nearby market and the thousand car horns of an Egyptian traffic jam, and stepped through an arch into a cool, dim hall. A veiled woman asked me to remove my sandals. When she shut the door, the din of the street was instantly silenced, and I stepped through the archway towards the mosque within.

The marble courtyard opened before me, wide as a skating rink, made of pure white stone which was smooth, clean, and cool. Ornate walls rose around the silent expanse, and three minarets towered high into the blue above me. I could hear myself breathe. A husband, wife, and their young daughter crossed the far side of the courtyard, making no more noise than the muted steps of stocking feet and the gentle swish of cloth.

Al-Azhar was founded in 970 AD, making it the oldest functioning university in the world. For more than a thousand years it had been the religious capital of Cairo, instructing over thirty thousand students a year in the Arabic language and the Holy Qu'ran. While it was originally founded as a mosque and a religious school, it expanded during the Islamic Enlightenment to encompass the fields of history, mathematics, astronomy, geography, and medicine. In the 1960s, it added faculties of applied sciences and engineering to its ranks, making it a full-fledged modern university, while at the same time preserving its ancient commitment to the teaching of the Islamic faith.

One of the elaborately-carved minarets split into a unique double-tower at the top: one side for the Shia, one side for the Sunni: the two branches of Islam. Inside, the mosque had two levels—the inner for the Sunni, the outer for the Shia. It was very rare to see a mosque built for both versions of Islam, and Al-Azhar was just that sort of creation. It symbolized the unity which the faith lost so many centuries ago.

The schism in Islam began very early after the founding of the religion, over a disagreement about the succession of leadership after the Prophet's death. The side that favoured family lineage, led by Mohammed's cousin Ali, eventually became the Shia. The side that favoured the ancient Arabic custom of election by the tribal elders became the Sunni. The feud soon developed into a bitter civil war. For the first time, Muslim fought against Muslim, and the Sunni army even spiked verses of the Qu'ran onto their spears, which made the armies of Ali refuse to fight. Ali was murdered by one of his own ranks, and his first son Hassan succeeded to the leadership. When Hassan was poisoned, his second son Hussein became the spiritual leader.

The split became official after the slaughter of Hussein during the battle of Karbala. Shia Muslims are always taught to remember the martyrdom of Hussein, and many today even flagellate themselves to symbolize the suffering he went through to defend the faith. His head, entombed in a massive silver casket, lies in the mosque across the road from Al-Azhar.

"So how was it?" Sean asked me, after we had met up and jumped in a taxi.

"It was. . .ok," I said. "The courtyard was amazing. But the mosque itself was—well, kind of unimpressive."

Sean nodded. "They always are."

My encounter with Mohammed had somewhat taken away from my ability to walk freely about the mosque and appreciate the building itself. But I had seen what I needed to see. The ceiling was low; the red carpet was worn and old. Further inside there was a slightly raised ceiling, lined by tiny glass windows stained in colourful floral designs. But none of this was designed to be seen by everyday believers. Most of the faithful would only see the low, dim interior, lit only by weak lamps which hung between small, cold pillars of stone.

Since I arrived in Egypt, one of the capitals of Sunni Islam, I had yearned to see a mosque of glorious construction. Sean and I had traveled Europe two years before, and gazed upon the likes of Notre Dame de Paris, the Florence Cathedral, and the Vatican in Rome. These giants took my breath away immediately when I ventured inside. But so far, in the Muslim countries I had visited, Egypt and Turkey, I found the mosques kind of. . .bare and disappointing. I longed to see a mosque to rival the lofty majesty of Notre Dame—a wonder built high to awe the faithful; a visual expression of the majesty of God.

It was for this purpose that Sean and I were headed to the Citadel, one of Cairo's main tourist attractions. We were off to visit the mosque of Mohammed Ali.

The Citadel was a massive stronghold built atop Cairo's highest hill by none other than Saladin—the Kurd who became Sultan of Egypt and Syria, the commander who beat back the Crusaders and recaptured Jerusalem for the Muslims. The mosque was built in the 1800s, while Egypt seethed under Ottoman rule. Mohammed Ali Pasha, then the governor of Egypt, commissioned the mosque to be built with one great dome surrounded by four half domes and four full domes, with two towering minarets. This symbolized the ultimate authority of the Egyptian Sultan, an open act of rebellion against the Turks.

The mosque stood tall and proud on the Citadel's highest point, it's bright silver domes shining in the sun, an iconic image of the Cairo skyline. After admiring the grand exterior and the sky-scraping minarets, Sean and I took off our shoes at the door, and stepped inside.

But the inside of the mosque seemed. . .hollow. The walls were a smudgy brown, giving the lofty interior a drab, empty feel. The cupola's patterns were barely noticeable in the dampened light. Large rings of wrought iron held lamps at just above head level, hung from the high ceiling on dusty chains which marred the view of the ceiling. Cross-hatched Islamic patterns ringed the walls. None of them were very colourful; faded patches of red and black were dotted here and there among the carved stone. I took a few photographs before realizing that none of them were really worth keeping.

Sean grunted in disappointment. "It's times like this I feel a little jealous of people like Salman," he said. "He knows this from far back in his child-hood; perhaps he can appreciate a beauty here that we just don't see. But this does not seem glorious to me. It just feels kind of. . .empty and foreign."

I left the Citadel that day disillusioned. Again, I could not shake the uncomfortable feeling that it was probably my culture talking—that my West-ern sense of aesthetics prevented me from see-ing the splendor in these towering mosques. But this thought could do nothing to improve my appreciation for a style that, to my eyes, was underwhelming.

I just didn't find mosques to be all that beautiful.

"When I came here with my family in 1999, I didn't see a single veil," Claudia told me. "Now they are everywhere. Things have really changed."

Claudia was Italian. She had already studied in Cairo at our school for six months by the time we arrived. She invited Sean, Anya, Salman, and I, as well as another Canadian student named Michael, to Al-Azhar park to watch the sunset. As we strolled along the path, she chatted with me about her experience so far.

"I think we have come to Egypt at a very special time," she said. "Because of George Bush and his wars, people here think Islam is being threatened. And they are responding. Egypt is one of the most Islamic countries in the Middle East."

I could see why Al-Azhar park was Claudia's favorite place in all of Cairo. A fountain bubbled up in a pavilion at the gate. Children laughed and taunted the jets of water, while young parents watched on, relaxed, amused and in love. White palm trees with sprouted up in symmetrical rows along paths of red and white stone which snaked throughout the park. In some places, a sluice had been cut in the center of them where a small stream flowed. The sound of trickling water whispered everywhere through the garden. Wherever we walked we saw lush grass, tailored bushes, and soft purple flowers. Al-Azhar park was a flourishing garden on the highest hill in the city, with a panoramic view of the whole landscape. Nestled in the center of hot, dirty Cairo, it was a green glade of paradise.

Claudia led us up the park's highest hill, where people sat watching the sunset. It was surreal to stand in this lush garden and gaze at Cairo's dusty buildings, rising up out of the parched streets below. Hundreds of minarets poked up from the skyline, some rising from ancient domed giants that had stood for centuries; others from humble ones that served only small neighbourhoods. The sun burned a deep orange. Egyptian lovers held hands and sat on the white walls, watching the sky, and the city that seemed so calm and still from such a distant height.

The other night, I had stretched out on the couch in my flat and flipped through the Qu'ran— reading random pages, rather than surah by surah. Like the Bible, the Qu'ran was originally remembered through oral tradition, and later composed into a written work by scholars. In the Arabic language, the Qu'ran has rhyme and meter. It is not just a book, but a long and elegant poem. It is this rhyme scheme that allows it to be chanted with such art, and to be memorized word for word by young Muslim students.

Two images, I noted, recurred in the text with great frequency: the images of heaven and hell. They are vividly described, in different language each time, but the details are always the same. The unbelievers, those who deny the punishment of God, 'shall be inmates of the Fire, where they shall dwell for ever.'[2] And when they are 'flung into its flames, they shall hear it roaring and seething, as

[2] Qu'ran, 2:280

though bursting with rage. And every time a multitude is thrown therein, its keepers will say to them: "Did no one come to warn you?"'[3]

But as for the righteous, 'they shall be lodged in peace together amid gardens and fountains,'[4] gardens 'watered by running streams, where they shall dwell for ever.'[5] Within such a paradise 'shall flow rivers of water undefiled, rivers of milk for ever fresh; rivers of wine delectable to those that drink it, and rivers of clarified honey. There shall they eat of every fruit, and receive forgiveness from their Lord.'[6]

Our group of expat Arabic students sat on the hill and watched the sun crawl lower; its last rays streaking across the haze of dust and fumes that sat lazily in Cairo's sky. In the dusk, we heard the rattle of one scratchy speaker—the call to prayer ringing from some distant mosque. As if summoned, the call exploded from every tower across Cairo, the City of a Thousand Minarets. The numberless voices blended together into a single, throbbing hum.

Darkness fell. Lamps flickered to life between the palms. As we continued through the garden and climbed a stone staircase, a great domed building of

[3] Qu'ran, 67:10
[4] Qu'ran, 44:50
[5] Qu'ran, 98:9
[6] Qu'ran, 47:16

polished stone rose before us, at the end of a path cleaved by a glittering stream. The building's walls were lit by the soft light of lanterns against the deepening sky, a miniature palace inside Eden.

Sean spoke.

"In the movie Lawrence of Arabia, Lawrence has a discussion with King Feisal. They were deep in the desert, and Lawrence spoke about how much the desert was home to Feisal's people. Feisal replied: 'We hate the desert. The desert is not our home. Years ago, the Arabs made their home in Spain. We still remember the gardens of Cordova. . .some of the most splendid gardens in the world. We are not fighting for the desert, but for the gardens of Cordova.'"

And immediately, the Arab obsession with the garden became clear. Here, in the center one of the dirtiest cities of the world, the Egyptians had reconstructed the gardens of Cordova. We were walking in an image of paradise, a vision of heaven from the Holy Qu'ran. A garden, watered by running streams.

4
TAKING SIDES

"Hey Kieran, look at this!"

Sean swiveled his laptop so I could see the screen. It was a news report about Lebanon.

"They're having an election soon," he said. "And it's looking *bad*."

The BBC said that Lebanon was the most tense than it had been in decades. After a brutal civil war which lasted fifteen years, the country had finally managed to regain stability in the 1990s. But now, in a country divided by hostile factions, President Emile Lahoud was about to step out of power with no clear successor to take his place.

Lebanon was our next stop. When Kristen and Nickie arrived, we were going to head there immediately after a few days in Egypt. Time was running short, and we were busily trying to contact people in the countries we were going to visit, to set up stories to film.

"Things are *tense* there right now," Sean told me. "I've emailed a lot of people and gotten no responses. All that anyone from Lebanon cares about right now is the election that's going to happen in two weeks."

I nodded. "And we're supposed to be arriving in three."

"God," Sean said, "imagine there is violence and they close the airport. They did that in 2006 when the Israelis bombed."

"That would be *awful*," I exclaimed. "We wouldn't get to see the place!"

"There might be violence," said Sean. "There might not. In this region of the world, you can never say for sure. But I have to see Lebanon. I *have* to see that country. I wonder if I should go early."

We both sat in silence and pondered the idea.

"Well," I said, "that would be useful. You could do some groundwork for our films. And you'd get to see the lead up to these elections."

Sean thought for a moment and his face lit up.

"Hell yeah I should go! Really Kieran, is there any reason for me still to be in Cairo?"

"Well," I said, "you still have a month of Arabic lessons. . ."

Sean scoffed loudly and marched out of the flat to go buy a plane ticket.

On our last day in Cairo, Sean and I decided to do some sightseeing. We set out in mid-morning, while the sun was climbing high, and began our walk down Soliman Gohar to the metro station.

"I met some Christian guys in the bar the other night," I told Sean as we walked down the metro stairs. "They were great. They even took me to their church, a Coptic one up the road from our house. I felt comfortable there; kind of like I belonged. They want to meet you. We should spend some time with them when you get back to Cairo."

Sean scowled.

"I would caution you against taking sides. We are in the Middle East—everyone's got a tribe. You should try to remain objective and not get involved in their little hatreds and local rivalries. You don't want to join a tribe."

We had chosen the wrong time to ride the metro in Cairo. A bulging horde occupied the platform. We squirmed into the forest of elbows and potbellies, and waited endlessly while trains arrived and departed without us getting much closer to the doors. Luckily, our destination was only a few stops away.

We were off to see Coptic Cairo, the old Christian quarter of the city.

Coptic Cairo was easily older than the city itself. Christianity has been in Egypt for two thousand years; when the religion first moved out of the holy land, Egypt was one of the first places converted. Christianity spread first among the Greek-speaking population, and then eventually to the whole country. It flourished in Egypt for six centuries before Muslim armies marched across the Sinai from Arabia, and conquered Egypt for Islam.

Somaia told us that when the Muslim general arrived at the central church in Alexandria, he spread his prayer mat in front of it and prayed three times towards Mecca. In doing this, he sent a signal to all of his followers: the Christian population of Egypt was to be respected. Though hundreds of thousands of Arab Muslims settled and built a civilization on the banks of the Nile, they attracted few converts from the Christians. The Muslims never compelled them.

This was in keeping with the teachings of the Prophet—that Christians and Jews, the 'People of the Book,' were always to be tolerated and accepted. The Muslims believe that Jews and Christians are worshippers of the same One God; that many of God's prophets had come in their time to reveal His truths to the world. These prophets were men such as Moses and Elijah, the great Jewish patriarchs of the Old Testament. Another such prophet was Jesus. Muslims believe the final prophet was Mohammed, and that his teachings were the last and most complete version of the Lord's revelations. Mohammed revered the cultures that had gone before him, and he forbade his followers to convert them by the sword.

To this day, hundreds of Christian communities exist all over the Middle East. The Christians that live in Egypt are known as Copts; the official language of their church is Coptic, a language derived from ancient Greek.

As we walked through the Coptic Museum, Sean and I passed dozens of Bibles in glass cases. They were works of art, with colourful images of the saints and martyrs drawn in the margins around the long tracts of Coptic script. As we walked through the historical progression of museum, we saw the Bibles of later ages, illuminated in the same way, but written entirely in the flowing script of Arabic.

"Do you think that was so they could preach to the new flock?" I asked Sean. "To their Arab converts?"

"It's probably so they could preach to their own flock," he replied. "I think it just shows how the language of Egypt changed over the centuries."

Eventually we entered the cathedral adjacent to the museum. The Hanging Church is one of the oldest and most famous in Egypt. The causeway was lined with long, beautiful mosaics—one of the half-blind Simon the Tanner, the saint who once lusted after a woman after seeing her thigh, and put out his own eye for his sin. Others were of the disciples and Christ, and still others were of the first Christian saints who lived as hermits in the desert, wearing hides and living on barely any food to practice their devotion to God. The colourful depictions, so carefully arranged, were quite a contrast to the imageless mosques of Islam.

But even so, we noticed Islamic influence on the great stone entrance to the church itself. Intricate, serpentine designs swirled symmetrically around a large cross carved in the center. Arabic words were inscribed in stone above them. The doors opened to reveal a high wooden church, with weaving designs of green, brown and yellow adorning every beam. Rows of icons stood along every wall: designs peculiar to Orthodox Christianity in which a religious scene and the clothes of the saint are sculpted of silver or gold, while the face and hands of the holy figure itself are inlaid as a flat painting. In front of each icon was an iron stand, where prayer candles stood fastened to the base by dribbled wax.

As in every Orthodox cathedral, the tabernacle—the holy compartment where the symbolic bread and wine is kept—was hidden from the public view, covered by long scarlet drapes. Images of saints were sewn into them: Mary, the virgin mother of Jesus, and Egypt's favorite saint, St. George, sitting atop his horse, thrusting his pike through the mouth of a dragon below. Egyptians prayed with their eyes downcast and their palms open upwards in front of these images, and then knelt and kissed the blood-red cloth.

"I do feel more comfortable here!" Sean remarked, with some astonishment. "I guess all those years of going to church have had some effect. But it's not the religion; I couldn't care less about Christianity. It must be just—pure familiarity."

Just as I was about to leave the Hanging Church, an Egyptian girl stopped me and said hello. I began to practice my choppy Arabic on her, but she only looked around nervously. It was probably not culturally acceptable, I realized, which made it such a strange and rare thing that a cute Egyptian girl would introduce herself to a Westerner.

"What's your number?" she asked.

I gave her mine, and she put hers into my telephone. "What's your name?" I asked.

"Merina" she said, and then ran away quickly, lest her parents see her talking to a foreign man.

"It's funny how in Egypt, the 'Christian quarter' means the liberal area."

Claire sat across from Sean and I on the sofa, fingering the strings of her guitar. She was an

Australian redhead—a traveler like ourselves who had landed in Cairo to study Arabic. Sean and I were over at her house that night to watch Egypt lose a football match with Tunisia. Basma, Claire's Sudanese roommate, cheered and laughed with glee every time Tunisia scored a point.

"It's ironic," Claire continued. "In Egypt, the 'Christian area' means a place where you can drink beer, and where women don't wear the veil and are allowed to have boyfriends. But in Australia or Canada, the 'Christian' part of town is the conservative, scary part of town that you don't want to visit."

Claire and Basma lived in an apartment in Maadi. They were all friends with the small crowd of expats which had formed around the nucleus of Drayah Arabic school. Salman and his Egyptian friend Ehab were coming over later, as well as Michael the Canadian, whose slightly brown complexion got him constantly mistaken for an Egyptian.

My experience in Egypt owed a lot to Michael. It was he that introduced me to Tamer.

In every foreign country I had visited, if I wanted to learn the language, it was absolutely necessary for me to get a good friend among the locals. Without this, all my classroom studying was for naught. Tamer was the perfect specimen. He was a burly, heavyset Egyptian of about thirty years of age, with a fake leg which swung about like a wrecking ball when he walked. Tamer's father ran a fruit shop about two minutes' walk from my house. Every night from seven until eleven-thirty, his father went home to rest, and Tamer performed the filial duty of sitting out on a chair, selling the occasional piece of fruit, and otherwise being bored out of his skull.

Every night he called me and pestered me to come sit out there with him, smoke a sheesha, and keep him company.

"What's your name?"

Tamer knew only two phrases in English. One of them was 'what's your name?' and the other was 'tomorrow.' I limped along in Arabic and the rest of the time communicated to him in sign language. He pointed to the large box of apples his father had stashed on the side.

"What's your name?"

"*Tufah*" I said, remembering the correct word. Very good, he nodded, and pointed to the bananas.

"What's your name?"

"*Mose.*" He nodded in approval, and pointed to the onions.

"What's your name?"

"Uh. . ." I stammered.

He slapped his forehead. "*Basal! Basal!*" He bugged out his eyes, and wiggled his hand beside his brain.

"*Styuupid!* You are *styuupid!*"

I laughed along with him. I didn't care to tell him that 'stupid' was actually a fairly strong word in English. I knew he meant it lightly.

Between customers, he showed me some of the things in his father's shop. Pasted the corner of the wall was a calendar with a picture of Jesus, and a photograph of the head of the Coptic Church, Baba Kurulis. He showed me a pocket-sized New Testament written entirely in Arabic. Then he made a drinking sign with his hand.

"You drink *birra?*"

Yes, I drank beer.

"Whiskey?"

Yes, I drank whiskey.

He got up and shuffled over to a corner, and pushed some boxes out of the way to reveal a litre and a half bottle of Absolut Vodka. I chuckled and shook his strong hand as he laughed greedily. But he did not serve any. With a nervous glance outside the store, he shambled back to the alcove and replaced the vodka, as though he were hiding a Playboy from an abusive father.

I looked at him quizzically. "Why?" I asked him.

His eyes darted left and right.

"Muslims."

As a Christian in Egypt, I had become part of something I had never been part of before—a persecuted minority. It gave me an immediate feeling of closeness. Around Tamer and his friends Romani and Imed, I felt a strong sense of belonging. It didn't really matter that in Canada, I barely practiced the religion—it was the shared culture that counted. Mixing with them was a breath of fresh air: no one told me it was a sin to drink a beer, no one preached Islam, and girls weren't categorically forbidden to speak to me.

Tamer, Romani, and Imed became my best friends in Cairo. They showed me tiny drinking holes where live bands played irritating music at appalling volumes, and scantily clad women danced for crowds of chubby, mustached males. They brought me to their homes in Shubra, a heavily Christian area of Cairo. We even went out together for beers on a bridge over the Nile, while the taxi man watched for police.

I thought it naive to try to 'remain objective,' as Sean had suggested. At that very moment he was in Lebanon, running around the streets of Beirut with a video camera, finding out that when he tried to film anything, he would be instantly interrogated by the army or the local militia, who thought him a spy. It was impossible, I realized, to be a dispassionate observer—no matter how you tried, you would always end up interacting with the surrounding environment. And what's more, I found that the more time I spent with my Christian friends, the more I learned about Egyptian culture, and the more Arabic I learned to speak.

But there was a darker side to this sense of community. Belonging was only one side of the coin. Carry on the conversation a little, and you would find hatred. The tribalism that Sean was talking about.

One night, Tamer invited me out for a couple drinks. I accepted readily, and told him I would bring some friends.

"Great! Michael, and Claudia! Bring them" he said. But then his face changed to a suspicious frown.

"But Ehab? Salman? Don't bring them. No."

He shook his finger and smacked his lips in disapproval.

"Muslims."

That night at Claire's house, Michael, Salman, Ehab and I decided to go out to a bar. We sat one Claire's couches for almost an hour debating on where to go.

"Maybe. . .Shubra?" Michael suggested.

"Shubra!" Ehab exclaimed in surprise. "No. Not Shubra. Let's go somewhere else."

Micheal turned to me and smiled. "Yeah, a lot of Muslims don't like Shubra. It's full of Christians. They all have this little cross tattooed on their wrists."

Ehab protested, and looked uncomfortable. He quickly washed his hands of this accusation. He didn't like Shubra because he just didn't like the bars there.

As we got ready to go that evening, my cell phone rang. It was Merina. I was used to her calling me numerous times to say hello, and to try to speak in Arabic even when I didn't really understand. Over a couple of weeks, she had managed to communicate to me that she was from a different town, Ismaili, and that I should take a bus there and visit her. But this time she called to ask me a very important question, a question she knew in perfect English.

"Are you a Muslim?"

Of course, I thought. Because if I was, you wouldn't be caught dead spending time with me.

"No, of course not, I'm a Christian."

I hung up the phone and sighed. This was indeed a new side of Egypt. Here in the Middle East, who you were as an individual mattered little compared to the tribe you associated with. I was a Canadian, raised in an environment of tolerance and acceptance. And I was beginning to feel the discomfort of living in a society where people of different cultures shook hands and smiled in the daylight, and muttered curses at each other in the darkness of their homes.

"Here my friend, have an orange!"

"You are not my friend. A friend would have offered me bananas."

Tamer chuckled and got up, shuffled awkwardly over to the front of the shop, and pulled down some bananas for Asharaf, his taxi driver. Asharaf always came by for a break from driving to drink some tea and perhaps smoke some sheesha. I was seated by the shop, with a dark shot of Arabic coffee and an over-sugared glass of lemon juice in front of me. Soliman Gohar street at night was quieter but still alive: dominoes clicked at the coffee shop next door, water pipes bubbled, and the odd car rolled past. We talked for a bit, Asharaf practicing his English and telling me how business was. Tamer roared at his pot-bellied cousin who worked in the coffee shop, who came scurrying out with a water pipe for each of us.

"Ok Tamer," Asharaf said eventually. "I have to go. I'll be back to pick you up at eleven-thirty."

"Ok my friend. *Ma'a salaama.*" Tamer said.

"*Ma'a salaama.*"

"I like Asharaf," I told Tamer once he had left. "He's great. I should hire him to go get Nickie from the airport in a couple of days."

Tamer sneered.

"I will get another cab driver for you. I will call him tonight."

I looked puzzled. "What's wrong with Asharaf?"

"He is not my friend."

"He's not your friend? But he's driving you home!"

"Yes, but he is not my friend."

Tamer's lip curled up into that signature sneer of distaste.

"Muslim" he whispered.

"But Tamer, Muslims are everywhere!" I said. "There are Muslims working there at the coffee shop. Muslims buy your fruit. Asharaf is a Muslim, and he's driving you home! You work with Muslims at your construction firm, yes?"

"Yes."

"And are they your friends?"

"No."

"Tamer, what's wrong with Muslims?"

He looked from right to left suspiciously, then cocked his finger like a gun and rattled it back and forth, shooting imaginary persons in the air.

Oh, I thought. Did the Christians here feel threatened? Threatened by the happy cab drivers, the cheerful waiters, the hospitable shopkeepers? Threatened by their colleagues and coworkers, by the poor labourers who helped them close their shops each night?

I returned to my apartment that night and lay awake in bed. In Canada, people of different cultures lived together in an almost seamless harmony. But in Egypt, multiculturalism meant that a thin veneer of tolerance covered an ocean of contempt. I was unsure of what to think of all this, and unsure of how to conduct myself around my cheerful, genuine, xenophobic friends.

I had discovered yet another side to the Middle East—a side that I wasn't really sure I wanted to see.

5

ONE MAN'S TRASH

"Ok Kieran, you sit up front and take still photos. I'm going to sit in the back with Zelika."

Nickie stroked her camera as though it was a pet. It was a bulky machine, obviously larger than any amateur would use, with a giant, intimidating lens. This camera would immediately get us respected as professionals wherever we went. She had given it the Muslim name 'Zelika' during her documentary work in southern Thailand.

"We have to be diplomatic," said Nickie. "Lots of smiles. We have to explain to them that we admire what they are doing, and that it helps the environment. Once they understand that we are not there to make fun of them or insult them, they will trust us and open up to the camera."

Nickie had arrived last night on a late flight from Vancouver. We made it home by midnight and she fell into bed, exhausted. But we were both up by the first call to prayer, getting ready for our first day of filming. We whizzed through the streets of Cairo in a tiny red car with a sewing-machine motor, piloted by Imed's brother. In the front seat sat John, a translator who we had hired for the day.

"So you guys are Canadian, right? Do you like Celine Dion? I *love* Celine Dion! *Titanic!*"

John was an Egyptian Copt of twenty-eight years who had studied English at the American University in Cairo. He was giddy with excitement to be spending the day with us. Every ten minutes he would make a swooning comment to Nickie ('how did you get so beautiful?' or 'Cairo is very happy to see you this morning'). Nickie smiled awkwardly and tried to be a good sport about it. As we ascended the ramp to the freeway that climbed over one of Cairo's traffic-congested neighbourhoods, John threw in a Celine Dion tape and blasted *'My Heart Will Go On'* at a volume that shook the windows. He turned it down periodically to talk to us.

"After this. . .perhaps you want to see the Cairo museum, or the pyramids? Do you want to see some truly *mysterious* places here in Egypt? Something truly *mysterious* for your film?"

He inflected the word 'mysterious' as though he were some sort of magician.

"Well," said Nickie, "only after we get what we need from Garbage City. We might have to come back tomorrow."

John looked confused. "Just the garbage city? You *only* want to make a make a film about the garbage city?"

He couldn't comprehend it. No Egyptian did. He had no idea why two foreigners had come all the way from Canada to make a film about. . .*this.*

The red car sped past Al-Azhar park and the Citadel. Eventually, we turned off the highway onto a road that led to a small community built in the shadow of the pale sandstone cliffs on Cairo's eastern edge. It was outside the city limits, where buses, taxis, and the normal citizens of Cairo never ventured. It was a place I had only heard whispered about amongst the expats that I knew from my Arabic school. The formal name of the town was Muqattam. But everyone I knew called it Garbage City.

The first day we settled into our flat in Dokki, Sean and I had gone through our kitchen with two scrub brushes and a vengeance. We cleaned every splatter of oil off the stove and the counters; we threw out every rancid bowl of food from the fridge, containers and all. At the end we were left with a spotless kitchen, and four bags of garbage which sat rank and stinking at the entrance to our house. I wondered aloud how we were going to get rid of them in a place like Cairo. I hadn't seen a dumpster yet. The whole street was littered with garbage, but I didn't feel right about simply pitching the bags unceremoniously out the window.

As if summoned, there was a knock at the door. When I opened it, a man was standing there in a long blue robe made of cheap, sturdy material; his head wrapped in an Upper Egyptian headdress.

"Garbage," he said in Arabic.

He carried by his side a large bag woven of reeds which was smudged with grime. As I picked up the bags of garbage, he seized them from my hands with the violence of a man who thought me unfit to dirty myself with work that belonged to his class. He thanked me, accepted a small sum, and left.

Every day, I had seen hundreds of men in orange jumpsuits sweep trash from the streets and pile it into trucks. Many garbage collectors regularly visited the apartment buildings on my street, carrying bags of trash out by hand. Originally, I thought this diligent work was a successful sanitation program of the Egyptian government. I had no idea how wrong I was.

In the 1950s, before the damming and the extensive irrigation of the Nile, there was a famine in Upper Egypt, the southern part of the country. Whole families abandoned their lands and migrated north to flee starvation. Cairo did not want these refugees, and there seemed to be no economic niche for them to fill. They settled in the hills in the outskirts of the city, beyond the pale of settlement for Cairo's mainstream citizens, and began to sort through the garbage dumps to make their living.

The garbage cities became an economic success. Within the next few decades, even more refugees fled northwards and settled in places like Muqattam. Large brick apartment buildings sprang up in the 1970s. The way of life had become permanent.

Each day, the men of the community and their sons traveled to Cairo and went around from block to block, collecting garbage. They were recognized by the security man of each building, and collected a small fee for their services—Sean and I paid four dollars a month. They brought the trash home to the women of the community, who sorted it. Plastic and bottles were sold to other men within Garbage City, who shredded them. Newsprint and paper were collected in bales or turned back into pulp to make paper. Metal parts and scraps were collected in a similar way. All of the recycled materials were sold back to Cairo's factories through middlemen. Finally, there was the food waste, which was fed to animals. Only two types of animals could ever survive on a diet of rotten food waste: goats and pigs. And since Muslims traditionally shun pigs as unclean, ninety percent of the citizens of Muqattam were Christian.

The city was probably the most efficient recycling center in the world. And it had come into existence long before the masses of North America had ever heard the term.

"I will drive you through in the taxi, but don't roll down the windows. The smell is terrible! We are not going to get out of the taxi. And *don't* take pictures. . .they don't like it. It is very dangerous here; they don't like visitors. Ok?"

On my scouting trip, I paid a taxi driver at the Citadel to take me there. As we entered, he rolled up the windows and lit a cigarette. I had no idea what could possibly smell worse than second-hand smoke in a confined space, but this was Cairo— everybody smoked. The taxi drove through the entrance to the city: a small passageway between two tall brick buildings. A pickup truck passed us on its way into Cairo, piled high with enormous, bulging white bags. As the streets opened wider, we began to see bales of trash piled up alongside all the buildings. Men in sweatshirts and rubber boots walked back and forth; women walked around in long, colourful, one-piece robes that I had never seen in any other part of Cairo. As we drove, some of the people smiled and waved at us. The driver returned the waves of the people he passed, wearing on his face a distant smile of pity.

"This is unbelievable," said Nickie, as our red car puttered through the mud streets of Muqattam. She trained her camera on a woman seated by the side of the road, folding old newspapers and placing them into neat piles. We drove past a shop with a jumble of miscellaneous metal parts piled high inside. Down the alleys, we saw entire streets covered in bits of paper, piled high for baling. Middle-aged women looked up from sorting food waste onto carrying trays; goats chewed repetitively and stared curiously at us. Youths watched us from the back of trucks packed high with cardboard bales. Children pointed and waved to us as we passed.

We passed a doorway on the left with plastic bottles stacked to the ceiling. Two men sorted through different types of plastic, and handed them in bags to men in the adjacent shop. Inside, a greasy machine roared to life, and one man piled bottles inside it with a snow shovel, another on the top leaned heavily on the mountain of plastic with a rake, jamming them down into the shredder beneath. Thousands of plastic shards spat noisily out of the bottom of the machine. After a few minutes, the men and gathered the plastic together in bags to ship out.

"These people. . .aren't poor!" Nickie remarked. "Look at those shops over there, and those women in that lovely clothing. They're doing fine."

The district had every amenity imaginable. There were cell phone stores, meat shops, and little grocery stores with hundreds of products. The only difference from the rest of the Cairo, besides the garbage, was the pictures of Christ and the saints hung reverently above the doorways, or crosses painted in whitewash on the walls.

We climbed out of the car. I got my watch strap repaired by a local watchmaker, who thanked me with a smile. We visited a bakery only to be given a free loaf of bread by the delighted women who worked there. We did not insult them by trying to pay for it, but rather thanked them with a smile. Men hailed me from countless coffee shops, asking where we were from, beckoning us to stay for tea, sheesha, or whisky. I shook many hands, and had to politely refuse their hospitality; we needed to film while it was still light out. Children rushed to play with us, and women greeted me and ask my name—something unheard of in the rest of the city.

Dangerous indeed. This was the friendliest place in Cairo.

"Here is where we make the carpets. Local women come here who want to learn to weave, and we teach them on our looms. We have seventeen women working here at this time."

Our interviewee was an Egyptian lady, about sixty years of age. She was plump and full of smiles, and she spoke excellent English, which was excellent for our film. Through our translator we had negotiated an interview with what we thought at first was a carpet-making factory. It turned out to be an NGO, a charity organization deep within Muqattam. It was run entirely by women.

"And here is where the carpets are completed. We get hundreds of bags of fabric from all the different textile factories in Cairo. They are pieces which the factory doesn't need. We take them, cut them into strips, and make them into colourful designs."

Nickie panned around a room of girls who sat working meekly around a large table. On the walls were splayed many wide carpets of truly original design. They were made of a woven fabric base, with hundreds of little strips of colour stitched into them. When we got closer to the girls working, some of them looked up, alarmed, and the rest of them simply didn't acknowledge us. They were too camera shy.

"Where do the girls come from?" I asked.

"They are from the street; usually orphans. We take them in here. Here, they can learn a trade."

"Who made this one?" I asked her, holding a beautiful red and white carpet on the wall.

She smiled a very motherly smile.

"This one was made by Miriam."

She called her, and Miriam got up reluctantly and stood beside the carpet for a photograph. She was a beautiful girl of sixteen years. Eventually, she broke into a wide grin, realizing that she was the center of attention.

"And Miriam will actually be leaving us soon," said the director, "she is going to be married!"

The director led us downstairs. We stood in a courtyard, home to the only tree I had seen so far in Garbage City. Nearby, we watched women mash up pulp in large, hand-pressed machines, and lay them in tubs of water.

"Here, we make paper. We take paper scraps from the village and soak them in water for many hours. Eventually, it becomes pulp. Then, we lay it flat and press it, and finally put it out to dry."

She beckoned to one of the women who worked there, who came over and showed us some of the large metal screens where the sheets of pulp were drying. We saw her take some dry sheets off the screen and cut the edges off, which she dropped back into another batch of wet pulp. The product was a grey, dry, grainy sheet of paper.

"We sell both the paper and the carpets upstairs. We also sell olives which we grow in our eco garden."

Upstairs, Nickie and I concluded the tour. We thanked them warmly for showing us their organization, and promised to send them a copy of any film we produced. As we sat in the back of the red car on the drive home, Nickie and I looked over our purchases. Nickie had bought a thick carpet, made of scraps of blue, white, and black cloth; I had bought a jar of olives from the eco-garden, as well as a small book, written by an academic from Cairo University who lived in their little town. I was excited. I was holding in my hands perhaps the first ever formal written history of Garbage City.

Back at the flat, Nickie and I relaxed and had some food, still bewildered by the cultural phenomenon we had just visited. I was still getting over the fact that thirty thousand people had carved out not only an existence, but even a relatively prosperous life from sorting the garbage of Cairo's twenty million people. Nickie booted up her computer, and began to load some of the pictures we had taken onto Facebook. We only chuckled at the comments they received.

"Wow, that must be really humbling to see people that live like that."

"Oh my god, that is so sad."

"How does seeing this stuff up close affect you? It must be so hard."

We couldn't really blame Nickie's friends. They hadn't visited Muqattam; they could only understand what they saw before them in the small borders of a photograph. They had not seen how well the people actually lived; they could not see the incredible service they were performing for the Egyptian capital.

But, as I flipped through my new book, I learned that life could be hard for the inhabitants of Garbage City. Alcoholism and drug addiction were problems there, and the rate of infection and disease was high, due to the constant contact with garbage. But worst of all was what I could infer from the reaction of our translator and taxi driver. The people of Garbage City were treated as second-class citizens by mainstream Cairo. They were marginalized, illiterate, and Christian. It suddenly dawned on me why my Muslim taxi driver was so afraid of the place; why he warned me that it was so dangerous there. For him, it probably was.

Yet Muqattam was, by now, an indispensable cornerstone of Cairo's existence. Bidden or unbidden, each day the citizens of Garbage City work on, collecting the trash of Cairo's twenty million souls, sorting it, recycling it, and getting paid at each step of the way. And un-thanked and unappreciated, they still continue to carve out for themselves a tenable existence in the hills to the east of Cairo, perhaps entirely unaware that their little community is an environmental miracle for Africa's largest metropolis.

6

ALEXANDRIA

I had forgotten how refreshing it was to visit the sea.

The instant stepped off the bus from Cairo, I filled my lungs with fresh, clean ocean air. I rolled down the window and smelled the holy scent of sea salt as we taxied through the city towards the ocean. The breeze whipped across my face, churning and cleansing the air around me. I closed my eyes, and breathed deeply.

As we walked along the white sidewalk of the Corniche, the road which lined the ocean, we watched the waves wash up on the stone below. The water shimmered and shifted from blue, to grey, to white, depending on the mood of the sky. And all the while we drank in the warm rays of the sun, and deep breaths of pure, delicious ocean air.

I had not known till that moment just how much Cairo's pollution bothered me. Coming to Alexandria was like waking from a long sleep.

As the sun glowed bronze on the horizon, the three of us sat down at an outside cafe. We had not expected to be chilly in Egypt, but Alexandria had a different climate than Cairo, although it was a mere three hours north. We sat at a table across from the ocean, zipped up our jackets, and slurped hot foam from the tops of our cappuccinos.

Nickie loved it here. And I think Kristen loved it even more.

My sister had flown into Cairo two days ago. I was late to pick her up, since I had been foolish enough to trust Asharaf, Tamer's friend the taxi driver, to actually show up on time. When I arrived, she shouted my name before I had even left the cab, and broke free of a circle of Egyptian taxistas who were crowding around her, accosting her, and hassling her for a ride.

It was her first realization of what it was like to be a young lady in Egypt with a head of blonde hair.

We spent the next day in Cairo. We had an obligatory trip to the pyramids, where we did our best to film the temple townies, despite Nickie's giant camera being disallowed at the door. The Egyptian government, we learned, was very wary of letting people film any side of the pyramids that might be viewed as negative by people back home. Tourism, after all, was Egypt's largest industry. But all the same, we met Aatif, the camel driver I had befriended a couple of weeks before, who had agreed to an interview. Although he was very happy to show us around that day, he was a little bit sad. His camel, Alex, had died two days earlier.

"That camel was with me for two years," he told me. "It's like losing a friend."

That night we went to Aatif's sister's place for tea and sheesha. His family served us biscuits until we were so full we literally had to stuff them into our mouths. Kristen and Nickie greeted Aatif and his brother-in-law without shaking hands, as custom demanded. While I was quite accustomed to settings such as this—a house with natte covering the floor, a blazing grill of charcoal sitting beside us for the sheesha, and our hosts all in long, flowing Egyptian dress—for my sister, this was a new world. Her eyes glowed with delight as we taxied back to my flat. . .she was in the honeymoon period of travel, those first exotic experiences in a new land which would be remembered forever.

The following day we were off to Alexandria, Egypt's ancient capital. The primary reason was to meet Nermine, an Egyptian girl Nickie had met on the internet. But we also wanted to visit the city itself. And I had been dying to see one building in particular since I arrived in Egypt.

"El Mektebah" I said to our driver. The Library.

We disembarked on the road behind the Biblioteca Alexandrina, the new modern Library of Alexandria. It was shaped like a massive coin which had been tilted into the earth—half of it was below ground level, and the other half sloped upwards towards the sky. On the curved, granite back wall were inscribed characters from one hundred and twenty different human languages. The roof of the coin was made of white metal, and had triangular windows, that gave the effect that it was made of dozens of gleaming white sails. In front, there was a wide, shimmering pool of water, which caught a perfect reflection of the library when it was still.

Postmodern statues littered the plaza around it. One of them was a liquid human figure with his arm raised, a copy of one I had seen before in Greece. 'Prometheus,' was its name: it was a statue of the titan from Greek mythology who had brought fire down from heaven as a gift to mankind. Across the street stood a provocative white sculpture of Europa making love to a bull. Within the library's glass doors lurked a hideous frame of twisted wire and mangled metal. All of this seemed to fit with the buildings' postmodern, space-age architecture. But there was one bust, standing right before the library entrance, which paid tribute to a more ancient, classical style of beauty.

'El-Iskander al-Akbar,' the inscription read. Alexander the Great.

Alexander who had founded this city over three hundred years before the birth of Christ. The young king of Greece and Macedon led a massive army eastwards against the Persian Empire, Greece's ancient enemy, and scored victory after victory. He conquered not only territory which Greece had lost to the Persians decades before, but vast new provinces as well, such as Anatolia and Syria. Before he went further east, his generals advised him to construct a giant navy to defend Greece, which was vulnerable to attack from the sea. But Alexander built no navy. Instead, he led his army south in a ring around the Mediterranean, conquering every port. Eventually, he reached the vassal state of Egypt.

In Egypt, Alexander was greeted as a liberator and crowned as a Pharaoh in a full coronation ceremony. He founded Alexandria on the shores of the Mediterranean, and rode eastwards against the Persian Empire, which he conquered in the name of Macedon. When he died at thirty-two, his fledgling empire disintegrated, and each of his generals received a portion over which to rule.

His most favoured general Ptolemy received the wealthiest province of the empire: Egypt, which was ruled from the new capital of Alexandria. It was his successor, Ptolemy II, who built the great Library.

The Library of Alexandria housed over a million books. It employed some of the world's first paid scholars, whose time was spent copying out scrolls in longhand. Ships that came into Alexandria's harbour had their books forcibly confiscated, and copies instead of the originals were given back to the ships owners. The Ptolemies once put an enormous sum down as security for the original works of Athens' most famous playwrights, and then kept the originals and returned only copies to Athens. The Library of Alexandria lasted for centuries without rival—it was the largest collection of written knowledge anywhere in the world, and the most renowned and revered international academy ever to have existed.

And then, for reasons lost to history, it was destroyed. Some accounts say it burned down in a fire that Julius Caesar's troops lit at the docks which spread to other parts of the city. Others say that it was destroyed in the attack of the Emperor Aurelian, three hundred years later. To this day, we do not know if it was destroyed on purpose, or if it was a tremendous accident. We do not even know the place where the great library once stood. And of the hundreds and thousands of scrolls within the ancient library itself, today, only a single one survives. Its original is housed in a museum in Vienna. A facsimile is on display in the collection of ancient books within the modern Biblioteca Alexandrina.

Built in 2002, the Biblioteca represents Egypt's attempt to restore Alexandria to its ancient academic heritage. Millions of dollars in contributions poured in from countries and organizations around the world. A European architect was hired to design the building: the sunken coin with a slanted roof of white sails. The Biblioteca's creators were criticized over the money spent on the ostentatious design, since it took away from the funds needed to build the library's collection. Today the Biblioteca holds about half a million books, and at the present level of funding, it will take a century to fill.

But as I walked around the structure, shooting pictures of this shining space ship, I wasn't convinced the size of the collection mattered so much right now. The ancient library rose to fame over hundreds of years; the modern library could do the same. What mattered more was the symbol—a great ancient library raised anew in the heart of Alexandria, a building with a design as bold and glorious as the concept itself.

"It is supposed to represent the sun of knowledge rising out of the waters. I studied it in university."

Nermine was a tall Egyptian girl with soft brown eyes and a welcoming smile. She wore an aqua-blue veil around her head, which matched the colour of both her sweater and her long, flowing skirt. She met us after dark in front of an ice cream store, we walked together along the Corniche. The wind had slowed; the night was warm.

"I adore architecture," I told her. "I've never studied it, but I admire it. Wherever I go, a lot of my photos are of incredible buildings."

"Yeah," she said. "Architecture, Queen of the Arts! I don't really pursue it in my line of work, but I studied it for years. It was my first love."

Her English was impeccable. She had lived in Germany for eight years, while her father was working there. She spoke both English and German with complete fluency.

"I'm always amazed," I told her, "that when I go to other countries I always meet people who speak English so well, but have never spent time in an English-speaking country."

"Well, it's a lot easier for us to learn English without going to Canada or America. We get all of your music and movies. And plus I practice by writing on the internet."

"I met Nermine on Facebook," Nickie explained. "She was a member of a group called 'Let's see if we can find 1,000,000 people who hate George Bush.'"

Nermine smiled. "Yeah. They found one million already. Now they are trying for two."

Nermine was the sort of person with whom you could feel completely comfortable after meeting for only ten minutes. I have met a few internet contacts in different countries, and in many cases people can be shy when you finally meet them in person. But not Nermine. She was open and inviting, and by the time we reached the end of the Corniche, she had us absolutely charmed. After buying a tasty Egyptian mixture of ice cream and rice pudding, we sat down at a cafe which was nothing more than a collection of plastic tables and one guy who made tea out of a little portable cart. We sipped the hot drink out of thin plastic cups, while waves crashed on the rocks just a few meters away.

And because of Nermine's relaxed and open demeanor, we soon fell right into talking about the one subject that everyone who had visited the Middle East before had warned me not to talk about. Islam.

"So. . .this might be a dumb question," I ventured, "but is it only Christian girls who don't wear the veil?"

"Not at all," she said. "Lots of Muslim girls don't wear it. It's a personal choice. I didn't wear the veil until I was twenty-two."

She pulled out her cell phone and showed us a picture from her early twenties, in a group of Muslim girls with uncovered hair.

"So, what made you decide to wear it?" Kristen asked.

"Well, my sister took the veil a year before I did. And I studied with her, because I never make a decision on anything until I study everything about it. I even stopped listening to Western music for those few months. . .I didn't want anything to influence my decision. Eventually I decided it was right for me. And it was crazy. . .as soon as I wore it, everyone started looking at me differently."

"But. . .you didn't decide to cover the full face," I said.

"No. The Qu'ran says that women should be covered from their head to their bosom, but I just couldn't go that far. We use our face so much in everyday interactions. . .I don't think I could really give that up."

Nermine's vibrant, sky-blue veil curled elegantly around her head. When I first arrived in Egypt, I found it strange, and almost unsettling to see large crowds of women wearing headscarves. By now, I found it beautiful. It was a striking way to present facial beauty—to surround the face with a field of brilliant colour. And by preserving the hair for the husband and the home, it made this beauty more rare, more special, and more sacred.

"This is just to wear around men who are not from your family," Nermine told us. "It's too bad you girls aren't here for longer. . .I would take you to some of the women-only beaches in Hurghada.

You should *see* some of the things our women wear there! It's like. . .California!"

Nermine told us that she had argued online with many Westerners about Islam and the veil.

"So many people think that we are forced to wear it," she said, rolling her eyes. "I constantly meet people on the internet who think that here in Egypt women aren't allowed to go to school or have jobs, and that our husbands beat us and keep us inside. I mean— really," she said, laughing. "Do I *look* oppressed?"

"Where we are from," Kristen said, "you can't get explanations such as this this. We see the Middle East through our media only. And you know how bad that is."

"Yeah," I continued. "I mean, we know that what we watch on the news is basically propaganda, even on some of the better stations. So we know what not to believe. . .but we don't have any other information to fill the void. In fact, that's one of the reasons we came to the Middle East. . .to see it for ourselves."

"Yes," Nermine said, "Nickie was telling me something about a film project, right?"

"Exactly," I said. "The idea is to document a different side of the Middle East. . .the things our friends at home don't see on CNN."

"Well," said Nermine, pointedly, "and what topics have you done so far? Camel men and garbage people? Are you going home to show *that* side of Egypt to North Americans?"

I opened my mouth to protest, but my tongue babbled and refused to make sense.

"Well," Nickie explained, "we're looking for personal stories. And in the end of the day, they have to be interesting enough to get on television."

"Right," said Nermine. "Well you could also show normal things too. That's what people usually don't see in North America. . .the normal life of most Arabs. They think that our countries are full of deserts and terrorists. . .they don't know that our lives and their lives are actually very similar."

I nodded. "Yeah, you should have heard the reactions we got when we told people we were coming here. The most common response was 'try not to get shot.' But really, it would be easier to get robbed in Vancouver than it is in Cairo! Egypt is one of the safest countries I've ever visited. Everyone just watches too much TV."

"You see, I think I'm kind of lucky," said Nermine, "because I get to see both sides. I watch CNN, and I also watch Al-Jazeera, Egyptian news, and other Arabic stations. The difference is unbelievable. I get to see what both sides show, and what both sides don't show."

"So what are some things that our media shows and that yours doesn't?" Nickie asked.

"Well, one thing that I think our people really need to see is the American soldiers in Iraq who really don't want to be there. When I first saw that, I was shocked! You never see anything like that on Arabic television. People here need to understand that a lot of Americans don't want the war at all."

"And what about the reverse?," I asked. "Like what are some things you would like our media to show about the Middle East that it doesn't?"

"Well, one of the things that they never seem to show is that our societies are actually cosmopolitan and tolerant as well. We have lots of Christians in Egypt. . .and we all live together just fine. We have for hundreds of years."

I sat silent for a moment, recalling Tamer.

"Well," I said, "I got the impression that Christians and Muslims here don't really like each other, but they just get along in public so there is no violence. I'm friends with a some Christians from Cairo, and they don't really seem to like Muslims."

Nermine sighed.

"Christians here are often like that. . .why? I don't understand it. But really, we accept them. It's in our religion. . .Mohammed forbade forced conversions. Really, I don't know why they have to be so racist sometimes. But not all of them are. I have many Christian friends."

"Hmm," I mused. "I guess first impressions can be misleading. I've met some Muslims too who don't seem to like Christians. . .I just thought that was the way it was."

"We feel a bond with Christians," she said. "In the Qu'ran, there is a surah about Mary, Jesus' mother. It is one of the most beautiful surahs in the whole book. Muslims love her. And," she noted with a smile, "in every picture of Mary I have seen. . .she is wearing the veil!"

Nermine explained to us that Christians had been around forever in the Middle East, and how Muslims have always shown respect to other People of the Book.

"We lived peacefully with Jews as well, for over a thousand years, until Israel came along. There were even Jews in Egypt. Really, I hate it when we see on Western TV that Muslims are intolerant. Some of them are, of course. But most of us are just normal, peace-loving people who are trying to do good."

"We're Muslims," she said, softly. "We don't bite!"

As the night wore on, we decided we should get back to the train station. Nermine got us a cab there, and translated for us when we were buying tickets. When she found out I had already paid for the cab, she became annoyed, since she felt that, as the host, she should have done it. It was one of those silly ritualized gratitude dances that I've played too many times to count, whose rules change from culture to culture.

Like a true Egyptian host, she stood with us on the platform, waiting to put us on the train. It was a full thirty-five minutes late.

She smiled. "Egyptian time," she said.

"It's a pity you aren't here longer," she told Nickie. "I have a lot of great friends here—friends who speak English too. We could take you out for a good time. . .to bars and places with live music. Really—I can show you young people with ripped clothing and crazy hair just like in Canada. . .and rock bands and everything. That's what you should be filming here. You should show North America that really, we're just like you!"

Nermine hugged the two girls. Nickie promised to send me back with a camera to film her suggestion. We thanked her for a lovely evening, all silently regretting that Nickie and Kristen couldn't be here for at least another day here to spend more time with her. My sister's eyes were shining. It was only her second day in Egypt, and I knew that Nermine had just made her trip that much more incredible.

"It was nice to meet you," she said to me.

"And it was truly a pleasure meeting you," I said back. "When I come back from this trip around the Middle East, I want to spend at least a week or two in Alexandria, so we can meet up again if you like. And have some more discussions."

"Absolutely," she said.

"So this isn't really goodbye," I told her, "I'll see you again."

7

UNDER MARTIAL LAW

From: gary_nelson@telus.net
To: kieran_nelson@hotmail.com; kristennelson@uvic.ca
Subject: Civil War in Lebanon
Date: Thu, 22 Nov 2007 08:47:47-0800

Mes chers enfants:

The CBC reported last night that open civil war in Lebanon is imminent. Imminent being TOMORROW (i.e., Friday). If Lebanese politicians locked in a Beirut hotel cannot agree on a new President by tomorrow, the country is expected to dissolve in civil war.

This was not the usual Chicken Little CBC report. This was Nahleh Ayed's report. She's there, she speaks the language, she's a marvelous correspondent AND she

*knows that when you want to find out about the pros-
pects of war, you interview the waiter in the (empty)
popular restaurant, the teacher in the (closing) local
school, and the politician (trying to put on a brave face)
in the only room the hotel that can be made available
for interviews for security reasons.*

*The Lebanese do civil war like no one else. Afghans
and Congolese don't hold a candle. All the pressures
of the Middle East are reflected there; allegiances and
alliances shift with a speed and complexity one cannot follow.*

My advice:

*Don't go there; don't even think about 'citizen journal-
ism' (which anyone with an AK47 will read as 'spy');
tell Sean to get his ass out while he can; and if it 'starts,'
whether by open street battles or simply an increase
in bombings and assassinations, be very, very careful wherever you go. Every conflict in the region that
I have observed has had unforeseen repercussions in
other countries. The US, Israel, Syria and Iran will all
be in the thick of it.*

Indeed, Lebanon was on the brink of civil war.
The election that was scheduled to be held was not
held. There was no candidate that every side in the
country could agree upon. The president stepped

down on the anointed day, and left the army in charge of the country. Sean was deep in Beirut, staying in a cheap hotel packed with amateur Western journalists. On his blog, he detailed every day of the lead-up to the election, including his plan to get smashed with his buddies if the succession wasn't decided by the day the former president stepped down.

I was in Cairo with Nickie and Kristen, following each new BBC internet report with grave seriousness. Beirut was our next stop, and a very important stop. Through some loophole in the visa system, the only way we could travel to both Lebanon and Syria without wasting time and money at embassies was to arrive at Beirut international airport and then take a taxi to Damascus. Without the entry stamp from that airport, we would not be able to see Lebanon or Syria. It was Beirut or bust.

But a civil war? I hadn't expected things to get this bad.

Civil war has been so frequent in Lebanon that was almost a cultural tradition. Every thirty years or so, the handful of tribes crowded together on this little postage stamp of land fight bitterly for political power and economic control. The most recent one began in 1979 and didn't stop for fifteen years. Beirut became a brutal battleground, divided block by block by Lebanon's many militia groups. It was a bloodbath, and civil society could barely function, but the Lebanese lived on.

The joke among visiting Westerners is that Lebanon isn't really a country in the first place. Lebanon is a piece of geographical shrapnel left over from the collapse of the Ottoman Empire, the Turkish state that united and governed the whole of the Middle East for five hundred years. When the Allied powers dismembered the empire in 1918, the province of Syria fell under French control. Long before, France had developed special ties with a group of Christians in Syria, called the Maronites, who lived on the slopes of Mt. Lebanon by the sea. The Maronites began to speak French and styled their religion after French Catholicism.

Revolt came quickly to the new nation of Syria. King Feisal had just waged a long and bitter guerrilla war against the Turks alongside the famed Lawrence of Arabia; he had been promised an independent Arab state under British guidance. When Syria was tossed to France as a bargaining chip, Feisal again mobilized his forces for war.

The Maronites saw their chance. They declared a holy allegiance to France, gathered armies to fight the Syrians, and raised a new flag on the slopes of Mt. Lebanon: the French tricolour with a Lebanese cedar in the center. After the war, the French cut them a piece out of Syria as a gift for their loyalty. They called it Lebanon, after the kingdom in the Bible which sent cedars to Jerusalem for King Solomon's temple. The constitution was set up to ensure that the Christians would always remain in power.

There was only one problem. The Christians weren't the only people there.

Today, Lebanon is a patchwork of half a dozen tribes. There are the Sunni Muslims, who have been there since time immemorial. In the Shouf mountains there are the Druze: a breakoff sect of Islam whose followers believe in reincarnation. There are the Orthodox Christians, who outnumber even the Maronites in population. There are the Shia Muslims, who were traditionally labourers on the large Christian estates. . .they remain Lebanon's poorest class today. There are Palestinians, refugees who flooded the country after the 1948 war in which the Israelis captured their land. And finally, there are the Maronites.

"The Maronites rule Lebanon through powerful mafia families," we were told by Andrew, a friend of my fathers from Canada who had married a Shia Muslim woman and settled in Lebanon. "They used to rule the country through their large estates of land. Now they've all moved to Beirut and bought banks and casinos. On the outside, this country is supposed to be a democracy. It's not. Every seat in the parliament is occupied by a mafia don. They say on the news that this is an election!" he laughed. "Not even close! It's a negotiation between the godfathers and the heads of the other factions. They are negotiating on a man that is neutral enough that they all don't have to go to war."

You could sense the tension even on the internet. The Western press smelled a sensation and flocked to Beirut. On the BBC, on the CBC, on CNN, on the Guardian, on Fox News. . .it was everywhere. Lebanon was going to erupt. Even Sean's blog started to take on a stormcrow tune.

And then suddenly it all changed. The 'election' was postponed again, until the godfathers could agree upon on a leader. And this time they found one. General Suleiman was chosen as a candidate for president. And suddenly, the press shut up. The CBC started running articles on the Annapolis conference. The BBC started running articles on the English teacher in Sudan who got arrested for naming a teddy bear 'Mohammed.' The international media, in an embarrassed moment, conveniently forgot what last week's sensation was about, and began to run Chicken Little reports on something else.

We bought tickets for Beirut the next day.

My first impression of the city was a crowd of about a hundred people waiting for arrivals in the airport. They were dressed very nicely in European-style clothing, and bumped elbows with one another waiting for their relatives to arrive. The rain outside was pouring down just like good old

Vancouver. After negotiating an overpriced taxi, we shuttled off to the hotel where Sean was staying.

The Hotel Talal was run by Zaher and Wessam, whom Sean affectionately called 'The Druze Brothers.' Wessam would always croon or sing in a pretty little falsetto; Zaher would make animal noises. Every once in a while you would come down to the fridge to get a beer, and you would here the soft mewing of a cat, or the rough grunting of a gorilla. They ran the Hotel Cheap, where they had cheap beds, cheap rooms, and cheap cervezas.

For dinner, we ambled down to a shop called Makhlouf's. 'Surly George' Makhlouf had a shop stocked with Christian insignia, little models of cedar trees to sell to tourists, a fridge full of pastries that were stale but which we ate anyways, and a sandwich iron that he would use to grill us two-dollar sandwiches on Lebanese flatbread.

In the warm common room of the hostel, we cracked open some cold ones and laid back to celebrate our arrival in the country. Some of us sat on the couches, while my sister typed away on the common computer. Sean told me how all of his friends had a roaring laugh over my father's email. With a beer in hand, he leaned on a table with one elbow.

"Dangerous? Oh yeah, it's totally dangerous. Right now we're in a country that's technically under martial law. How unsafe do you feel?"

The next day we did some sightseeing. We jumped in a cab and shuttled off to Baalbek, the wonderfully preserved ruin of an ancient Roman temple. It was a two-hour bus ride there from the capital. On the way, we passed a high bridge that had two large sections missing. Dozens of twisted pieces of rebar poked out of the shattered concrete.

"Bombed by Israel" said Sean.

In 2006, the Israelis bombed Lebanon and invaded most of the south of the country. But it wasn't the Lebanese state they were attacking, it was Hezbollah. Hezbollah is a guerrilla organization that emerged in the Shia population of southern Lebanon in the 1980s, while the Israelis were occupying parts of the country during the civil war. For the past twenty years Hezbollah has waged a guerrilla campaign against the Israeli forces—during the Lebanese occupation and after the Israelis retreated, often attacking across the border and abducting soldiers.

In July of 2006, Hezbollah showered rockets on an Israeli settlement, and attacked two armoured vehicles with anti-tank rockets, killing three people. They abducted two soldiers of the Israeli Defence Forces. The IDF retaliated strongly, ordering air and artillery attacks. They blanketed the south of the country with bombs, along with targets in Beirut. They even bombed the bridges out of the Shia communities so that the people could not escape.

My Maronite friend Najat was there during that war. She and her father were about to cross a bridge in their car, when she heard a screeching in the sky. "Dad, they're bombing us!" she screamed. She watched as a bomb destroyed the bridge in front of them, right where they would have been two minutes later. For five or ten minutes, she told me, it was Armageddon. Bombs rained all around them, but miraculously missed their car.

That was enough for her. Beirut airport had been bombed, so she taxied to Syria and flew to Dubai, where she has been working ever since.

On the way past the bridge, I asked a soldier who was in our microbus why Israel bombed it. I got a sneer that turned politely into a dark grin. "That's not really a question I can answer. That's a question for the Israeli High Command."

Baalbek was red, vast, and spectacular. It was totally deserted; the tourist high season was in the summer. It was cloudy and cold, but it was still fantastic. In a similar archeological site in Italy or Greece, everything would be fenced off, and there would be multiple guards around telling us not to touch this, and to be careful of that. But this was Lebanon. Baalbek was our own personal playground. We could climb on anything we wanted to, move stones around, and photograph the whole experience.

The ruins were colossal. All that is left of the temple is six massive pillars that seem to reach to the sky. The Romans, with nowhere near our level of technology, built buildings as high as most of our large structures out of materials thousands of times heavier. And they did this with a wave of their hand—they took some model city in the Italian heartland and copied it all over the Mediterranean. I had visited the same ancient town in France, Italy, Egypt, Greece, and Turkey. Here it was again in Lebanon. A leftover fragment of an empire that had long since crumbled.

Outside, the Temple Townies were having a bad season. They swarmed us, peddling postcards, keychains, guidebooks, and Hezbollah T-Shirts. We bought some. We chose between yellow and black, and went off smiling to each other, having just funded terrorism in a very touristy way.

In the microbus on the way back, we debated prices with the cabbie, and Kristen and Nickie turned towards the windows and pretended not to notice the man in the front seat who sat staring at them greedily. I peered out the window and studied the countryside in the fading light.

Something had bothered me deeply on the way to Baalbek. It was all the bullet holes.

We had driven through a fair amount of Beirut before reaching the highway. Along the way, I saw evidence of the civil war. So much evidence in fact, that I felt like a complete green tourist for remarking on it. There were bullet holes everywhere. The sides of any building over twenty years old were pock-marked with holes that ranged from the size of a coin to the size of a fist. This was not only the case on important buildings on major routes. This was true of simple homes that were tucked away in the corners of neighbourhoods. Shop owners would pull down metal curtains to lock their stores for the night, and the curtains would be riddled with holes. There were bullet holes covering the building across the street from my hotel. . .and when I looked closely, I realized that there were ample bullet holes on my hotel itself.

Downtown Beirut, on the other hand, was a plethora of new buildings. I had never seen so many construction cranes in one place. Twenty years before, the area in between Christian West Beirut and the rest of town was a flat gravel patch laden with shrapnel. Since the days of peace, developers had bought up the land, and were building on it so as not to lose their investments, despite the imminent civil war.

A few of the buildings downtown did not just have bullet holes. They had bomb holes. Large, gaping holes the size of a car had been blown through the wall by some rocket or grenade. The buildings had long since been abandoned, and stood rotting in the center of town—grim visual reminders of past violence.

Across the street from our hotel was a place called Martyr's Square. In it stands a monument: a statue of the goddess Liberty with four dying young men. It was built by Lebanon to commemorate four martyrs who died trying to gain independence from France. But a closer inspection revealed something far more eerie.

The entire statue was shot up. The goddess Liberty looked like a pasta strainer. One of the young men had the lower part of his arm blown off, and a fist-sized hole in the center of his back. There are bullet holes in the cheeks and the temples of the dying men, giving the frightening impression that they are dying because they were shot.

The statue chilled me. I had never before seen a more perfect accidental symbol of a country. A monument to independence riddled with bullets. An independent Lebanon that barely keeps from tearing itself apart.

Yet, to walk along the street, you could never tell. There were women dressed in high fashions adorning the bars, French businessmen sipping cappuccinos in the cafes, and Makhlouf was constantly selling sandwiches. Everything seemed normal, albeit a little tense.

I thought for a while about the dozens of faces I saw waiting at the airport, and a chill crept across my skin. They all seemed so normal: well-dressed, content, waiting for their loved ones to get off the plane from Egypt. Yet just one week before, how many of those people were ready to murder each other in the name of their respective tribes?

8

OUR FAVORITE REFUGEE

Ahed was a refugee from Syria, so I heard. But it was difficult to remember this when I met him. I shook the hand of this stocky, smiley, twenty three year-old while Sean led the way through the back streets to some tiny local drinking hole. Ahed would have been mistaken for a local on the streets of Vancouver or New York. He spoke excellent English, and sported a black hooded sweatshirt and jeans much like any Western youth. The only discrepancy, as Sean pointed out with a laugh, were his black dress shoes with long, pointy ends.

"You should see the suit he's got to go with those clown shoes!" Sean said. "He looks sharp. Made some Lebanese women crazy at the club the other night."

Ahed took this with good humour. We ordered some Almazas, the cheap and tasty local brew. Within minutes they were trading jokes about the most recent characters to darken the doorway of the Hotel Talal.

"So, today Steve came up to me and told me all about the interview he had with somebody whose name I had never heard," said Sean. "So of course, I ask 'oh, who is that?' And then he hands me a book on Lebanon written by the guy. I love how he probably practiced the whole thing in the bathroom before he talked to me. I can't *stand* that guy!"

Steve was a chubby, bearded Floridan who took a pause in his undergraduate degree to come to Lebanon to pretend to be a journalist. If you talked to him for thirty seconds you realized that he was out to become the world's next great expert on the Middle East, and that he was very self-conscious of everyone's opinion of him. He was the kind of guy that would pretend to read a magazine while listening to every word of our conversation, and still be too daft to realize that we noticed him doing it ages ago and started making up wholesale lies for amusement. Just that morning Sean and I had convinced him that my father was a high-level operative for Canadian intelligence.

"Hey Steve, come in here!" Ahed hollered to him once, when we were all sitting on our beds in our dorm room. We had just been poking fun at his gullibility, and I was wondering aloud how long it would take before Steve eavesdropped just at the moment we were deriding him. But Ahed decided it would be funnier to put his foot right in it.

Steve appeared at the door. "Hey guys, what's going on?"

"We just got an interview with Amin Gemayel!" said Ahed.

"Really? You did?" Steve was shocked. Amin Gemayel was the head of the fascist Christian party, and its corresponding militia. He was a Maronite godfather, and one of the most powerful men in Lebanon.

"Yeah! We just talked to his aides and they say they want to put him on an American TV station."

The four Canadians in the room shot each other nervous glances, in disbelief that Ahed was concocting this embarrassing lie. We were sure that Steve would see right through it in a matter of minutes, and find out that he had been the laughingstock of our troupe for some time. All of us sat on our beds and studied our computer screens while Ahed constructed this fairy tale.

Ahed wasn't a terribly good liar. But Steve never saw through it. He was drooling with jealousy by the end of it, and begged to be invited along.

"We'll have to talk it over with the security. They will want your name and passport number.

They may have a maximum number of people that they will let in. We'll see Steve, we'll see."

Steve left back into his own room to spend some time alone with his inferiority complex. Ahed closed the door to our room and laughed himself sick.

Yes, Ahed had natural charisma of sorts. He ordered another Almaza, and had to shout over the din of the bar to tell me he an Italian joke that he knew. Sean slapped himself in the face and muttered. "Oh my God, I've heard this one *so* many times!"

Ahed was a Greek Syrian. He came from a community of Greek Orthodox Christians in Damascus. He explained that his great-grandfather lived in Ottoman-occupied Greece, and he and much of his community settled in Damascus while the Ottoman Empire was still alive and well. Then, in 1918, the Great Powers divided it up, and Ahed's family became citizens of Syria.

"So," I explained. "My friend Nickie is here with her giant camera. We have tentative contracts with a few news stations: Current TV in California, Real News in Canada, and maybe even Al-Jazeera English. We are making short documentaries to sell to these stations, and we are looking for personal stories. Would you be willing to do an interview, Ahed? Do you want to go on camera and tell what happened to you in Syria? You might even be on TV."

"Sure, why not?" he said with a grin. We clinked our beers together.

Sean talked to the Druze Brothers and secured the use of a hotel room. We chose one in the corner of the building that had plenty of light. Kristen went and found a chair for Ahed, Nickie sat preparing her camera: fitting together its many parts, and getting the microphone ready. I sat on the bed, conspiring with Sean about the questions we were going to ask and how we were going to ask them.

Ahed came in and sat down. We rolled camera.

"Could you please introduce yourself for the camera?"

"My name is Ahed al-Hendi, and I am from Syria."

"Could you explain why you are in Lebanon?"

"I am here as a political refugee from Bashar Assad's government. I am wanted by the secret police, and I am here applying for refugee status from the United Nations."

"What did you do in Syria to become wanted by the police?"

Ahed started into his story. A few years ago, during the beginning of his university studies, he began to be interested in politics. His parents ignored it for a while, but eventually they intervened. They sat him down and told him not to go into politics. Everyone in Syria who goes into politics, they said, either becomes a corrupt official that works for the regime, or they go to prison for opposing it. That's just what happens.

He understood. In that difficult moment he decided to give up his interest in politics, and pursue something else. Perhaps he would follow his older brother's example and become an engineer.

Then, his close friend Hussam and seven others were taken by the Mukhabarat, the infamous Syrian secret police. They had established a pro-democracy human rights group in their university, and they were arrested, sentenced for conspiracy against the state, and jailed. Ahed went into politics full tilt.

He began to meet and conspire with members of the Syrian opposition. The 'Syrian opposition' is a broad name for anyone in the country who supports a democratic state, and who wants the end of Bashar Assad's Stalinist regime. While his friends were being interrogated in one of Syria's dungeons, Ahed was busy at work. He wrote against the Syrian government, in English and in Arabic, on different websites under an assumed name.

And then, one day, he signed into the wrong net cafe. It was run by an Iraqi refugee. . .one of two million who have fled Iraq since the American invasion. This man was trying to get residency in

Syria, so he collaborated with the secret police. Ahed used the cafe a few times to post his writings to the net. And then, one day while he was sitting and typing, the Mukhabarat arrived. The Iraqi had provided them with screenshots, printouts of his writings. . .all manner of evidence that Ahed had indeed conspired against the government.

And Ahed was taken away, intimidated and interrogated by the secret police, and thrown in solitary confinement for over a month.

"They let me have a cell. . .only one meter and a half square, no light at all, and only a bit of food once a day. Once I begged the guards to even open the food slot, so that I could have a bit of light in the cell. They refused.

"They arrested me at the same time as my cousin. He was in a cell close to mine. One day, they took him out and tortured him. They did this close to my cell, so that I could hear it all happen. They have so many types of torture in the Syrian prisons. Sometimes they pull your fingernails, sometimes they beat you with electrical cables. And they have this chair they call the German Chair, because it was used for torture by the Nazis. I don't know what they did to my cousin, but he cracked. They would have tortured me too, but they got all the information they needed out of him.

"They told my family I had been killed. Dead in a car accident. My family grieved for a long time, until I finally got out and contacted them. Who does this? Who tells your family that you are dead when you are not?"

Eventually, they released him. Outside, he was as devoted as ever to the downfall of Bashar Assad. Three months out of prison, he realized that unless he left the country, the same thing would happen again. He went into exile. With his father to send him money abroad, he left for Jordan. Then he began to fear the Jordanian police would deport him. . .so he made his way to Egypt and stayed in Cairo. During this time he continued his activities against the Syrian government. He drew scathing political cartoons and posted them, again under an assumed name. He continued to write.

Ahed eventually wrote some things against the Egyptian government, and fled Egypt as well. He ended up in Lebanon—on Syria's doorstep. Lebanon, he said, was a lot more democratic than Syria. Since they were forced out in 2005, the Syrian army no longer has had a presence in Lebanon—although it is absolutely certain that they have more than a few spies roaming the streets. Yet Ahed felt safe here, and what's more, his father got a chance to visit him.

Now, he has chosen a new life. He applied for refugee status at the United Nation High Commission for Refugees office in Beirut. And ever since he has lived in Beirut, waiting for the decision to come through. He said he wanted to go to America, where he has family.

Ahed struck something in me. Here was a man who had fought for what he believed, and for this, he gave up his home—the ability to be near his family and friends for his whole life. Now he worked on towards his goal, the downfall of Bashar Assad, with his head held high, laughing and joking the whole way.

The interview finished. As I returned to my room, I began to wonder what the Syrian government might think of the footage we were taking.

"We just took sides" I said to my friends, when we returned to our hotel room.

By filming what we had just filmed, we had tacitly declared ourselves friends of the Syrian opposition, and opponents of the Syrian regime. It was another reminder that it was impossible to investigate the region without becoming involved in the local politics. But we felt comfortable with this—the tyrannical regime had tortured our friend, and we felt right in opposing it. And besides, we now had a piece of a story on film, and we needed to pursue more footage to make it complete.

That night we went out drinking. Ahed put on a fine-looking black suit and some cologne.

"When I wanted to impress the people at UNHCR," he said, "I thought perhaps I should buy a suit. So I bought this, and I went to the interview. And they said 'oh. . .you look like you're doing just fine. . .you're a refugee, you say?' So the next time I went, I did not wear this suit."

He punched me in the shoulder. "I don't look like a refugee, do I?"

We went to the bar and each ordered a drink that almost overflowed with vodka. Discos balls lit up clouds of smoke in the dark club packed with Lebanese youth, all clad in avant-garde European fashion that clashed with our own. We danced and drank and enjoyed ourselves that night. But the whole while, I couldn't shake one surreal thought. Ahed's sense of humour, his smiles, and his easy personality almost made one forget that within him lay a past marked by suffering, and a violent resolve.

One thing he said during the interview stood out.

We asked him if he was afraid that the Mukhabarat would find him in Lebanon. He said no, but he was careful who he talked to. He looked at the camera with an honest grin.

"But, if they come for me again, really, I hope they shoot me and finish the job. Really, I would rather be shot than go back to the prison. Because, when you are in the prison, you really wish to die."

9

EVA KURDISTAN

We found Ahed across the street, chatting on his mobile phone.

"I spoke to the family" he told us. "They said we should come."

We were off to film our next group of contacts. These were Kurds. . .a people whose traditional land is divided by the borders of Syria, Turkey, Iraq, and Iran. They are ruled by Turks, Arabs, and Persians, yet they are a people and a culture unto themselves. On the street we shook hands with Sirwan, a lanky youth of twenty-one, and Jihad, a balding man in his mid thirties. Ahed led us on a walk across Beirut to the family's house.

"We just have to act normal, and unfazed" my sister said. There were soldiers and policemen patrolling the streets on foot. Nickie was carrying her camera in her beer cooler, and I was bringing the tripod.

"Exactly," I said nonchalantly, "I'm just taking my tripod for a walk."

Kristen laughed. Nickie didn't.

We expected the worst when we went through a certain checkpoint. Gates barred the way, and razor wire was stretched across what was otherwise a very normal street. The checkpoint looked very out of place—the deserted street was lined with yuppie cafes; it could have been in central Seattle or Montreal. When the soldier opened Sean's computer case, Nickie looked tense. We knew we were all going to get searched. The soldier flipped open Nickie's beer cooler and saw the giant camera. Then he waved us on with a bored grunt.

We were led into a corridor to a shabby-looking building, with cement instead of tile on the ground floor, and water pooling in the murk. Our party climbed a long stairway in near-pitch darkness. There was a musty smell. That's right, I thought. This is where refugees live.

The door opened, and we were welcomed in by a middle-aged man and his wife, and by their two young daughters. The apartment was well lit; it was covered with furniture and fine carpets. The man and his wife were well-dressed, and they clearly lived comfortably. I nodded as another stereotype vanished in smoke. That's right. This is where refugees live.

We all sat down, and father launched right into his story—Ahed translated. Soon they paused, and Ahed leaned over and asked me "when do you want to begin filming?" I looked up at Nickie. She was as dumbstruck as I. . .we had not even introduced ourselves.

"Well. . .right away!"

I introduced myself first of all to the father. He told me he was Ibrahim, and then he introduced his wife and his very polite children. Ibrahim got up and offered everyone a cigarette. . .which a few of us had to continually refuse throughout the evening. His wife and daughters scuttled away to the back room to change into traditional Kurdish clothing for the film. Nickie pieced together her camera.

Sean and I looked at each other. Zelika's familiar red light blinked on and off. Nickie's eye signaled me to begin.

"My first question is, please tell us who you are and why you are in Lebanon."

"My name is Ibrahim, and I am a Kurd from Syria. I left Syria four years ago, because of the insecurity there. Now I am in Beirut, and my family is applying for refugee status in a Western country."

His wife answered the same. Sean and I kept the questions rolling.

"You see, in the Middle East about four years ago, there was a program called Star Academy. This was like your American Idol, only for the Middle East. My daughter Eva at this time was sixteen, and she was the top of her class. The class was voting on the two singers in Star Academy, and they wrote the names of the two singers on the board. One of them had the first name of Bashar. . .you know, just like Bashar Assad, the President of Syria.

"After the competition was done, she got up to erase this name from the board. And a girl from her class had a father in the secret service. She reported that my daughter had erased this Bashar's name from the board. Eva was hauled away and interrogated by four branches. . .all four branches of the Syrian secret service. They said she had publicly spoken against president Bashar Assad by erasing his name."

"Later, they arrested me, and interrogated me. They accused me of raising my daughters to hate the state. They asked why my daughter had done this. I was very afraid; afraid for my family, and afraid they would put me in prison."

He explained more. He was a member of the Yikati party, which the state was against, and he had participated in the Qamishly uprising. The Yikati party fought peacefully for the rights of Kurds in Syria. . .and was an illegal organization.

The Qamishly uprising went unnoticed in the Western press. It began at a soccer match when the team from a predominantly Arab city was playing the local Kurdish side. A large portrait of Saddam Hussein—whom the Kurds despise for gassing their people in northern Iraq—was displayed above the ring. The announcer began to hurl racist insults at the Kurdish crowd. A riot ensued. Meanwhile, the television informed the whole city that two children had been killed in the arena. . .this made throngs of worried parents flock to the center of town. Syrian plants in the audience began to throw rocks and bottles to accelerate the violence. The riot police arrived, including men standing on APCs firing Kalashnikovs into the crowds. By the end of the day, 37 Kurds lay dead in the streets.

Kurds across the country rioted. It was the year 2004.

After her arrest Ibrahim's daughter was terrified and traumatized. She was expelled from school. She lost her entire opportunity for an education because the government wanted to scare some local Kurds. Perhaps they were using her to strike at Ibrahim for his political activities. He considered his other seven children, five of them younger than Eva. He feared for his own freedom; he feared for their future. It was time to leave.

"We hate Lebanon" the mother explained, her head wrapped in a black-patterned Kurdish shawl.

"It is not our country. We have no family here. We want to go to Denmark, that is where my sister lives." She smiled and chuckled. "I can tell you, if I knew we would go into exile, I would not have had eight children!"

One of Ibrahim's daughters was married in Saudi Arabia, another was in Dubai. Eva was at work, they explained. . .she would be back later that night. Ibrahim's two sons were asleep in another room, and his two daughters has long since evaporated into the kitchen.

Ibrahim spoke.

"When my son was born I wanted to call him Azad. Azad is a Kurdish name. Yet when I received the birth certificate, there was no 'Azad,' but 'Mohammed.' Now his legal name is Mohammed, but everyone calls him Azad." He shook his head and smirked. "We cannot even name our children in Syria."

His daughters appeared at the door with tea. Tea in the Middle East is often an excuse to drink excessive quantities of sugar. We gulped it down with difficulty and smiles.

"My name is Jihad, and I left Syria because of political activity."

Jihad and Sirwan were also Kurds. Jihad was a born writer, and through websites and newspapers he had written out against the Syrian regime. Both were members of the Yikati party. . .it seemed that every self-respecting Kurd was. Sirwan left Syria of his own accord, and while abroad he signed a statement in solidarity with Alan Johnson, the BBC journalist who was kidnapped by extremists in Gaza. This caused rumblings at home. The secret police began to question his friends in Syria about his activities. Sirwan decided to stay in Lebanon rather than risk going home.

What fascinated me about this situation was the loose chain of trust that got us to take these people's stories on camera. Nickie often told me stories of how many hours she had to spend with someone before they had enough confidence in her to open up on camera. Yet here, we built trust with a snap of our fingers. Sean had spent three weeks with Ahed, and the rest of us had just met him. Ahed knew Jihad and Sirwan, and Sean had only briefly met them. Jihad and Sirwan knew the family. That chain of contacts, plus the Kurds' wish to tell the world their stories, produced the incredible chemistry of that room. We conducted a full interview, with the excited cooperation of nine refugees, just miles away from a country that would jail them all for such confessions.

For them to be there was a risk. Meeting foreigners they didn't know was a risk; giving away information about their lives and their identities was a risk. For refugees, almost everything in life is a risk.

And some risks, they believed, were worth taking.

After the batteries ran out on the camera, Nickie plopped some small Canada pins into Sean's palm. We distributed them as small thank-you gifts to our film subjects. Someone disappeared into a room and emerged with honorary pins of the flag of Kurdistan. They pinned them on our shirts and embraced us.

They asked if we wouldn't mind staying for dinner. Of course we accepted. "Prepare to get fed to death" I said to Sean. A tablecloth was brought out and laid on the ground. And within minutes it was laden with Lebanese flatbread, a thin cousin of tzatziki, chick-pea soup, plates of fresh vegetables, and two heaping plates of steaming meat dumplings that I affectionately named 'Kurdogies.'

We tucked into the delicious meal. As expected, the wife wanted to see Nickie and my sister leave with bulging tummies. They refused politely, while I tapped my own gut in satisfaction. As Sean wolfed down a third portion, Sirwan commented on his thin Asian frame and its disproportion to his boundless appetite.

A discussion ensued after dinner. We talked a bit more about the Kurds and their objectives. The family liked all things Kurdish except two things: they did not like the PKK liberation group in Turkey, and they did not like Saladin. They did not like the PKK because it used violence. They were peaceful people. Sean even asked them if they wanted a free Kurdistan one day.

"We simply want our rights to live as citizens in Syria. We don't want our own country. . .Syria is fine. We want to live there and have basic human rights."

Sean pushed them on Saladin. He was the most famous Kurd in history: he led the Arabs to great victory against the Christian armies during the Crusades. They hated him. They said he was the reason that the Western powers came and divided up Kurdistan in the shape of a cross. . .for beating back Europe's armies eight hundred years before. Sean's face dropped in disappointment. I think a little part of him died. Sean loved Saladin.

Suddenly came a knock at the door. In walked the star of the show: Eva, finally back from her job in Beirut. She was twenty now, and stunningly gorgeous. She was a bit flustered to see the house filled with people she didn't know, and her dad briefed her on the situation while Sean and I conspired on questions. Nickie set up Zelika, and we got ready to shoot.

The light blinked; the camera rolled. Everyone went silent. All eyes in the room went to her. She looked at us warily, unsure of her new interrogators.

"Could you please explain who you are, and why you left Syria?" I asked.

"My name is Eva. . .and. . .I don't know why I left Syria." She stammered, and studied the ceiling. The light glinted in her half-born tears. Her father spoke to her to reassure her. Then the answers came.

"I erased the name of someone from Star Academy from the board. One week later I was taken to the station and interrogated. They did not care that I was a child; they intimidated and frightened me like I was a grown man. To this day I am afraid when I see soldiers. The soldiers took over my class. . .the students were so afraid they could not even bear to explain the mistake. Before this incident, I was the top of my class. After it, I was expelled from school. I have seen all my friends graduate university, but I cannot. Because of this."

He tears were obvious now. In between translations, she stared me right in the eye, with her brave and pained smile. It ruined me. I was some stranger from Canada who ambushed her in her home with a giant camera and very personal questions. She didn't even know me. . .and here she was, telling all. I stared at the floor.

Sean spoke. "All these men were chased away for political activities, but you were the only one here who was punished for something totally innocent. Is this common?"

"Of course." she replied. "Because we're Kurds."

She had never done anything political in her life before this incident. Now she goes to rallies in Lebanon against the Syrian government. She works as a secretary in Beirut. One day, she said, she hopes to pick up where she left off. . .to finish her studies at a western university.

Nickie had a question before we turned off the camera. "What did you want to be when you were sixteen?"

"I wanted to be a fashion designer for the clothes on TV." She smiled bravely as she recalled the vanished dream. Again, she stared right at me.

At the end, I approached her. Her eyes were dried, and the pain fled her face as she shook my hand. I tried to apologize for the awkward and difficult situation we had put her through. . .but my Arabic failed me. I couldn't be elegant. . .all I could muster was a bumbling smile, an apology, and a thank you. She scribbled her email address for me.

When we left, the whole family walked down the dark stairwell to see us go. They left us with an invitation to come back and eat Kurdish food whenever we liked, and to please take our film and tell their story. They parted from us on the street, and I walked home with downcast eyes. I had the paradoxical feeling that we had just gotten our best footage yet, but we had to extract it by making that girl relive her painful and embarrassing memories.

I looked at her contact information. She had given me her telephone and email, despite that fact that I spoke no Arabic and had to write to her in English. As I read it, I understood the full effect of her treatment by this paranoid police state. Like everyone in that room, the state had meddled in her life, narrowed her future, and changed her from an indifferent civilian into a moral activist.

Her email said it all.

It was eva_kurdistan.

10

SLUMWALKING

"Is that it?"

I pointed to a place on a map of Beirut, a few kilometers south of the hostel.

"That's it" Sean answered.

"The real thing? Not something named after it?"

"No, the real thing."

We were seated at a coffee shop down the hill from the Hotel Talal. A half-eaten bean mash with some torn flatbread sat neglected on a plate in front of me. I sipped a syrupy excuse for a cappuccino to nurse my hangover. Kristen's eyes, as well as Sean's, were only half open; they could not wait to go back to the hotel and lie in bed for the remainder of this cold and breezy day. Nickie was the only one of us that looked sprightly.

I folded up the map. "Well that's where I'm headed today. It's only a few hours until dark, so I'd better take off."

I left the cafe and began to walk up the hill towards the road that would take me to my destination. My head was aching, my tongue dry, my limbs heavy. The night before, we had all gotten stupidly drunk in a Lebanese club known as the O18. I ordered a gin and tonic, and the bartender filled the glass more than half full of gin and added a tiny shot of tonic and a lime to the top. The night ended in a swimming blur; Ahed tried to kiss my sister, Nickie lost her wallet, and somehow I learned that the whole club we were in was built atop a mass grave.

It was fitting that the next day was grey and rainswept. I walked along the road in a warm jacket I had used in the Yukon and closed-toed sandals. My feet were shivering, and I tried not to think about them. Somehow it had entered my head that I was too poor to buy real shoes, which I probably wasn't. Or perhaps I just didn't want to admit to myself that the sandals I bought to walk around the Middle East were woefully inadequate when I arrived and realized the place wasn't nearly as hot and sandy as I had expected it to be.

The rain floated down in light drops as I entered Martyr's Square. The shot-up monument to independence and the blue-domed mosque were far across the street, behind a barricade of barbed wire. Escalades with tinted windows drove by, churning up puddles of water as they passed. Across the road, a soldier in green fatigues stood atop an armoured personnel carrier, leaning his arms on his gun and looking miserable and bored.

On my right, I passed the beige headquarters of the Phalangists, the fascist Maronite Christian party of Lebanon. It was diagonally across the road from our hotel; we had a really good view of it from the balcony. Two guards in military fatigues looked at me sternly as I passed. I kept my camera firmly in my pocket.

The Phalange party, whose name derives from the word 'Phalanx,' was founded by Pierre Gemayel, an athlete who competed in the Olympics in Berlin in 1936. During his stay, he was inspired by the Nazi party, and later returned to Lebanon to found the Phalangists on the principles of "God, the Nation, and the Family." The Phalange militia was one of the most powerful and heavily armed during Lebanon's civil war. His son Amin Gemayel, now well into his seventies, leads the party today.

A giant banner on the west face of the building showed the picture of a man of about forty years of age in a sharp suit, with the red and white flag of Lebanon fluttering behind him. This was Pierre's other son, Bashir Gemayel, who had briefly been president of the country in the early 1980s. During that time of fierce civil war, when the complex politics of Lebanon became almost impossible to understand, Bashir led the Phalangist militia, and coordinated its movements with the Israeli Defense Forces and the Syrian Army, which had both occupied Lebanon to try to restore order. Bashir was a strong leader, and millions of Lebanese looked to him to end the ferocious violence of the time. But on September 14, 1982, only weeks after being elected, Bashir Gemayel was assassinated in traditional Lebanese fashion—by a massive bomb. He was mourned across Lebanon. And the Phalangist leaders, furious and heartbroken, plotted a brutal act of retribution against the Palestinians, whom it was later revealed had nothing to do with the assassination in the first place.

It was the site of that act of retribution which I was going to visit today.

The day after the assassination, the IDF occupied West Beirut and surrounded the Palestinian districts. Their commander invited the Phalangist militia to enter the refugee camps of Sabra and Shatila, to destroy terrorist havens. Throughout the night, the Israelis lit up the camps with flares, as the Phalangists went from block to block, shooting everyone they could get their hands on. Whole families were lined up against a wall and executed. When they finally left, thousands of Palestinians lay dead in the streets.

The Israeli commander was a very shrewd man. He had mastered the art of being ruthless toward his enemies, and at the same time washing his own hands of the blood guilt. His name was Ariel Sharon.

I had no idea what I would actually find at Shatila, if I ever found the place. My map told me to keep walking in one direction, but all I found was a tangled maze of highways and overpasses. Beneath one of them, I came upon a massive tent city, long since abandoned. The wind blew the tent flaps back and forth; forgotten barbed-wire barricades stood at strategic points to guard the entrances.

Sean had told me about this place. Just a few weeks before, hundreds of Shia Muslims camped out here to await the results of the 'election.' If the tribes negotiated a leader who would govern only for Christians and Sunnis and leave the Shia disenfranchised, there would have been another civil war. For just as the Christians and the Sunnis have their organized militias, so too do the Shia. Theirs is known as Hezbollah.

"Excuse me, can I see your camera?"

A member of the Lebanese military approached me, after I was done photographing the tent city. He asked for my passport, which I also gave him. He took a look through my photos before deciding that I was not a spy. I was getting fairly used to this; it happened wherever I went.

When he let me go, I continued on the road to Shatila. Rain wisped down and soaked my feet and the bottom of my pants. The city grew shabbier and shabbier the farther I got away from West Beirut. I could have taken a taxi, but I didn't want to. In Cuba I learned the virtue of walking through slums when I left tourist-tailored Old Havana for a stroll through the more hidden parts of the city: where the street paving had long since disintegrated, where the real Cubans lived. Here in Lebanon, I was all too conscious that I was spending most of my time in pristine and shiny West Beirut, the side of town people thought about when they called it the "Paris of the Middle East." I knew there was much more to this city than the affluent Christian district, and I wanted to walk through the rest of it.

Bullet holes covered the local buildings, large and small. I was numb to seeing them by now; they were simply everywhere. The civil war had ended only some fifteen years ago, and I suspected it would take many years to erase all the evidence from the face of the city. And as I photographed a tiny yellow house with a tiled red roof whose wall had been splattered with bullets, I wondered if the residents of Beirut, given the way that violence recurred in Lebanon, considered fixing bullet holes to be simply a waste of time.

Eventually, I reached the place designated 'Shatila' on the map. It was a massive traffic circle, in the center of which was a giant Shia mosque. After I took some photos of it, a military man in a cubicle accosted me and asked to see my camera. He gave it the required inspection, while I smiled and waited patiently. Eventually he smiled, handed back my camera, and let me go on my way.

Whatever Shatila really was, I knew it wasn't just a mosque in a traffic circle. I walked towards some of the surrounding city—after all, I was there to see the former refugee neighbourhoods: the site of the massacre. I knew I was totally out of place, and that they had probably never seen tourists there before. But I didn't care. I was used to it.

The light was fading—if I wanted any photos of Shatila, it had to be now. I got some of somebody's fruit shop, and some children juggling a soccer ball in the street. I got a decent photo of a political poster of some Shia martyr on a wall, and also one of a barbed wire fence protecting a residential building. Was this where Palestinian refugees lived? Maybe.

My hangover begged me for food and drink. I stopped off in a nearby tiny shop and looked around at the cheap Egyptian-manufactured chocolate bars and bags of chips. The toothless shop owner smiled and shook my hand with the traditional weak Arab handshake. I paid for my food.

I turned around to see that a wall of people had assembled. I recognized the owner of the fruit shop.

They were all staring at me with frightened shock on their faces and mouths agape. I smiled back.

"Hello, what's your name?"

The crowd pushed the lone English-speaker over to talk to me. He introduced himself as Ibrahim; he looked about nineteen.

"I am Kareem" I said, using the Arabic version of my name.

"Ok, Kareem" he said with a polite smile. "Where are you from?"

"From Canada."

"What do you do?"

It would be dumb to say that I was a writer, or that I was a filmmaker, when indeed I was part both. Writers write things; filmmakers make films.

"I'm a student."

"Can I see your camera?"

He looked through the photos. Then he handed it back to me and smiled.

"Ok, Kareem. Thank you. Here, not a good place for photo. You see, Hezbollah is here, and if they see you taking photos, they will come and make big problems for you. Ok? Not little problems. Big problems. No more photo, ok?" I nodded in agreement. No more photos.

Hezbollah. I shuddered at the name.

Though listed as a terrorist group by the United States and Canada, Hezbollah is slightly more complex than that. It is a militia that protects the Shia of Lebanon, a neighbourhood police force that keeps law and order in Shia areas, and a political movement that fights for the rights of an oppressed people. The Shia have been the underclass in this country since time immemorial; yesterday's farmhands, today's street sweepers. To claim a political place, and to defend themselves from Israel and Lebanon's other tribes, they formed Hezbollah. They were a dangerous group, and armed to the teeth—and here I was snapping photos on their turf.

I said a big smiley apology to the shocked locals who were still crowding around the store, mumbling in Arabic amongst themselves, and staring at me with a frightened perplexity, as though I had no inkling of the severity of what I just did. I guess I didn't. I walked out still talking to Ibrahim, who was smiling.

"Are you Lebanese?" I asked.

"Yes, I am from Lebanon."

Drat, I thought. This wasn't even the Palestinian part of Shatila.

I went with Ibrahim next door to a net cafe to send some emails. I wanted to sit down and eat my chocolate, and I wanted refuge from the cold drizzle. I still stupidly believed that I was not in danger. I should have gotten out of there as fast as I could.

After twenty minutes, Ibrahim came in and got me. His face fell.

"Kareem, Hezbollah is here, and they want to talk to you."

"What is your name? Where do you come from?"

I was standing in a dark, sheltered corner near the entrance of some building. A yellow light glowed the in background and dimly illuminated a staircase with chipped and peeling paint. In front of me stood a short and stocky man, about five foot six, who had a protruding nose and hard, pinpoint eyes. He was wearing a grey jacket zipped up to the base of his chin, and a two-day growth of beard. He looked about thirty-five.

This was a Hezbollah underboss.

He had two youths circling me, smiling and translating, for he spoke only Arabic. Ibrahim stood in the background looking concerned. The underboss regarded me with a cold, stern glare.

"Passport?"

"It's in the hotel."

It was in my pocket. I handed him a photocopy of my passport from my wallet.

"Let me see your camera."

I handed him this too, flipping it on so he could see the photos I had taken. I held my breath, hoping they would not offend.

"What hotel do you stay at?"

"The Hotel Talal."

"Who did you come here with?"

"Three Canadians."

"What were their names?"

"Sean, Kristen, and Nickie."

I bit my lip. I knew I had just compromised the group's safety. But early on the conversation I had made a decision to tell the whole truth. If I hesitated for just one second to make something up, even a false name for my sister, that would be the end of me. He would sense a lie, and then I would be taken somewhere for a darker, more thorough interrogation, somewhere in one of these dingy apartment buildings in the center of Shatila, where the Lebanese police had no authority; where Hezbollah ruled without rival.

"Where is the Hotel Talal?"

I pulled out the map from my pocket and spread it up against the cold concrete wall. The youths translated.

"Here."

"How did you come to Shatila?"

"I walked."

"You *walked*?" He stared right at me, his eyebrows drawing tighter. "You *walked* all this way?"

He had an aggressive stare, as though trying to ferret out a lie. I swallowed, taking refuge in the truth.

"I walked all this way."

"Who do you know in Shatila?"

"I don't know anyone in Shatila."

"Why didn't you take a taxi?"

"I wanted to walk."

"Show us the way that you walked."

I pointed my route out along the map.

"What is your job?"

"I'm a student. A university student."

There was a pause. The youths talked to him in Arabic for a bit, he did not answer back. He flipped through the pictures of the camera. I remained there with an innocent half-smile on my face. I couldn't break my countenance. This was bloody serious, but I knew I had to remain cool. That was the only way out, the only way back home.

"What hotel are you staying at?"

"The Hotel Talal."

Didn't he already ask me this?

"Who did you come to Lebanon with?"

"Three people. Canadians."

I was sure he had asked me this. Didn't he believe me?

"What were their names?"

My thoughts raced. Were my answers not good enough? I told him the truth for the love of God!

"Don't worry, don't worry, nothing is wrong! Don't be afraid!"

The two youths danced around me like butterflies, smiling and patting me on the shoulder. Damn it. I had let my guard down, and showed my uneasiness. I swallowed and smiled back, willing myself to retain composure.

"How did you come to Shatila?"

"I walked."

I wanted to run. I thought through what might happen if I sprinted from the spot. I would lose a student card, a map of Beirut, and a digital camera. I could make it to the highway without being caught—unless—unless the underboss had a gun. Don't run, I told myself, don't be stupid. Stay where you are. You aren't a threat to them, don't act like you are. They will soon realize it and let you go.

"Who do you know in Shatila?"

"I. . .don't know anyone in Shatila. I know him."

I pointed to Ibrahim. The agent looked at him. Ibrahim got shaky and his hands begin to jerk. He spat out some Arabic and quickly washed his hands of me. He only met me when I arrived.

"Why did you come to Shatila?"

Good question. Why the hell did I come here?

"Um. . .well, I am a history student. I heard that twenty years ago, Ariel Sharon did a very horrible thing here. I wanted to see it because of that."

The youth translated for the agent. It elicited no reaction, like every other response I gave him. He was still looking through the rest of my photos, trying to ascertain my identity. I prayed to every god I knew that he would not ask me to step inside for a minute. Up the stairs to any one of these houses meant possible kidnapping, torture, or murder. . .or maybe nothing but a scarier interrogation. I would have to choose whether to sprint on the spot, or follow them in. I did not want to make that choice.

Finally, his face softened. It was the first change I had seen in him the entire time. He did not smile, but he relaxed. I relaxed. He gave me back my camera.

"No more pictures. It's dark now. You should probably go back to the hotel."

I went back to the hotel.

"You did *WHAT*??"

Nickie and Sean were furious.

"Well, I had to! I'm sorry guys, I know it compromised you, but I needed to tell the truth. If I had made up a lie that might have been the last thing I ever did. We can change hotels if you think we need to."

Nickie and Sean and Kristen were seated on their beds, staring at me. Nickie had set up the camera so we could catch this important moment of the trip on film. And now I was suffering my second interrogation of the day.

"Kieran, you went to Shatila and just snapped photos of whatever," Sean chided. "What the *hell* were you *thinking*? My friend Sam dragged me and some friends around Shatila last week. He *forbade* us to take any photos, and he kept flinching and looking behind us. He was terrified that one of us was going to get grabbed and stuffed into the back of a car, and we'd never see him again!"

"I. . .I didn't kn—"

"Yes you *DID*, Kieran!" Nickie snapped.

"Sean told us about this when you were still in Cairo. And you didn't experience it yourself, but we have to trust each other on a trip like this. This isn't Vancouver. . .you can't just take pictures of whatever you like! You know you can't even take photos of the areas of downtown that the military is protecting. . .and they won't kill you if you try. This is *BEIRUT*, Kieran!"

I sat there, stupid-faced, while they read me the riot act. I deserved every word. In the end, we did not switch hotels, we reasoned the Hotel Talal was locked at night and that was probably enough.

When our conversation ended, Nickie went over to the door, and packed up the camera. When she was there, she glanced into the hallway. Steve, the chronic eavesdropper, had been standing in front of our door listening to us for the past twenty minutes. When Nickie saw him, he turned towards the nearby sink and pretended to wash his hands.

11

DOWN THE RABBIT HOLE

"My name is Mahmoud Homsi, and I am from Syria."

The man was short, fat, and balding. He sat in a chair across from Ahed, in a suit with a tie, and a montage of Syrian propaganda behind him.

"I was a member of the Damascus Declaration."

"Can you please explain to the camera what the Damascus Declaration was?"

"The Damascus Declaration was a group of intellectuals who came together in 2004 to produce a document on Syrian democracy. It argues that the rule of Bashar Assad is undemocratic, and that Syrians deserve a type of government that does not deny them their human rights."

Homsi had left Syria a few years ago, fleeing political persecution. He was hiding in Lebanon.

Ahed told us one day that he could get us an interview with a real member of the Syrian opposition. . .a politician, not just a normal refugee. And, in pursuit of footage for our Syrian piece, we packed up our camera gear the next morning and followed him.

We rolled up to a swanky hotel and were ushered inside. We were led up to an opulent suite, with velvet furniture and brass candlesticks. A chandelier hung above the table; the floor was made of fine hardwood. Behind Homsi, as a film backdrop, was assembled a flag of Syria, and large poster boards of photos of members of the Syrian opposition that had been arrested or expelled from the country. On the table in front of him, had been placed an old black-and-white photograph from the twenties, the last time the Syrians had a chance at democracy.

"Please don't film any of the hotel," asked Homsi's aide, in perfect English. "We cannot give any clue to where Mr. Homsi is. You can film the place we prepared, but nothing more."

Nickie gulped. I took one look at his elaborate display and froze. Kristen and Sean both noticed my widening eyes.

"What's wrong?" they asked.

"Ok. . .guys I think we need to have a group chat after we're done this. Kristen. . .don't go on camera. And while the camera is rolling, don't say a thing. I don't want you to be a part of this."

Homsi walked around his posters, gesturing to different members of the Syrian opposition.

"This man, a Syrian politician, is dying of cancer. They have the equipment to treat him in Lebanon, or in Jordan. . .but the government won't give him the visa to leave the country." Homsi beckoned to the different photos, showing us the portrait of each man who had been condemned to misery or death for speaking out against the regime.

Finally, as Nickie's camera time was winding down, Sean and I got to the question that we really wanted to ask.

"How do you think that real change will happen in Syria? What is your hope for the Syrian government."

He drew himself up. "I am hoping that the international community will put pressure on Bashar Assad and the Syrian government. When that happens, the Syrian people will demand their human rights."

That's what I thought. No plans for revolution. No hidden caches of arms, no plans for a general strike, no intentions to march a giant crowd into downtown Damascus and sit there until the government changes their tune. Just get the "international community" to frown at Bashar Assad, and he will fold instantly. And lo, there shall be a new springtime of democracy in Syria.

Alright, I thought, things are wrapping up. Put on your biggest smile. Shake the fat man's hand.

"Thank you, my friend. That was excellent, really excellent."

He spread his arms wide and grinned. "You are excellent! Thank you so much for coming!"

"So how was it?" Ahed asked us outside.

"I didn't really get to ask him very good questions" Sean grumbled. "It was. . .well, it could have been better" said Nickie. Kristen agreed.

"It was excellent" I said. "It was really excellent."

"WELCOME!"

We sat down in a Lebanese restaurant called Le Chef. It served great lentil soup, and cheap hummus. And Le Chef himself, the tall and friendly owner, stood at the door and boomed "WELCOME!" in a voice that sounded like a robot using a bullhorn. Ten minutes after we sat down, when people were pleasantly eating and conversing, he would shout it when no one was entering the restaurant, and when no one on the street was even near enough to hear him.

"WELCOME!"

We had taken a taxi back to our hotel's area. Ahed had left us to go inquire at the UNHCR office as to the status of his refugee claim. We ordered food and sat. The silence was loud.

Sean turned to me. "Well, I've pretty much heard everybody's opinion on today. I'd like to hear yours."

"That interview was *appalling!*" I said. "I felt used. I felt absolutely used. The instant I saw his little propaganda display in there, I realized we were in too deep. I just wanted to get out of there!"

"Okay good!" Nickie said. "Because outside the hotel, you said—"

"—yes, because I didn't want to let on that we were really uneasy about that interview! Did you hear the answers he gave us to those questions? What substance was there at all?"

"I know." Sean scowled. "That fifty-year old man answered our questions by explaining to us the value of human rights! He didn't say a single practical thing. . .he just sat there and lectured us on democracy. It was patronizing!"

Nickie groaned. "After I was done, I just wanted to take that tape and throw it out the window!"

"Look," I said. "Like it or not, we just took sides in a war. A war between the Syrian government and its people. And what's worse. . .we just stumbled into this. Nickie took sides in a war in Southern Thailand when she was filming there. But she knew about it beforehand; she had read up on the conflict, and she was prepared to take that risk. But this? We came to the—"

"WELCOME!"

Le Chef was at it again. I slapped myself in the face.

"We came to the Middle East looking for personal stories. . .for interesting people to film for Current TV. And with every new interview, we were slowly pulled further down the rabbit hole. . .and now we are carrying footage on us that could get us killed! I mean, a few refugees is *nothing* compared to that man. He is a serious politician, and the government is *scared* of men like him. Come on! These are the Syrians we are talking about. These are the men who killed Hariri!"

Sean told us a story he'd heard sometime during the past few weeks. The year before, in 2006, a Canadian girl wandered into the city of Hama in Syria. She started taking lots of pictures, and she started asking the locals which parts of the city exactly were cannoned by President Hafez Assad in 1982. She disappeared, and has never been heard from since. Some say she was kidnapped by a local. Others say that the Mukhabarat took her. They say that she was hurt so badly in prison that they realized they could not release her or there would be political hell. But whatever happened to her, it is unlikely that she will ever be found.

This story weighed heavily on our minds. Here we were, about to go to the same country, with the same secret police. And we had just done something much worse than ask the locals about a massacre that happened twenty years ago.

I spoke.

"Guys, after today, one thing is clear. We have to talk to some people to see if it's even safe to go to Syria anymore. Perhaps we should just fly to Jordan. And for sure. . .we are mailing *all* our footage home. If we have *anything* on us at the Syrian border, that puts us in serious danger."

"Well, we have Daniel," Nickie said, "the contact that Marc gave us. He's coming from Syria and he'll be here in two days. We can—"

"WELCOME!"

"I'm seriously going to *kill* that guy!" I muttered.

Nickie continued. "We can ask them whether they think we really did something stupid, and whether or not we should fly to Amman."

"Ok," said Sean. "Another thing we should be thinking about is what sort of footage we want out of Syria."

"Well, we need B-Roll. We need stuff that isn't interviews. But we can get some of that with your tiny camera, Kieran. Also, we have gotten all our interviews heavily from one side of the issue. We should find a pro-regime opinion. We can probably interview someone that supports the regime."

"I don't know about that" said Kristen. "Think about it. Four conspicuous white kids show up from the Western press, which is already known and feared in Syria by the government. And they show up to a government spokesman, and start asking a lot of happy questions about how great Bashar Assad's regime is? That is going to red-flag us in no time. And whatever we do, we *don't* want anyone to be watching us. Not the secret police, not the normal police, not the border patrol—*nobody*!"

We all knew that she was a hundred percent right. We nodded, and studied our empty plates. No one spoke.

"WELCOME!"

"Okay," I said. "We need some breathing time. This has been a difficult day, and we all need some time to consider what has just happened, and how to proceed from here. Luckily, Daniel is coming in two days and we can ask him for advice. He knows better than us. But at the same time, let's keep this to as *few* people as possible. No emails, no phone calls. The only power we have right now is power over this information. But we do have to talk to someone—Daniel, I guess. I mean, Sean's right—we can't just descend into paranoia. But at the same time. . .it's not paranoia if they're actually after you."

Nickie spoke.

"Right. I think we can calm down. We have quite a few things going for us. We're still somewhere quite safe, and we still have time. Let's use some of it to think. And then, we find someone who knows firsthand. They will be able to tell better than us what our situation is. We talk to Daniel."

12

THE ROAD TO DAMASCUS

The December mornings in Beirut were freezing. Rain sluiced down and flooded the storm drains, and began to flow in a stream down the side of the road. I had no idea just how cold and wet it would be to travel the Middle East in the winter. The sky was as grey as the sea, which I could see easily from our hotel balcony. The suburb of Gemmayzeh sprawled behind me, with its bullet-splattered apartments and faded paint.

My friends awoke, showered, and made their way to Makhlouf's for our morning dose of coffee. We got the camera ready, and Nickie and Sean slipped on two red T-Shirts, printed with the words "Draw the Line 2007." They were protest shirts for a rally going on in Beirut that day. . .perhaps the only rally that the military would ever allow.

"Alright," Sean said. "Time to go find out if any-one in the Middle East cares about climate change."

It was perhaps the first protest of its type in the region: a demonstration about the threat of global warming. Downtown on the Corniche, the road that runs parallel to the ocean, there were about a thousand people carrying balloons and wearing the same red shirts as Nickie and Sean. It looked like any protest I had seen in Canada. People of all ages were there—children in their parents' stroll-ers, boy scout teams, and teenage deviants strum-ming guitars. Organizers had tables set up with free bottles of water and information leaflets in Eng-lish, French, and Arabic. There was a large banner hoisted above and a speaker system beneath it blar-ing rock music. The rain had passed, and the sun peeked through the clouds and warmed the air.

The crowd grew larger. I was impressed at the numbers—a similar protest in a North American city might have drawn as many. But this was Bei-rut, in a fragile Lebanon whose president had but a fortnight ago stepped down from power and left no one in his place. Yet these people felt no dan-ger, and Lebanese of all backgrounds assembled to show their support for action on climate change.

Beefy, stern-faced soldiers in military fatigues lined the streets. They stood scanning the crowd with folded arms, talking into microphones that hung beside their faces. And the press coverage was overwhelming. At least a dozen professional video cameras and at fifty photo cameras were trained at the crowd. Beirut news stations were there, along with people from local newspapers in every language, and even some from the international press.

And we were among them.

"So why did you come out here today? Why does climate change matter to you?"

Sean and Nickie took turns holding the camera, and we all got a chance to conduct an interview. Kristen proved to be a natural at it; she led the way through the crowd to seek out ever more interviewees. Sometimes we got answers based on science, sometimes we got slogans. But the most telling answer we got from a frizzle-haired sixteen-year old carrying an electric guitar which was blasting out sound from an amplifier that he hung on his hip.

"Al Gore has convinced us that if we don't act on climate change soon, there will be disaster."

This comment struck a chord with us. Al Gore's film *An Inconvenient Truth* was released in the summer of 2006, and by the winter of 2007 the people of Beirut had heard his message. It made us realize the power of the very cameras we were carrying.

We began to notice a few people in the crowd that seemed to be far more interested in the people taking pictures than in the protest itself. These individuals looked otherwise perfectly normal, but they would study the crowd of reporters carefully and snap pictures of each one of us. Intelligence agents. I suppose it would be naive to think we could bring two large cameras to a protest in Beirut without having our photos taken by spies.

The protest began with a speech by someone over the loudspeaker system, and a tremendous cheer. A wall of red-shirted demonstrators marched forward, carrying a large yellow banner bearing the words 'ACT AGAINST CLIMATE CHANGE' in English and Arabic. All of them sang and shouted slogans for about fifteen minutes, after which the group energy its lost steam, and the crowd simply marched patiently in one direction towards the finish line. We interviewed the organizers, and then stopped for a quick meal.

Afterwards, Sean wanted to show us something. We walked away from the waterfront until we reached a certain bend in the road. The building on the left had been hit with incredible shrapnel. Many balconies were broken through, and all the facing was stripped off. Across the street, another building was caved in, and around it was the rusted, twisted frame of a workers scaffold that had all been bent and warped in one direction.

Sean pointed to a patch of new asphalt on the road, about the width of a house.

"There it is. That was the bomb that killed Hariri."

Rafik Hariri was an incredibly popular leader in Lebanon. While the Christian mafia godfathers are more powerful overall, infighting amongst the families makes them disorganized and disunited. Hariri was a political leader of the Sunni Muslims, who are more politically organized, and form a good part of Lebanon's middle class and wealthy elite. The Sunnis are the middle ground between the Shia and the Maronites, and this makes them good bargaining partners for international disputes.

Lebanon not only has its tribal rivalries, but it is the focal point of many international interests as well. The Israelis want to stop Hezbollah and militant Palestinian groups residing within Lebanon. The Americans desperately want another ally in the region. The French want to keep trading with it. And the Syrians want it back.

For thirty years, the Syrians kept a military contingent in Lebanon to keep the peace. This of course meant that Bashar Assad's army was, for a time, controlling all the security in the country. Although many Lebanese politicians were pro-Syrian puppets, some resisted. Rafik Hariri was a strong, anti-Syrian Prime Minister under a pro-Syrian President from 2000 to 2004. He strongly opposed Bashar Assad and his firm grip on Lebanese politics.

One day in 2005, Hariri drove his car around that certain bend near the Corniche, where hundreds of kilograms of explosives were waiting inside a truck. The explosion killed twenty-one, wounded a hundred, destroyed the road, and splattered shrapnel on three buildings.

Tens of thousands took to the streets. Sunnis, Christians, Druze, even Shia marched together in Beirut, demanding the end of Syrian influence in Lebanese politics. And the Syrian army did not put down the demonstrations with force, as they had in the 1990s. They were forced to leave and relinquish control of the country to the squabbling mafia parliament. In Lebanon, this was known as the March 14 Movement—in the West it was known as the Cedar Revolution.

I looked at the damaged area, and imagined the force of the explosion needed to smash up two buildings and rip up a giant section of road. I felt a chill. This was the doing of the people that exiled Ahed and Eva. The Syrians.

"My job is. . .dodging the Ministry of Information."

We were seated across the table from Daniel and his gorgeous Syrian girlfriend, in a swanky nouveau-chic Lebanese restaurant. When the girl ordered, she got a hard scowl from the waiter as he recognized her accent. She lit a second cigarette.

She worked in Syria for a small newspaper, just as her boyfriend did. Daniel was man from Britain in his late twenties, and he had decided to settle in the Middle East. He worked for a Damascus English-language magazine. We had gotten their contact through a friend of ours, and we had met to discuss the dangers of filming in Syria.

"If you want some government opinions, we have some contacts you can talk to. But you have to get a minder."

"What's a minder?" asked Nickie.

"It's an employee of the Ministry of Information. He will accompany you to observe exactly what you film and what you ask the people you interview. They will make sure you don't film anything illegal."

"Wow."

"That's the way the Ministry of Information does it. You need to get a letter from your TV station, and then you can apply at the border for a journalist visa. Then they will check everything and you'll be just fine."

"But. . .then we couldn't film anyone from the opposition?"

She laughed. "The minders are lazy and usually go home at four o'clock or five. You'll be free after that to do what you want. Just don't do anything in a hotel. . .hotels report directly to the Ministry. Nothing will happen to you, but whoever you talk to will get arrested and brought to prison."

"What if we just went and decided not to tell the Ministry at all, and then just film in secret?" I asked.

"That. . .could work. They don't really search you at the border. But if you get caught, they'll probably take away your footage and your camera. You probably won't go to jail. The worst that could happen is that you'll get deported. But the people you film will have serious consequences if you get caught. So you really have to be careful."

I lowered my voice. "Now. . .we did an interview with. . .well. . .Mahmoud Homsi the other day. We would like to know if he's really wanted by the government, and if this might get us into a lot of trouble."

She chuckled. "No, Homsi actually lost a lot of credibility in Syria before he went into exile. They don't really care about him any more."

We talked on. We would have loved to interview her, a Syrian who worked in the Syrian media, and ask her about the level of censorship in her profession. But we could never get her to go on camera. It was out of the question. For her, it would mean suicide. But off camera, she had no problem giving us her opinion on the situation in her country.

"Most people in Syria don't want the alternative to come to power. They know that if it's not Bashar Assad, it will be some Islamic extremist regime, so they would rather stick with the secular Ba'ath party. They know it's corrupt, and they know that the Mukhabarat tortures and imprisons people, but they don't want the alternative."

"And do you think there will ever be change in Syria?"

"Yes" she said. "You see, in the 1980s, they flattened a city. And when your government does that, you really learn to shut up and do what they say. But inside, it makes you crazy and it makes you hate them, and you wait for times to change. This is what happened to all Syrians. And the government can sense this. . .they've even liberalized enough to let the Islamists speak again. They are letting them speak so that the Syrian people can remember the alternative to this regime. But I don't think it will last forever, not without some change."

She was referring to the Hama massacre of 1982. Syria's dictator, Hafez Assad, was constantly defied by the Islamic brotherhood in the city of Hama. One night, the brotherhood kidnapped and shot some officials, and tried to launch a revolution in the city. Assad's response was to seal off dozens of square blocks and cannon them without mercy. Later, when it was mentioned to him that he must have killed 20,000 people, rebel and civilian alike, Hafez Assad laughed and responded: "No, I killed at least 50,000 people."

Hafez died in 2000. His son, Bashar, is now the ruler of the country.

We exchanged emails and telephone numbers with Daniel and his girlfriend. We thanked them for their help, and went off to the hotel to discuss our decision. Would we leave tomorrow, or the next day? Would we notify the government and get a minder in Syria, or try to film the opposition on the sly? It would all depend.

In any case, we had a few things to do first. We called up the editor of a local English language newspaper, a Canadian expat from Montreal named Marc, and he agreed to an interview the next day, to talk about the Shia and Lebanese politics. Nickie sent a letter to her Canadian TV station, and we talked about making doubles of our compromising photos footage to mail home in case of trouble.

After a short chat, we decided that the six or seven days we had in Syria would be nowhere near enough to get a minder, find a translator, talk to government ministers, and then do our own work incognito after 5pm. Instead, we were going to slip in below the radar. We would pack Sean and Nickie's camera deep within our bags, and collect any street footage we needed with my small, tourist-sized video recorder. We would tell the border guards we were there for tourism, and interview a member of the Syrian opposition in secret.

Kristen ran up the stairs and smacked open the door with a rude awakening for all of us.

"A car bomb went off in Beirut this morning. It killed a general."

We sprang up, rubbed our faces, and logged on to the hotel's wireless. A car bomb had gone off in Beirut. It killed a general of the Lebanese army, a Maronite Christian who had led a brigade that flattened a Palestinian refugee village a couple weeks before. To our indescribable relief, the bomb did not kill general Suleiman, who was the only reason Lebanon was delivered from another civil war.

We emailed everyone at home to tell them we were fine. The bomb went off in a part of Lebanon far away from our hotel, and there were no immediate calls for retaliation or war. I called up Marc and told him the news.

"Wow. Well, then you guys have lost my services for the day, then, I'm afraid."

It was time to leave.

We began to pack. We still needed to mail our footage to Canada, pay the Druze brothers, get a cab to Syria, and say goodbye to Ahed. I went out to throw some CD's in the mail. The army was in the streets. At least five times as many troops showed up than had been posted there in the previous days. Army jeeps, tanks, and other APCs filled the square. Men in green fatigues with submachine guns stood uneasily on every street corner.

I went down the street to suck back a coffee and one of Makhlouf's sandwiches. George Makhlouf gave me a warm welcome, and began to make my breakfast and inquire how I liked Lebanon so far.

"Did you hear what happened this morning?"

"No, what?'

"A car bomb went off and killed a general."

Indeed, even as I spoke, a military vehicle was driving slowly down the street, barking instructions in Arabic for the owners of vehicles to please remove them from the sidewalk. The army was about to set up a barricade.

Makhlouf threw up his hands in exasperation.

"You see? This is the only Christian country in the Middle East, and they want to take it from us!"

After packing, Sean and I stood from the balcony of the hotel Talal and watched the sunset. The Phalangist headquarters across the street was on lockdown. There were dozens of soldiers, a few APCs, and barbed-wire barricades. No car could get near the place. Makhlouf had long since closed shop, and someone had moved his brother's hot dog stand from the street so that the army didn't crush it.

When the military wasn't looking, we raised our cameras above the balcony and snapped highly illegal photos of the Phalangist headquarters. A line of sleek black and white Escalades pulled in, all with tinted windows. There were about twenty in all. Men stepped out of them in dark, expensive suits.

Amin Gemayel had called an emergency meeting. And the godfathers had arrived.

After the light faded, we slapped Ahed on the shoulder, hoping to see him again in America, as long as his refugee papers came through. We piled our bags into a taxi bound for Damascus.

It was time to cross our fingers and make our way to Syria.

13

THE LONG-NECKED ANIMAL

Our cab driver was Armenian. He told us this with all the English he knew. He had a comfortable car and a cross with prayer beads hanging on the rear-view mirror. An image of the Virgin Mary was engraved into a small ceramic on the dashboard. Damascus was only a two or three hour drive from Beirut. Right before the Syrian border, he stopped at a local store and bought a carton of Malboros, which he packed under the seat.

Nickie's giant camera, like Sean's, was buried deep in her backpack. And those backpacks we buried in the deepest part of the taxi trunk. We stopped at the border crossing and walked into a dark office lit by weak florescent bulbs to buy our visas.

"So," said Nickie. "The visas are fifty-four dollars. And I think the idea is we give them sixty."

She looked at me intently. Our freedom was at risk, never mind her camera. Calmly, with her eyes, she was telling me that if I made even the smallest attempt to dodge this ritualized bribe, she would rip my face off.

I smiled happily and gave the sixty dollars to the border guard. He pocketed the extra and gave me a stamp.

"Welcome to Syria."

There were about eight guards loitering outside by our parked taxi. Only one of them had the energy to pop open the trunk. Inside, he found four traveler backpacks, all the same size. He zipped open Kristen's pack, saw laundry, and became bored with the whole project.

We drove on to another checkpoint for a passport check.

Our taxi driver rolled down the window.

"As-salamu alaykum" he said.

The guard looked in and saw the cross swinging beside his head.

"As-salamu alaykum" he said back.

'As-salamu alaykum' is a Muslim greeting. It is actually the first part of a Muslim prayer—it means, literally, "the peace of Allah be upon you." My Egyptian friend Tamer once scolded me for greeting him in this way. Christians don't say that, he told me. They say *'masaa al-khayr,'* which means 'good evening'. Christians didn't speak amongst

themselves the way Muslims spoke amongst themselves.

The border guard leaned forward and stared our driver menacingly in the eye.

"As-salamu alaykum" he said. *"As-salamu alaykum!"*

Each time he repeated it with more force, and each time he leaned a little bit farther into the car and his stare got more aggressive.

"As-salamu alaykum!"

The driver's eyes went wide. His hand darted under his seat, where he wrested free a pack of Malboros and gave them to the guard.

"Masaa al-khayr." He waved us through.

I had wondered what those cigarettes were for. The driver had come well-prepared.

Once safely in Damascus, we checked into the local sheesha bar and ordered a water pipe and some tea. We were exhausted: physically and psychologically. And now that we had taken refuge in the corner of a warm shop, surrounded by cushions of cheap red fabric, we could finally relax. We began to debrief about the experiences of the past few days.

"Too bad we couldn't get that interview we wanted with Sam," Sean said.

Sam was a nineteen year-old Sunni Muslim that Sean met in Lebanon. Sam showed him and some friends around some of the fractured suburbs of Beirut. He was connected to a Sunni neighbour-hood watch group in his part of the city. Naturally, we followed this lead and tried to find this group; hopefully to get some stories of life inside the conflict-ridden city. It didn't turn out as we had planned.

"Yeah," I said. "Sorry Kristen and I bailed out. It was just that the farther he led us into that neighbourhood, the more unwelcome and out-of-place I felt. Then he started asking if we had our passports and other ID cards, and telling us we couldn't film this and we couldn't say that. . .I just got a really bad vibe. Kristen and I wanted out."

Sam had taken us to the door of a building where part of the 'neighbourhood watch' was located. He shook hands with a greasy-haired under-boss in a big black jacket, and I had a nice flashback of my experience with Hezbollah. Kristen was looking nervous. We decided not go inside, and instead walked right back out to grab a taxi for the hotel.

"No, it's alright Kieran," said Nickie, "I was going to recommend that you bail. The interview went alright, though, but the guards confiscated the footage in the end."

"'Neighbourhood watch' indeed," said Sean. "That was a full-blown militia group. When you ask them directly, they say they have no weapons. But then they tell you that if the Shias ever attack they would come from the south, and there would be a sniper on top of every building. He showed me on a map. . .his Sunni neighbourhood, surrounded by hostile Shia neighbourhoods. He pointed out that they wouldn't attack from the north, because if they amassed any forces there the Christian militias would take them out. And slowly, I began to see how the delicate chess game of Lebanese tribal warfare is played in the streets of Beirut."

I took a sip of water pipe. Peach-flavoured smoke flowed into my mouth. I passed the pipe to Sean.

"You know," I said, "in consequence-free Vancouver, it's really easy to read about the problems of the Middle East, and ask why these people can't all just make peace. But tell that to Sam. He would laugh at you. In fact, if I was a Sunni born into his position, or a Christian born in West Beirut, I would probably think exactly the same way. The other tribes are out to kill you, and you have no choice but to stick with your own."

Sean nodded. "The more time you spend in Lebanon, the more you start to see things through their tribal lens. And this is why I wrote you earlier saying that I wanted to get out of there. Every day I was seeing more and more of the logic to their factional thinking. It started to scare me."

He paused to take a pull on the pipe. The water bubbled softly.

"Lebanon easily has the most complex politics in the Middle East; I could argue the most complex in the world. You want a historical comparison for Lebanon, Kieran? It's like those Christian crusader states surrounded by an ocean of Islam. The Christians there are barely holding out."

It was a huge relief to be in Syria. Instead of Lebanon's warring tribes, Syria was dominated by a monolithic government, where order was maintained by the army and four different branches of secret police. While we had to worry about who was listening when we spoke, we were at least free from the fear of violence on the street, or from invisible tribal boundaries that separated from one block to the next.

"So. . .when do we talk to Rachel and Adam?" Nickie asked.

"Why don't we do some tourist things first?" said my sister. "We need to see Old Damascus and there's a crusader castle I want to see too. We can talk to Rachel and Adam towards the end of the week, and then perhaps leave the next day."

Rachel and Adam were our code names for our two opposition contacts inside of Syria. We obviously couldn't say their real names openly when we talked about them. We developed code names for a few other things, borrowing freely from Harry Potter and the Lord of the Rings. Bashar Assad was called 'He-Who-Must-Not-Be-Named,' or Voldemort for short. The Mukhabarat became the 'Dark Riders,' and general everyday soldiers became known as 'orcs.' Mahmoud Homsi became 'Mr. H.'

"So yeah, we should take precautions," said Nickie. "Our cover story is that we are filming environmental topics for Envirospeak.tv. But let's remember that nobody knows we're here, and even if we do get caught, the worst they will do is deport us. So really, we can relax and not be too paranoid."

Sean took another pull from his peach sheesha. "I seriously hate the feeling of paranoia. I can't live my life thinking like that.

We had calmed down quite a bit from the Homsi interview.

Old Damascus has its charm.

The massive old city, reputed to be the most ancient in the world still in use, was ringed by colossal stone walls which were many meters thick. As we approached the entrance, we came upon a giant green statue of Saladin, riding high upon his horse.

'Salah ad-Din,' known to the English-speaking world as Saladin, was the leader of the Arab forces that took back Jerusalem from the Christians during the Third Crusade. He fought against King Richard the Lionheart from England, who campaigned there eight hundred years ago while Robin Hood was busy picking off his deer in Sherwood Forest. Saladin, who ruled the Arab peoples from Egypt to Syria out of his capital Damascus, marched his army into Jerusalem and took back the third holiest city in Islam.

The statue of Saladin was turbaned and rode with his sword high. Two soldiers on horseback flanked him, with the symbol of an eagle engraved into their shields. Behind his horse sat two European knights, exhausted and defeated, with crosses sewn into the baldrics on their chests. They were Raynald de Chatillon, and Guillame de Montferrat, the two former kings of Jerusalem and its nearby regions.

Saladin was a remarkably tolerant king. He treated the People of the Book with respect. Christian rule ended in the region, but the Christians and their churches remained in their places, and the priests were allowed to worship. The Crusaders slaughtered Muslims left and right when they rode through Jerusalem; Saladin left the Christians alone.

Old Damascus begins with a giant *souq*. The walled city is entered through a tremendous archway, which is packed with people on any day of the week. The cobblestone street is lined with shops selling cushions, fabrics, spices, and highly-sugared Middle Eastern candies. We bought ice cream cones covered with pistachios for a dollar each, dodged tourist vultures, and walked around crowds of praying Muslims that overflowed the local mosques. It was a Friday.

We entered the Umayyad Mosque. It was a giant Byzantine Church that had been converted.

The same thing had been done to the Santa Sofia in Istanbul. I told this to some Muslims I knew back in Egypt, and they snickered at me and refused to believe it was true.

Nickie and Kristen were directed to a certain room where they were given appropriate attire. The appropriate attire was a brown, baggy cloak that swallowed their faces, and looked like it was washed about once every couple of weeks. The girls rolled their eyes and dressed into their monk-costumes, covering their brilliant blonde hair with cowls.

Saladin's grave was in the back. I expected to find a brilliant mausoleum adjunct to the church, but instead there was a small marble room, with dust collecting on the walls and in the corners, and a wooden coffin with an arched top—much like the coffins I had seen of honoured sultans in Turkey. A green shroud was draped over the coffin; it was adorned with elaborate Arabic writing. But the red carpet in the place was stained and faded, and the whole thing had a musty smell. In an open closet off to the side, Saladin's vacuum cleaner was sprawled out so it could be with him in the afterlife.

"They really didn't do a good job of Saladin's tomb," Kristen said. "After all he did I expected them to honour him a little more."

I laughed darkly.

"Well after all, he was a Kurd."

We continued to the very corner of the city, along a maze-like network of streets, with asymmetrical houses jammed up beside one another. In places, the street paving had been completely ground up, and there were shirtless workmen shoveling mud and gravel. Large patches of water pooled beneath the husks of broken concrete buildings. We walked along precarious plank bridges to our destination.

We found the church which claimed to be built on the place where St. Paul was lowered from the walls of Damascus in a basket to escape the Jewish authorities. Paul was one of the two leading figures preaching the Christian religion after the death of Jesus. He would preach to Jewish communities, telling them that the saviour had come and there was a new law now to follow. The Jewish elites repeatedly tried to kill him for preaching blasphemy. . .and was even once stoned by a crowd, and dragged out of the city by his disciples who found to their surprise that he was still alive. Paul continued to work all of his life to establish an organized Christian religion. By the time he died, Christianity was preached in a network of churches that spread from Greece to Jerusalem.

This was five thousand years after the birth of Judaism. And six hundred years before the birth of Islam.

We took photos of the stone stele of Paul on the church walls. . .him being lowered in the basket to safety. And of course, tucked in the corner of the church, they had a giant basket woven of reeds; large enough for a man to sit in.

As the day went on, I began to notice more and more the constant presence of Syria's leader, Bashar Assad. His photo was hung in every second shop. He is a tall, mustached man who is often depicted in strong, set-jaw photographs. They show him in a white or black suit, often with the black, red, and white colours of the Syrian flag flowing in the background. Some posters were of a military Bashar Assad, dressed in fatigues and secret-service sunglasses.

I realized that although a lot of Syrians had his photo in their shops to demonstrate their good behaviour to the authorities. However, there is no way that so many people would have hung his picture up if he was indeed widely hated and enjoyed no popular support. Some shopkeepers clearly genuinely believed in the man.

"If there were free and fair elections in Syria tomorrow, Bashar Assad would win 90% of the votes."

In Lebanon, our Montreal-born friend Marc, an editor for a English-language Lebanese newspaper, had explained a few things about Syrian politics.

"Everyone knows that if Bashar were to fall, the only other option would be a radical Islamist government. And no one in the country wants that."

"I hope that one day there will be a democracy in Syria."

Deep within an Irish pub in Beirut, Ahed once had an argument with Andrew, a middle-aged Canadian friend of my fathers.

"You can't have democracy in Syria," he replied bluntly, with a smile. "The conditions aren't right for it. It's like trying to grow. . .citrus fruits at the north pole."

"Yes, but we are making the conditions for it."

"Do you know how long it took for the conditions to be right in the West when we had a society like Syria's? About five hundred years. I'll talk to you in five hundred years if you like. Syria has a Western model right now: the Stalinist model, and if they ever dropped that, they would take on their own model—Islamic fundamentalism."

Ahed smiled and answered the man without rancour.

"You see, you think exactly like my parents. They didn't think they could change Bashar Assad because the only change would lead to Islam gaining power. That's why they didn't want me to go into politics."

Assad rules Syria through not only his power agencies like the Mukhabarat, but also through his family and five other elite Damascene families. He stifles the press, and individual Syrians censor themselves so they don't appear a threat to the government.

In front of the gates of Old Damascus, there is a giant poster of Bashar against a white background, smiling in a dark suit, and extending his hand out in front of him in a regal gesture of openness. Beside him was written, in English and Arabic, 'Syria Believes in You.'

Ahed was telling us that Bashar has an abnormally long neck, and his nickname in Syria is the Giraffe.

"Yeah, so when the Syrians actually want to talk about a giraffe, they can't say it because they are afraid the Mukhabarat is listening to their calls. So instead of 'giraffe,' they say 'the long-necked animal.' Tell me, how are you going to expect political change out of a people that are too afraid to say 'giraffe' into their cell phones?"

Control over information in Syria was very high. Which is why I was really happy when I saw that the young guy running the net cafe had a cross around his neck. He was a government-hating minority, and he probably didn't have too many Mukhabarat probes on his computer. To our surprise, Facebook, which had been banned across Syria, still operated in this little cafe.

But all the same, Ahed and I had an MSN conversation that was something out of 1984.

"Hey, you know your Greek friend?"

"Um. . .my Greek friend?"

"Yeah, your Greek friend that you met in Lebanon?"

I paused, wondering who on earth he was talking about. Ahed didn't introduce me to any other Greeks.

"You know, the guy who took you to see the Kurdish family?"

I caught on. He was talking about himself.

"Yeah, I was wondering about him. Did he go downtown to the bureau today?"

"He did actually."

"And what was the result?"

"The result was positive."

I raced back to the hostel to give my friends the news. Ahed had been accepted for refugee status by the UNCHR office in Beirut.

14
ALI ABDULLAH

It was time to be tourists for a while.

Crac de Chevaliers is a castle northwest of Damascus. It was built by crusaders almost a thousand years ago to guard the trade route from the Holy Land back to Europe. It is one of Syria's few tourist attractions. We didn't have much time in Syria, and this was one thing we had to see.

And, like many things in the Middle East, it took us two tries before we actually succeeded.

We flipped open our guidebook and found the name of the station for buses going north. Our taxista, however, had different ideas. As I limped along in Arabic, he communicated to me that buses went north from another station. But we insisted that our guidebook was right. We rolled up to the station, only to find out two things: the buses went

south, and it was Friday, and everything was closed.
Our taxista threw up his hands and started lectur-
ing us in Arabic.

"Well, that's what you get when you trust the
Lying Planet," said Sean.

In a different part of the world, we would have
always taken the taxista's advice. But this was the
Middle East. And in the Middle East, we were constantly plagued by what we termed 'Arab directions.'
If you ask a random person where the embassy is,
or how to get to the bus station, he will never, *never,*
tell you that he doesn't know. Instead, he will look
confused for a moment, and perhaps indicate some
direction. Then he will shout at his cousin in the
shop across the street, who will call someone else on
the phone. And in the end, the team of people that
have assembled to help you will form a consensus
and point you in the opposite direction. When you
come back after forty-five minutes, and tell the guy
the embassy was nowhere close, he will open his
cell phone and call someone else, and without even
blinking point you in a different direction.

Someone who receives Arab directions with
a Canadian cultural understanding will often find
themselves bent over the table of some coffee shop,
crying into their folded arms, and wishing to God
that they could have three hours of their life back.

The next day we assaulted the correct bus
station with renewed vigour. That's when we

discovered that trying to get a bus in Syria is like wrestling with a giant octopus. The station was an open-air parking lot with shacks set up to sell bus tickets, packed with bustling people. It was like a great bazaar. To get a bus ticket, we needed to join a crowd of men who had all crushed themselves against the glass of one ticket-seller, bunching themselves into a compact, odorous ball and holding their passports aloft. The ticket salesman would take one passport, and with agonizing slowness, copy out pages of information on each person. Buses would ritually depart an hour behind schedule, often with frustrated Syrian men still elbowing each other for tickets.

It took us a full two hours of culture shock to realize that the only way we were going to get there was to each drop twenty bucks on a taxi. We found a driver, an Iraqi, who agreed to take us all the way.

Two hours later, we were stuck on some remote Syrian hillside, our Iraqi bent over a tiny stream with half a milk carton cut into a vessel, collecting water for his steaming radiator. Syrian yokel children in dirty clothing stared uncertainly at us from the side of the road. After thirty minutes of running between his car and the stream, our driver's car sputtered weakly to life, and we were on our way. He threw a tantrum and laid on the horn when I refused to pay him twenty American more than we originally negotiated.

Sigh.

We walked the last few hundred meters up to the crusader castle, rubbing our foreheads, trying to laugh off the dismal headache that is the natural consequence of Middle Eastern transport.

The castle was magnificent. It was built on the crown of a giant hill, and it rose imposing and impregnable above the land. Inside of the outer wall was an even higher citadel, built up with tremendous slanting walls. We walked through long, dark passages which used to be stables or kitchens; at each corner there would always be a large circular room with holes in the roof. This type of architecture will never be replicated again. It was built precisely for battle with the technology of the Middle Ages. The holes in the ceiling allowed warriors to hurl projectiles or boiling water onto invaders who had taken the lower level.

From the walls the countryside looked gorgeous and green, even in winter. The rolling hills were covered with olive trees and pale rocks, and the landscape was dotted here and there with townships. A quaint mosque in the village below belted out the call to prayer on a weak and tinny megaphone. Temple townies swarmed below and hawked postcards and guidebooks.

A mere mortal cannot describe in words the quality of the meal we had inside the castle's restaurant. After a lavish line of dips and steaming bread, there came teeming bowls of salad and plates of cooked vegetables. After this, half a grilled chicken arrived for each of us, stuffed to bursting with buttery garlic, and all washed down with tall, foamy pints of beer. Compared to the standard restaurant food in the Middle East, this was an island in the storm.

We bussed back to Damascus in the dark, and crashed into our hotel beds, too tired even for our customary tea and sheesha. We needed to rest. We were meeting Rachel and Adam the next day at noon.

It is pretty difficult for four Westerners to stand on a Damascene street corner and appear nonchalant. There was no outdoor cafe even that would provide decent cover. Nickie and Sean rolled their eyes when I dragged a few chairs out from inside a local store, which bewildered the shopkeepers who had just sold me coffee. The stakes were high. If we aroused any suspicion at all, we might put Rachel in grave danger, as well as ourselves.

Across the street, we spied a woman who did not look like she was walking in any particular direction. I was struck by her European appearance: she had light skin and sandy hair, like so many Syrians. She looked like she was in her mid-twenties. And, like most women we saw outside of Egypt, she was not wearing the veil. She crossed the street and introduced herself, albeit a little uneasily.

I understood. It took a lot of courage to come and meet us.

She led us through some back alleyways and we climbed the stairs to her apartment. We made sure no one saw us enter. Once inside her two-room flat, Nickie up the camera on the tripod, and I closed the window blinds to ward off any watchful eyes. We took a seat on the couch; Sean and I discussed the questions we planned to ask Adam when he arrived. Rachel brought us some water and lit a cigarette. Smoke curled upwards to the ceiling, and the loathsome odour of burning tobacco filled the room.

In the intervening time, we waited with the camera turned off. Rachel told us a bit about what it was like to be an opposition member in Syria.

"The internet is the greatest thing for the Syrian opposition! This is where we collaborate and where we do all our activities. This is where we write. This is where we associate."

"Yes, but the internet isn't all safe," said Nickie. "When I open my gmail in Canada, it says 'https'— the extra 's' stands for 'secure'. But here in Syria it doesn't do that. And of course Ahed went to solitary confinement because he signed into the wrong net cafe."

Rachel nodded. "Yes, we can't use msn because we know it is being watched. A few of my colleagues were arrested, and during their trial the Mukhabarat brought printouts of an msn conversation to accuse them. We have to talk very guardedly on msn."

I told her about Ahed's acceptance for refugee status. She smiled and said she already knew.

Kristen had a question.

"How do you live with. . .paranoia? Are you ever afraid that the Mukhabarat will come for you?"

I wondered this as well. She had risked her freedom by coming to find us on the corner and getting us this interview.

"It is just something we have to accept. I know that perhaps today, perhaps tomorrow, the Mukhabarat will knock on my door and I will be arrested. I can do nothing about it except continue what I am doing. We are not running from them. All opposition expect to be arrested one day."

"And how does that change because you are a woman?" I asked. "Are you afraid to be arrested?"

"Actually, it is easier to be a woman in the Syrian opposition. Women are very rarely arrested. And if we are, we are not treated worse than men in the jails."

I shuddered to think of what any treatment would be like in those places. Interrogation, solitary confinement, mental torture, physical torture. Endless waiting without a single bit of contact from your family or anyone else you knew. I admired her bravery. The risk we four were currently taking felt truly small in comparison.

There was a knock at the door. I held my breath—imagining the unthinkable for a brief second. Rachel opened it and a heavy-set man walked in a grey hat and a grey trench coat. He was in his late sixties and he had a bushy moustache dusted with grey. He smiled, greeted us in Arabic, and settled down on the couch. This was the man we had code-named 'Adam.'

With the help of Rachel's translation, we began.

"My name is Ali Abdullah, and I am from Damascus. I am a member of the Organization for Human Rights in Syria, and I have written many things against the regime of Bashar Assad and the Ba'athist Party."

He had a grandfatherly smile, and he was charismatic on camera. He had just given another interview the day before.

"Could you please tell us about the times you were arrested, and why?"

Ali explained. He had worked in Tunisia as a journalist covering the Palestinian cause in the 1970s. During his time abroad, the wind changed and the Palestinian Liberation Organization fell out of favour with the Syrian government. Yet Ali Abdullah continued to give his support. When returned to Syria in 1994, they arrested him as he was walking off the plane. He spent six months in jail incommunicado.

In 2000, he joined the Organization for Human Rights in Syria and was elected as a member of the Administrative Council for one year. He was a founding member of several committees to revive civil society in Syria. In May 2005, he was arrested following an interview with the Attasi Forum for Democratic Dialogue. He was tried before the Supreme Security Court and was released after five months in a presidential pardon for 190 prisoners.

In March 2006, Abdullah was arrested after participating with his son Mohammed in a protest against the abuse of families of political prisoners by police. In prison, at age sixty-five, he was tortured by being having his hands slammed repeatedly in a door. He spent six months in prison with his son, after being tried before the military court in Damascus.

On the day he was released the third time, he went to pick up his clothes. When he called the name "Abdullah", the prison guard him brought him a pile that he didn't recognize immediately. Soon he realized it was his son's. Without him even knowing it, his other son Omar had been arrested and thrown into the same prison.

Omar was given five years for founding a pro-democracy youth forum with other university students. He will be released sometime in 2012.

"Why don't you leave Syria?" I asked. "Why don't you fight the government from abroad?"

He chuckled. "So I would say things abroad, and leave people in Syria to face the consequences? No. I can't do that, that isn't right. I have to be here to face the consequences myself."

His cell phone rang. He said something in Arabic, and Rachel's mouth dropped in astonishment. But the camera was still rolling, so we continued the interview.

"How do Syrians censor themselves?" I asked.

"Each Syrian has two personalities. One is the personality he shows outside, to everyone else. This one agrees with the government, and doesn't care about politics. But the other personality is shown only to friends and family. That is the side that criticizes the government, that is discontented with his country. But in the street, or in the newspaper, most Syrians have learned to keep quiet."

There was a pause. Sean had one last question.

"Are you proud of your sons?"

The man's expression did not change. He nodded slowly, and looked us all in the eye. "Yes" was all he said.

We stopped the camera. Rachel explained the phone call that caused alarm.

"They arrested Fida. Fida is a woman, about Ali's age, who signed the Damascus Declaration." Rachel's voice was grave, yet measured. "They are cracking down on the opposition. They had about thirty people arrested a few days ago, and half a dozen yesterday. And, here I was telling you that women rarely get arrested!"

I looked at Ali Abdullah. This man, advanced in his years, had taken the news with an amused smirk. His face was otherwise unchanged. A wave of heat flushed through me as I fully comprehended the courage of these Syrians. They faced the constant threat of arrest and they didn't blink. They continued their work, despite all the pressure; numb to emotions such as fear or paranoia. As I looked at Ali Abdullah's calm composure, I got the chilling impression that for him, arrest, detention, and even torture was. . . .something unremarkable.

We departed silently, giving each other high-fives as we left Rachel's alley. We had just conducted a our best interview yet. And with every passing block, we grew more and more confident. We had just wildly broken the law, recorded testimony against one of the most pernicious governments in the world, and no one had noticed. It was such a relief to get back to the hotel and pack our bags. We would soon climb into a taxi and make our way across the border to Jordan.

For Ali Abdullah however, things were a little different. He was arrested by for the fourth time only two days after giving us our interview. While we shuttled across Jordan in a taxi, he was rotting in a Syrian military prison.

15

THE HASHEMITE KINGDOM

We were leaving Syria. It was time to hold our breath and pray for the best. Nickie tucked the tape with the Ali Abdullah footage in the deepest pocket of her bag, and we packed her bag as before in the deepest bowels of the taxi trunk.

Our taxista stopped at the duty free shop at the border. He got out and rushed inside, explaining with gestures that the stop was mandatory. When I went into the store to get some chocolate, I saw him at the cashier cradling six cartons of American cigarettes in his hands. Back in the taxi, he opened up special hidden compartments underneath each seat, and began to unwrap the cartons and stuff the cigarettes inside. Malboros cost more in Jordan, and our driver fancied himself an entrepreneur.

He crumpled up the ball of cigarette carton wrappings and tossed them out the window. At that very moment, a car full of Syrian police pulled up right in front of us. The window rolled down, and an angry officer leaned out and confronted our driver.

"*Jawez!*" he barked fiercely. "Passport!"

I took a deep breath. I looked back at the others. Nickie's face was stoic. This was surreal. We were minutes away from fleeing this paranoid dictatorship once and for all, and our confounded driver, greedy for a handful of American dollars, had brought the Syrian police down on us. No doubt they would search every cranny of our car for smuggled cigarettes. I could just imagine the looks on their faces when they found something even more incriminating.

Our taxista made an eloquent defense before the cops. He protested passionately, waving his hands and arms, leaning outside the window for greater emphasis. The police got out of their car. Our driver lit the ignition and hit the gas.

My pulse was pounding. The car sped up as our driver made for the border checkpoints. What was he doing? Did he not know the police could bring him down with a simple phone call? He was mad!

The cops raced past us on a secondary road, then pulled right in front of our vehicle and stopped, partially blocking our path.

A full-body argument ensued. I haven't the faintest idea what was said. Our taxista leaned out the car window and gave an exasperated speech, waving his arms in the air like a maestro conducting a mad symphony. The policeman shouted and flailed his arms in response. I clutched my remaining American bills quietly in my pocket, wondering how much I had left for a possible bribe. And the way they were shouting at each other, I started to wonder if a bribe would even do the trick.

Our taxi cranked the wheel and piloted the car over the curb and onto the sand. He was back on the road to Jordan. As we left the police in our dust, I shook my head in disbelief. No one can defy the police like that and get away with it! Two or more checkpoints were coming up, teeming with guards. I dreaded the moment when the hammer would finally fall.

But the moment never came. To my infinite bewilderment, nothing happened to us at all. They did not even bother to search us. We stood in line for our exit stamp behind a small, fur-wearing Kazakhstani, and then ambled back to our taxi in peace. The last checkpoint waved us through.

We all cheered with relief, wondering with delight why on earth we were so lucky. As we drove the next few kilometers to the first Jordanian checkpoint, we leaned against the car doors and relaxed. In Jordan we were safe.

But we weren't there yet. Our taxista jumped out of his car when he had to stop at the end of a long line, and walked up to the border to negotiate something. I didn't understand, so I followed him. I came upon a very different shouting match than the one I had seen take place earlier. My taxista was waving his hands in a crowd of frustrated taxistas, looking desperate, while a corpulent border guard turned his face away and refused to listen to them. Minute after minute, the taxistas argued and gesticulated; the fat man swiveled about with indifference.

"What's the problem?" I asked a nearby woman whom I overheard speaking English.

"The border closes at three. It is five past three. They are trying to get through."

I was about to panic when the lady explained to me that the border was closed to cars, not to individuals. I called my friends and we entered the office and received our entry stamps. The taxista argued forcefully in protest when we pulled our bags out of the back of his car. He shouted at us when we paid him only half price, since he had taken us only halfway. He kicked the dust and swore, and skulked back towards his car. I chuckled. We left him with a plantation's worth of tobacco lying useless in the belly of his taxi.

Jordan was to be a short trip. Above all, I wanted to see the southern city of Petra—a city where tremendous buildings had been carved right into the mountainside by an ancient people. It was basically the only tourist attraction in Jordan, although there were a few others that the state desperately tried to advertise. Our taxi dropped us by a bank machine in Amman, and we took out some money before continuing our journey south.

"One and a half American dollars to the dinar!" I remarked. "I hope these things stretch."

They did not. Jordan was expensive to the point of absurdity. Coming from Syria, where street prices were as cheap as Egypt, this was an unwelcome change.

"Why is it so expensive?" I wondered aloud. I looked at Sean. He had studied the Middle East extensively in university, and we constantly probed him for facts. He replied with a wry smile.

"It's entirely artificial. The dinar is pegged higher than the dollar by the government. There's no massive industry to create such high prices. There isn't a *drop* of oil in this country. Almost all of their revenue comes from American aid. Hundreds of millions of dollars a year."

"Really! Why do they get so much?"

"Think about it. One third of Jordanians are Palestinian. One *third*. In 1948, this is where most of the refugees fled. And it was the only country in the Middle East to actually give Palestinian refugees citizenship. The Americans are making sure they have nice, comfortable lives here in Jordan so that they don't think about going back to Palestine."

I looked at my dinars. On the twenty, there was a picture of the Dome of the Rock, the third holiest site in all the Islamic world. This mosque was in Jerusalem, built directly on the foundations of the ancient Jewish temple. It was the only time I had ever seen a monument from another country depicted on a national bill. The top of the bill read 'The Hashemite Kingdom of Jordan.'

Jordan had been a kingdom ever since the Ottoman Empire was parceled up by the European powers in 1918. The French and British created monarchies in many of the resulting nations of the Middle East. King Faisal, whose revolt in Syria against the French failed miserably, was installed in Iraq as a King by the British. The Red Sea coast of the Arabian peninsula, known as the Hejaz, was governed by Faisal's father, from the Hashemite clan. He had a dream of uniting the entire Arab world under Hashemite monarchs. The slow brother of the family, who was thought by all to be mentally deficient, was given the throne of the new nation of Transjordan.

It didn't work out precisely as planned. King Faisal in Iraq died of a heart attack. His father heard about his sons death, and went clinically insane. The Hejaz was overtaken by the house of Saud, and the country was absorbed into Saudi Arabia. And the only Hashemite kingdom that survives today was the one governed by the 'mentally deficient' brother, who turned out to be an apt ruler after all. Today, his great grandson King Abdullah governs the country, whose name has been shortened to Jordan.

It was getting dark as we packed into a taxi and made our way south to Wadi Musa, the gateway to Petra. I spent plenty of time arguing in abysmal Arabic with a taxista who simply didn't *want* to understand that we wanted to find a restaurant and we didn't want to pay twenty dollars American each for a meal. Frustrated and tired and famished, I gave up and implored him to go straight to Petra. We would skip the restaurant.

He pulled into a restaurant. I didn't know whether to laugh or scream.

He slapped me on the back and walked in with us. He was joking the whole time, and now he was giggling at my exasperated face. We sat down at a grungy-looking table inside. The restaurant was large and over-lit by white florescent lights; the walls were a putrid shade of pink. Dozens of Arab men sat staring at my sister and Nickie, powerless to resist gazing on this blonde phenomenon that had just walked through the door of a Jordanian truck stop.

But the place was filled with the succulent smell of cooking meat. Large racks of greasy, blackened chicken were being pulled off a barbeque the length of a room. We ordered some of this, and it arrived with hummus and flatbread, salad, and four ice-cold Cokes.

The food was nothing short of sublime. Some of the best food in the world is cooked in roadside stands.

Petra has one of the greatest entrances of any ancient city. It begins with a kilometer hike through a long chasm—a path lined by cliffs of red stone, known as the *Siq*. The *Siq* winds from the temple town of Wadi Musa to the beginning of the city of Petra. When the red stone cliffs finally open, a wonder comes into view: a building many stories high, made of pillars in Greek style, carved into the side of the mountain. It is designed for no other purpose than to awe the traveler, ancient or modern, who enters the city for the first time. It is called the Treasury, but this was a false name given by some British archaeologist who fancied that this was where the Egyptian Pharaoh kept his treasure. Most people know it as the place where Indiana Jones found the Holy Grail.

An ancient people called the Nabateans created the city. All of the hundreds of stone caverns dug out of the rock faces were tombs, not houses made of stone. Houses were constructed with temporary materials that have long since vanished.

The largest of the tombs were those for the city's ruling families.

Petra's wealth came from it's position on the camel route from Arabia and Asia into Europe. It attracted the attention of one empire in particular, whose monuments it bears today. The main causeway of Petra is a Roman road. There is a Roman amphitheatre, Roman temples, Roman pillars, and a Roman forum. It was an imperial outpost of the eastern provinces of the empire, and of course generated great wealth in taxes.

We strode down the main road. Sean and I drooled at the sight of ancient temples; Nickie and Kristen were enjoying a day of pure relaxation. We climbed together up a staircase of hundreds of stone steps. On the top of the city, bathed in sun and surrounded by a deep, cloudless sky, was an altar carved into stone. It was called the High Place of Sacrifice. We looked around and breathed—the whole ancient city could be seen from the height of that peak.

What an excellent break Petra was. There was no Mukhabarat, no Syrian opposition, no interviews, no border guards, no danger. We climbed to the edge of a nearby peak and looked down at the city. Below us, dozens of Bedouins with camels walked up and down, pestering tourists for a ride. When the first one hailed me and offered me his camel saying "Bedouin Ferrari," I was charmed and couldn't help but laugh. By the time the seventh one did it, I was thoroughly annoyed. Along the stairway to the High Place of Sacrifice sat little Bedouin children with cardboard boxes of red rocks. They were selling them for one dinar each.

"I mean, they're *rocks*" said Sean. "Do they really think I'm going to pay them a dollar for a *rock*? I could pick one up if I wanted!"

Since Cairo, we had all learned to laugh off the temple townies, the thriving underclass that makes money by hawking trinkets or offering camel rides to the tourist population. They annoyed us constantly whenever we found a ruin worth visiting; we had to learn how to deflect them and not be irritated. But the other side of the coin was also obvious to us—that these were a tremendous community of poor people, whose young were sharp enough to bargain prices in seven languages, and were fed and clothed entirely off the change that tourists threw away without thinking.

Two Bedouin youths lay on a mat just a hundred meters from where we sat. They were napping in the sun and had long since abandoned their hawking duties. My sister spoke.

"So who are the Bedouins exactly?"

Sean answered. "Bedouins are more Arab than the Arabs. They were the original nomadic tribes who roamed the desert during the time of Mohammed. They were the people who first converted to Islam and then conquered this whole place."

Fourteen centuries ago, Mohammed converted the Arab tribes and marched on Mecca. When the Prophet entered the city, he had all the monuments of polytheism destroyed, and proclaimed the pre-eminence of Islam. Thereafter, as the Arab world spread to Egypt, Syria, Palestine, and beyond, the Bedouins found themselves no longer nomadic. They now lived in cities, farmed for food, and mingled with the populations they conquered.

Some tribes, of course, remained devotees of Islam but never lost the old nomadic ways. I looked at the youths sleeping near us, in tattered T-shirts and dirt-covered jeans, their faces darkened by constant exposure to the sun. From Egypt to Syria to Jordan to Palestine, these Arabian Gypsies roam, herd goats, and continue their ancient life in a new world dominated by city-dwellers.

As I walked out of Petra later that night in the fading light, I was passed by half a dozen of them, whipping exhausted, sweat-drenched horses in front of their carts. They were swarthy men, whose poverty was obvious in their ragged clothing and rotting teeth. How sad, I thought, and how ironic, that this nomadic culture was the seed of the Arab peoples and all of their achievements. And now they skulk about the wilderness and the temple towns of the Middle East, disenfranchised by their own descendants; living on the outskirts of a world of cities and agriculture that has left them behind.

We checked out of the Hotel Iceberg, whose shower felt like a glacial stream, and whose rooms were so frigid that they were impossible to be in without lying in one's bed under the minimal supply of bedding. Of course, this was one of the places highly recommended by the Lying Planet, and we were too happy to leave.

We piled into a van for Amman that day. The hotel owners explained this would be the last day we could take the van for a while, because of the Hajj. The Hajj is the yearly Muslim pilgrimage of people to the holy city of Mecca, which the Islamic faith commands all members who are able to make the journey to accomplish at least once. The beginning of this pilgrimage is a holiday across the Muslim world, even for those who are not making the journey.

We didn't need to stay in Jordan any longer, and we were off to Israel. A Palestinian cab driver in Amman agreed to drive us to the King Hussein bridge—the border crossing into Israel—for thirty dollars American. The trip took three hours. When we arrived, I rolled down my window and a Palestinian guard smiled politely at me.

"No. Is not open. It's Christmas!"

My mouth dropped as I stared at the border guard.

"No, my friend. We came all this way. It's ok. . .we'll walk." I got out of the taxi and prepared to get out our heavy bags for the walk across this sun-scorched bridge.

"No." Another polite smile. "Is closed. It's Muslim Christmas. No open."

I was enraged. Then why was he even standing there? We were gaining access to the West Bank: Israeli-controlled territory. The border was run by Jews. And this fool had to patronize me with a big smile by telling me it's 'Christmas', as if white people were unable to understand what the Hajj was.

"So. Where do you want to go then?"

I looked daggers at the taxista. It dawned on me that he knew all along this bridge would be closed today. And he sat there with a straight face and withheld the information because he knew he could get money out of us on the way there, and money to take us to a hotel on the way back.

We had him drive us to a nearby town. When we only paid him forty dollars American, he jumped out of the car and shrieked and ran after us. He chased us into the hotel and raised hell with the staff because he was only able to cheat these white men for ten dollars above the price they negotiated. He wouldn't leave.

I had to walk into the serene hotel and examine the pool so as not to explode. I left Nickie to deal with this one; thank god she did. She ended the conflict by adding five dollars more, and walking to the door and holding it out like she would a carrot to a bad donkey.

The donkey left. And my headache immediately decreased by half.

Nickie treated all of us to the hotel. We were so relieved. It had wireless internet and laundry services, as well as a lovely restaurant downstairs. It was heaven. For a few dinar more, Nickie and I were driven off to a spa nearby made from a natural hot spring. In the hot, sulfurous water we watched the sun go down. Thank god for that evening. Nickie had told us that we really needed to recharge our batteries for what was ahead.

Our spa was at the base of a large hill. We had stopped on the way down to take a picture of the landscape. Our driver pointed out the formations to us on the plains below.

"That is the Jordan river, and that, is the Dead Sea."

We stared. Before us stretched the most contested land of all, our final destination on this journey. Across the Jordan, beyond the Dead Sea, lay Israel and Palestine. Tomorrow, the King Hussein bridge would be open, and we would finally enter the land that all of us had waited many years to actually see.

16

DISNEYLAND

'Disneyland' was Israel. Daniel had told us this at the chic, avant-garde restaurant in Beirut. It was a traveler's codeword for a country's name that was taboo to speak in Arab society. Arabs, as a rule, called the place 'Palestine,' in solidarity with the people they saw as its rightful owners. I always thought this might be the cause of some serious confusion when they got down to discussing the finer points of politics, such as who fired rockets into whose territory, or who flattened whose city in retaliation. But for our purposes, when spoken over the tables of cafes, or walking down the road, Disneyland was Disneyland, and that was that.

We first saw the bright white-and-blue flags, emblazoned with the six-pointed Shield of David, flapping in the breeze as we crossed the King

Hussein Bridge, and officially exited the nation of Jordan. Here, nomenclature played another trick on us. The King Hussein Bridge is called the Allenby Bridge by the Israelis, after the last British commander in charge of the Mandate of Palestine, before the British army pulled out in 1948 and the bloodbath began. The bus lurched to a stop in front of a drab, squat building, which was guarded by steel-faced Israeli soldiers in olive fatigues, carrying black, businesslike automatic weapons. As we got off the bus, darker-skinned Palestinians in florescent orange vests cheerfully hoisted our bags on their shoulders and humped them over to a conveyor belt, where they disappeared one by one into the bowels of the border compound.

"See the division of labour going on here, Kieran?" Sean said wryly.

I nodded. "Does Emily like this?"

"NO!" Nickie and Sean spat together, in a threatening, parental tone.

I flashed them a wide, sarcastic grin that had once gotten me tossed out of math class for impertinence. They rolled their eyes and glowered. 'Emily' was my camera; I had just asked them whether or not it was kosher to take pictures, knowing full well that it wasn't. We had been forewarned to take no pictures whatsoever of any Israeli military installations, especially checkpoints such as this. The two of them were on edge about my compulsive photo-snapping after my little escapade in Shatila.

We stepped through the mother of all metal detectors, and Israeli soldiers met us at the other side and waved magic black wands over our bodies to check for concealed guns. They were efficient and dispassionate. All of them were in their early twenties or younger, and most of them were female. Sean muttered to me under his breath that they were probably allotting the less strenuous physical work to the women: Israel, like most militarized nations, has mandatory conscription beginning at age eighteen.

Inside the checkpoint was a giant white waiting room, filled with Westerners looking bored or nervous. Most of the people here were in their twenties or early thirties, shabbily-dressed, and looking like they would have a tall backpack on their backs if the Israelis weren't busy inspecting them We recognized a couple we had met in Syria, who were traveling by motorcycle across the Middle East.

"How long have you guys been waiting here?" Kristen asked when we took our seats.

"Only two hours!" they replied. "Some people here have been waiting for more than five."

I sighed and realized that the Israeli government was going to thieve a traveling day from us. We had given them our passports at the entrance, and now we simply had to wait until they called us.

Up at the entry wickets, there was a shift change. Some plain, humourless girl soldiers had come to replace the plain, humourless ones going for a break. They sat there chatting dryly, making a show of not caring how many people were waiting patiently to get into their country and spend their tourist dollars. The girls who were leaving were lighter and looked European; the girls who were replacing them were darker and looked Ethiopian.

Since its birth, Israel had been a nation of immigrants. The country was established as a homeland for the Jews, since in the aftermath of the Second World War and the Holocaust, it seemed the only way the Jews could ever be free from persecution would be to have a nation-state all to their own. After the United Nations resolution of 1947, which divided British Palestine in half—one part for the Jews, one part for the Palestinians—boatloads of immigrant Jews streamed in from around the world. Many of them were from Europe, where they had been imprisoned or relocated under Nazi rule. Thousands came from lesser-known diaspora communities, in places like North Africa or the Middle East. Thousands came from Ethiopia, where a community of Jews live who claim to be descendants of the Queen of Sheba and King Solomon. And some came from a community of black Americans from Chicago who claim that they are the rightful heirs of the tribes of Israel. All of these disparate peoples make up the population of the modern Israeli state, which absorbs thousands and thousands of new immigrants every year.

Sean explained to me that the army is the chief tool used to homogenize these new arrivals. In the Israeli Defense Forces, or IDF, everyone learns a common language: modern Hebrew. Everyone learns cooperation and discipline regardless of one's individual background. And—perhaps most important for the Israeli state—everyone learns the military mentality of constant vigilance against an omnipresent enemy.

The motorcycle couple was called to the wickets for questioning. They spent nearly twenty or thirty minutes arguing with the Ethiopian girl soldiers. They were planning to go to Iran, and they were desperately hoping to avoid getting the kiss of death on their passports.

"The kiss of death," Sean said, rubbing his hands. "I can't wait to see what it looks like!"

The 'kiss of death' was the Israeli border stamp: to receive it was to be barred from entering many of the countries of the Middle East. The Arab nations had not accepted the UN partition of Palestine, and when the British left in 1948 they immediately declared war on the Israelis. In what became known as the War of Independence, the Israelis fought valiantly and checkmated the Arab armies, displacing millions of Palestinians, and doubling the size of

Israeli-controlled territory. All that was left of the nation of Palestine was quarantined within two tiny territories: a jelly-bean shaped piece of land called the West Bank, on the border of Jordan; and the twenty-mile wide strip of coastline known as Gaza, on the border of Egypt.

Since that day, all the Arab nations have refused to recognize Israel's existence except for two: Jordan and Egypt, who signed a peace treaty with Israel after a war in 1973. It was this treaty that made it possible for me to travel back to Egypt after the journey was through.

Now a family came out of a consultation room nearby. The middle-aged mother was near tears; her dejected teenagers skulked out behind her, followed by a husband who patted her on the shoulder ineffectually. They had been refused entry. This caused a twitter of concerned whispers to break out among the foreigners who sat nearby; I took refuge in the opposite corner of the room, and dived into a book that I had lifted from the hotel in Jordan. My frustration was rising, and I did not want to contemplate the possibility that we could have come all this way just to be refused entry. Our wait was nearing four hours, and the only form of weak revenge I could think of was to trash this fascist little country on my blog and convince my friends not to come here.

"Nelson? Kristen Nelson?"

The girl soldiers were calling for my sister. Nickie was called to the wicket with her; Sean and I were called to the next wicket. They asked who we were traveling with, and where and how long we would stay in Israel. We responded with true answers, and one rehearsed lie.

"We are going to Jerusalem, Tel Aviv, and Haifa."

No Israeli border guard wanted to hear that we were going to Palestine.

The soldiers searched our bags and found nothing offending, except for a mosque-shaped alarm clock that Sean had bought in Syria, which wailed the call to prayer. They didn't even seem to care that Nickie had a huge camera; they didn't ask one question about what she wanted to film and why. In the end, it was simple, and I wondered why a four hour wait was really necessary. But we hoisted our bags on our backs with glee, for we had finally arrived.

"So now that we're in, where do you want to stay?" I asked.

"Let's go to the hotel Faisal," Sean said. "It's on the Green Line. In the guidebook, it says 'come for the politics.'"

It was shocking how small the country was. Barely an hour passed between the border and the moment we first saw the beige and white towers of Jerusalem come into view. Another hour and we might have reached the sea. Our taxi dropped us a hundred meters from the Damascus Gate, one of the giant stone entrances to the walled Old City. The Damascus Gate marked the site of the Green Line, the invisible boundary that separated the Israel and Palestine. I noted how even the roads conformed to this fact of political geography: here the road from West Jerusalem and the road from East Jerusalem both curled north and diverged towards their respective sides, separated by a large green fence. Only on foot could we cross the line.

East Jerusalem was Palestinian; West Jerusalem was Israeli. When Israel was first born, almost all Jerusalem was Palestinian, with only a small enclave of Jews in the Jewish Quarter of the walled old city. Now the Jews dominated West Jerusalem, and had ringed the outside of East Jerusalem with settlements. Although Tel Aviv was nominally the capital of Israel, the Knesset, the Israeli parliament, was in West Jerusalem, as well as most of the government ministries. There was no question: Jerusalem was the Holy City, the beating heart of the Jewish faith, the shining gem of the Israeli heartland. The Israelis wanted it all to themselves, and the Palestinians, for whom the city was equally holy, would resist them to the last man.

I smiled as we humped our bags up the cold cement flight of stairs to the Hotel Faisal. Our hostel, only a hairsbreadth inside East Jerusalem, was practically in the dead center of political ground zero of the Arab-Israeli conflict.

"Where's Sean?" Nickie asked, once we had all unpacked our bags and settled into our rooms.

"I told him to go," I answered.

"You told him to go? Without us?"

"He dropped his bags and then just stood there looking forlorn. I could see he just couldn't wait. He's wanted to see it all his life."

"See what?"

"The Western Wall."

Nickie, Kristen and I left the hostel while the light was just beginning to fade. We stepped down the uneven stone steps through the Damascus Gate, and then fought our way through a bustling crowd of Arabs. Men were packing up portable falafel grills and shutting shop on the steps leading down to the labyrinth of covered walkways that was Old Jerusalem. We passed Muslims selling hordes of sweet pistachio candy, or copies of the Qu'ran and plaques of its verses in Arabic calligraphy; we passed Jews selling small statues of Moses, menorahs, and colourful little skullcaps; we passed Christians as well, their shops packed wall to wall with icons of Jesus, Mary, and the saints; there were gilded bibles, and crucifixes hanging in bunches, waiting to be sold. Upon first glance, I could see no physical differences between the shopkeepers, be they Muslim, Jew, or Christian. All of them had dark hair, light brown skin, and the same facial features I saw in all the peoples of the Middle East. The only differences I could see were in their clothing, or in the religious paraphernalia which adorned their shops.

We followed rusted signs in Hebrew and English down the long cobblestone streets of the old city. Here and there we passed places where the paving stones were giant, yellow, and uneven: plaques told us they were the remnants of the old Roman roads which had once run throughout Jerusalem. We passed the Via Dolorosa, the path along which Christ carried the cross towards his place of crucifixion. And finally, by following a group of Orthodox Jews with skullcaps and white tassels dangling below their clothing, we made it to our destination, the holiest site in all of Judaism. The Western Wall.

IDF soldiers watched us carefully as we passed through metal detectors, and we stepped down into a courtyard lit with floodlights, above which was hoisted a large Israeli flag. Dozens of Orthodox and Hasidic Jews, sporting round black hats and long beards, were lined up against the wall, praying. At the right moment during their incantations, they would bob their heads rhythmically in the direction of the wall, in one of their most ancient rituals of prayer. Just like every mosque, the wall was sexually segregated for reasons of modesty; just like every mosque, the female half was smaller. Kristen and Nickie went to one side, while I went towards the other, and donned the obligatory paper skull-cap which the gatekeeper handed to me.

In the soft yellow light, the giant stones looked smooth and ancient. It was easy to see where the stones of antiquity ended, and modern construction began. This was the last remaining wall of Solomon's Temple, the holy resting place of the Ark of the Covenant, the great golden casket that the Israelites had carried before them during their wanderings; a symbol of God's promise that they would one day posses a land of their own. In the year 70 AD, the temple was sacked by the Romans, in response to the Jewish tax revolt. The Romans expelled the Jews from Palestine, and thus began the two-thousand-year exile of the chosen people. They settled in communities all across the world: in the Middle East and North Africa, in Europe and Eastern Europe, and especially Russia. Some even made it as far as India and China. Over the years, a few filtered back into Palestine, which the Arabs had long since conquered. The shining Dome of the Rock, and the Al-Asqa mosque were built on the very place Solomon's Temple once stood. All that was left was the Western Wall.

For years even after the founding of Is-rael, the wall, which lay deep in the heart of

Palestinian Jerusalem, remained sealed off from most of the Jewish believers. Things changed in 1967, when the Arab nations secretly prepared for war, to oust Israel from the Middle East once and for all. Things didn't quite work out as planned. In what became known as the Six-Day War, the Israelis made preemptive air strikes against Egypt and Syria, destroying most of their air force while it was still resting on the ground. And in order to ensure the security of their tiny strip of land, the Israelis pushed forward to the banks of the river Jordan, and occupied all that remained of the Arab nation of Palestine. And Old Jerusalem, which before had been closed to all but the Arabs, was now finally controlled by Jewish soldiers. The Jews, for the first time in two thousand years, were in possession of the last remnant of Solomon's Temple.

The stones of the wall itself were worn smooth by centuries of touching. In the cracks between them, I could see dozens of little scrunched up bits of paper. This was another timeless tradition—to write one's most desired prayers on a small sheet of paper, and press it into the cracks of the wall.

It was a ritual I had come all the way across the Atlantic to perform.

In a nearby enclave, I scribbled my wishes on a small scrap of lined paper. I bunched it up as tightly as I could, to leave room for the next people who came to leave their prayers. And before I stuck it into the cracks on the wall, I closed my eyes and relaxed, and meditated on my requests.

"What's your name?"

I opened my eyes, my train of thought disturbed.

In front of me was a Hasidic Jew, perhaps forty years of age, with a glowing orange beard. He grasped my hand in his.

"Um. . .Kieran."

He began to pray. He bobbed his head in front of me, incanting some rhythmic lines in Hebrew, all while keeping a firm hold on my hand.

"Name again?"

"Kieran."

He continued. Here I was, an obvious gentile, visiting the Jews' most sacred site—and this devout man was uttering a blessing on my behalf. I was utterly charmed.

"You have twenty shekels for the Synagogue?" he asked, once he had finished.

"What?" I blurted out.

"Please sir, just twenty shekels!"

I walked away from him rudely, deeply offended that he had interrupted my prayer to petition me for money.

Over by a different part of the wall, I again closed my eyes and blanked my mind. I fingered my crumpled little petition in my hand, breathed deeply, and began to pray.

I was just about halfway through when I felt a hand grasping mine. I opened my eyes to see *another* Hasidic Jew in front of me, of the same short stature, this one with a great black beard.

"Excuse me. What's your name?"

I did not make the Synagogue twenty shekels richer that night. And by the time I left the Western Wall for the hostel, I had finally managed to find a moment to pray at this most holy of places. In a nearby enclave, out of the reach of the pan-handling *Haredim*, I stood still, relaxed, and whispered my requests. And then, finally, I approached the base of the wall, its massive boulders worn smooth by centuries of touching, and closing my eyes, I clasped my little crumpled page within my fingers, and pushed it between the cracks.

We awoke the next morning in the frigid yet authentic atmosphere of the Hotel Faisal. It was run by Osama, a chubby Palestinian with one withered hand, and his cousin Ali. As the day began to break, the dozens of young travelers from a myriad of nationalities stirred to life. We rose and washed ourselves in his freezing showers ("hot water, twenty-four hours!"), and waited patiently to brush our teeth in one of the two working sinks.

We strolled outside and walked back towards the Old City, the sun shining high above the Damascus Gate. There wasn't much question of where we were going to go. Our maps of Old Jerusalem showed that it was divided into four quarters: the Christian Quarter, the Jewish Quarter, the Muslim Quarter, and the Armenian Quarter. Today, we were visiting the Christian Quarter, and the Church of the Holy Sepulchre.

The Church was arguably the holiest site in all of Christendom. It was built, supposedly, on the very spot that Christ was crucified. It stood tall and dusty, almost entirely obscured amongst the buildings of Old Jerusalem. It would be easy to miss, were it not for its two shining silver domes. Unlike the Dome of the Rock, or the Lutheran Cathedral up the road, from the outside, the Church was visually unimpressive.

But then we stepped inside.

At the entrance of the church lay a large, flat beige stone on a dais, worn smooth as butter. A glittering mosaic on the wall behind displayed what it was. It was an elegant message—a scene wrought out of tiny coloured shards of ceramic—which needed no words and no translation. It was a scene of the dead Jesus, his skin pale, the stigmata upon his flesh, being laid on a rock and wrapped in a shroud by his weeping disciples. This was the rock, according to legend, on which Christ was prepared for burial.

Christian pilgrims surrounded me, gathered around the stone, and crouched silently, and touched their forehead to the soft stone. They were so silent you could hear them breathing. As this scene unfolded before me, my skin tingled. Some early Christian sympathies from my childhood burned to life within me, and I bowed and touched my forehead to the stone. It was though I was animated by an invisible force. In that moment, everything cynical within my soul—a full decade of atheism—vanished into smoke, and an inner voice told me that here, I was to bow, and pray, and give reverence to this most sublime and ancient place.

What followed next was surreal. I was walking through a dream.

We wandered slowly through the deep, silent Orthodox church, with its high-vaulted ceilings and its glowing beams of light. Crowds of pilgrims walked past with their eyes cast about them in awe, rapture upon their faces, many shedding tears of solemnity. We paused briefly before a Catholic mass being held in one of the church's many enclaves. A white-robed priest was speaking about the place we were standing.

"When they buried Him, it said, they buried him in Calvary. Calvary was a quarry in the time of Jesus, a field of white stone. After a crucifixion, they would take down the body, and place it in a tomb they had cut in the rock nearby. And if you will notice, inside the tomb of Christ, the stone is entirely white. . ."

For a brief hour, I was back in the early days of Christianity, when thousands of pilgrims queued for their turn to touch one sacred relic. I knelt to touch Golgotha, a piece of the rock upon which the cross was raised. As we wandered downstairs to a vast subterranean chamber, with a great mosaic of Christ's face upon the floor, Sean and I traded a Bible I had brought, and solemnly incanted passages from the story of the passion; pieces I had known since childhood, pieces I knew so well I could almost recite them by heart. Yet here, in the sanctum of such a place, they shook me to my core, and in some way that I cannot comprehend, I became like a child again, awed by the sanctity of the ground on which I stepped.

And finally, after we had visited all of the great cathedral, we walked to its heart, to a circular room beneath a great silver dome. Long shafts of light reached down from the ceiling, catching the glowing dust. And here, in the center of all, we paid homage to the central symbol of that ancient place, encased in a small wooden building. Deep within, we knelt down, folded our arms across a tiny altar of milk-white stone, and said a prayer in the very tomb of Christ.

When we left, the sunlight and the midday heat broke the spell. I had to stand for a moment and blink; reluctantly, my mind drifted back from dream to reality. And in that moment, I realized the subtle power that Jerusalem had held, for so many thousands of years, over the minds of men.

I understood why the Israelis had done everything they could to capture and keep this polis, the jewel of the holy land. I understood why they had fought for the city and conquered it; why they had divided it and peopled it with Jews; why they fenced off the eastern half with settlements; why they had split it off from rest of Palestine by a wall. I could understand that somehow, the Israelites could never have their nation. . .without Jerusalem.

And I understood why the Palestinians, the inhabitants of one of the most sacred and ancient cities in all the Islamic world, somehow knew that the loss of Jerusalem is the loss of themselves.

We rounded the street to last landmark that we had wanted to see. The Lutheran Cathedral was almost a contradiction in terms, considering the Lutheran commitment to humility and modesty. Inside was sparse and unadorned, with its curved arches and bare simplicity. But we had not come to see the building itself, but its tower.

Upwards and upwards we climbed, on hundreds and hundreds of white stone stairs. Through miniscule windows we stole snatches of rooftops as we climbed, higher and higher until our breath was short and our legs ached. Yet still we pressed on. When we finally reached the top, the landscape of Jerusalem exploded into view. We saw it all: the thousand pale rooftops of the Holy City, the silver domes of the Church of the Holy Sepulchre, the midday sunlight glimmering in the hypnotic golden skin of the Dome of the Rock. Before us, we beheld the Temple Mount, the prize of the Holy City; before us, we beheld the pale stonework of Sueliman's walls against the dark foliage of the Mount of Olives. Breathlessly, we stood silent and motionless, drinking in the splendor of the moment.

And I opened my Bible and read, in a voice I was barely able to keep straight after climbing the stairs, a passage from Isaiah.

"Nations will come to your light,
    and kings to the brightness of your dawn.

Lift up your eyes and look about you:
    All assemble and come to you;
    your sons come from afar,
    and your daughters are carried on the arm.

Then you will look and be radiant,
    your heart will throb and swell with joy;
    the wealth on the seas will be brought to you,
    to you the riches of the nations will come.

Herds of camels will cover your land,
    young camels of Midian and Ephah.
    And all from Sheba will come,
    bearing gold and incense
    and proclaiming the praise of the Lord.

All Kedar's flocks will be gathered to you,
the rams of Nebaioth will serve you;
they will be accepted as offerings on my altar,
and I will adorn my glorious temple.

Who are these that fly along like clouds,
like doves to their nests?

Surely the islands look to me;
in the lead are the ships of Tarshish,
bringing your sons from afar,
with their silver and gold,
to the honor of the Lord your God,
the Holy One of Israel,
for he has endowed you with splendor.

Foreigners will rebuild your walls,
and their kings will serve you.
Though in anger I struck you,
in favor I will show you compassion.

Your gates will always stand open,
they will never be shut, day or night,
so that men may bring you the wealth of the
nations—their kings led in triumphal procession.

For the nation or kingdom that will not serve you
will perish; it will be utterly ruined.

The glory of Lebanon will come to you,
the pine, the fir and the cypress together,

to adorn the place of my sanctuary;
and I will glorify the place of my feet.

The sons of your oppressors will come bowing
before you; all who despise you will bow down
at your feet and will call you the City of the
Lord, Zion of the Holy One of Israel."[7]

After the sun had set, we relaxed, exhausted and famished, upon Osama's cushions at the hostel. Outside, the world was dark, and the walls of Old Jerusalem could barely be discerned against the deepening sky. I sat wordless, staring into the deep orange glow of a brazier that Ali had set burning near my feet. Sean slowly sipped a cup of tea, and Kristen and Nickie stared, lost in thought.

Little by little, the room began to fill with travelers. Osama's hostel was unique to probably any hostel in the world: it served a free meal at eight o'clock every evening. By the time Osama's skinny cousin had hauled the massive cauldron onto the common table, the room was packed to bursting. There were hippie Americans, unshaven Germans, chattering Japanese, and a middle-aged Austrian in patched clothing who sat meditating in the corner of the room, with a walking staff hung with dozens of colourful charms balanced across his knees.

----

[7] Isaiah: 60, King James Bible.

Osama sat beside us and contemplated the brazier. When Nickie struck up a conversation with him, we learned he was a documentary filmmaker; the hostel was merely a side job. He seemed very interested seemed in our film project, especially in our intentions to go north to Ramallah and interview some patients at a torture clinic the next day.

"Anything you need," he said "anything *at all* that you need—I will get for you! Just ask."

We noticed one freckle-faced girl, perhaps twenty-three, snapping dozens of photos during the evening meal. She took wide shots of everyone who was there—of Osama, the guests, and the staff—with a camera unusually large for a tourist. She took one of Ali while he was serving her. When he looked up with raised eyebrows, she snapped three more in rapid succession, blinding him with the flash. Ali almost dropped the bowl he was holding and cringed, smiling nervously at her. She giggled and smiled, like it was all a joke.

"I don't like that girl" said Osama, watching her intently. "She asks too many questions."

I understood. Israel's security service was everywhere, especially in corners of East Jerusalem where the IDF did not have Jewish contacts. It was entirely possible that she was a member of Shin Bet, the Israeli internal spy agency.

And if she was, she was doing a really bad job of hiding it.

17
MENTAL HEALTH

"How soon can you get here?" Amjad asked, his voice polite but firm.

"Well we are in Jerusalem, and we can be on a bus within half an hour." I was awake and groggy, pacing over Osama's cold floor in my bare feet, speaking into the little blue cell phone we had bought.

"Half an hour? Ok. It's just that we have cases waiting for you right now."

"Now? Ok. We'll get moving right away."

"Yes, please do. A few of them have left, because they are afraid of appearing on camera. So it's important that you get to Ramallah as soon as possible."

I roused my friends, and we all got out of bed and groggily began to prepare as fast as we could. I stuffed my tripod into an oversized back-pack, and Nickie stuck her camera equipment into a beer cooler for the inevitable Israeli check-point. We all made sure we had our passports on us. I waited outside and bought a falafel sand-wich, which the Palestinian vendor stuffed with hummus and every type of vegetable, including red cabbage, and munched on it while waiting for my friends to appear. Once they finally came, we walked up the road two blocks to the station, and boarded a bus for Ramallah.

Ramallah, the de facto political and economic capital of Palestine since the segregation of East Je-rusalem, had an entirely different landscape. The apartment buildings were more run down and mis-shapen; flecks of garbage littered the streets; the traffic moved slower and was more chaotic. It was immediately obvious that it was an Arab city.

We descended from the bus a few steps from the center of town—a large square with four great stone lions posing in the center—a gift to the city from Yasser Arafat. As we turned the corner and walked up the bustling street towards our destina-tion, I saw posters of the man pasted on the cement walls of abandoned lots, many of them peeling or damaged by water. Some showed his face imposed over a photograph of the Dome of the Rock. Even dead, he was still their hero.

Yasser Arafat was the leader of one of the many Palestinian guerrilla factions which mushroomed to life after 1948, when the Palestinian exile truly began. While many of these splinter groups sought patronage from Arab countries, Arafat would have none of this. He founded a movement called *Fatah*, meaning 'conquest', which was dedicated to the liberation of Palestine by Palestinians alone.

Arafat became the champion of the Palestinian cause after he successfully resisted an Israeli invasion at the Palestinian town of Karameh, which in Arabic means 'dignity.' He rose to become the chairman of the Palestinian Liberation Organization, and umbrella group for all the splinter guerrilla factions of the Palestinian resistance. Due to his many failures in the political hornet's nest of the Arab world, the PLO under Arafat was chased out of Jordan into Lebanon, and then out of Lebanon into Tunisia. Yet despite all of his mistakes, none of them ever seemed to stick to him, leading the New York Times correspondent Thomas Friedman to term him 'the Teflon Guerrilla.'

Late in his life, things began to change when Bill Clinton opened up negotiations between the PLO and Israelis during a series of conferences which would eventually become known as the 'peace process.' But whatever the offer laid on the table by Israel, be it a political filibuster or a real concession, Arafat stuck to his guns. The Palestinians wanted three things: for the Israelis to cease the military occupation of the West Bank and the Gaza strip, for the right of return for all Palestinian refugees, and for Palestinian control over East Jerusalem. And of these three conditions, Jerusalem was the one that the Israelis would never, ever put on the table.

Talks broke down in the Bush era, when the hawkish Ariel Sharon was elected President of Israel, when Western militancy came back into fashion, and when the definition of 'terrorist' became slippery and malleable. Arafat died in 2004 at the age of 75. A cause of death was never revealed to the public, and right-wing Western magazines speculated that he had practiced sexually deviant habits and contracted AIDS. He was succeeded by Mahmoud Abbas, who is now president of the Palestinian Authority, an organization that now exercises limited authority over some areas of the occupied territories. All Arafat left Palestine was a few corrupt political organizations which had already been thoroughly infiltrated by Israeli spies, and a legacy of perpetually frustrated peace conferences which the Israelis use to stall for time while they build more settlements on Palestinian land. That, and his unifying image, which continues to be mounted on posters throughout the West Bank, to give hope to the young Palestinians that one day, eventually, victory would be theirs.

"It's right up here guys," Nickie said, and pointed to a large building in front of us which had

'TRC' marked down the side of it. As we went in, we made our way through a small crowd of youth wearing black and white Palestinian *keffiyehs*, and stepped onto the elevator.

We had arrived at the headquarters of the subject of our next film project: The Treatment and Rehabilitation Centre for Victims of Torture.

"First, could you please introduce yourself and tell what role you play within this organization?"

"My name is Mahmoud Sehwail, consultant psychiatrist, and the founder of the TRC."

Amjad, the heavyset psychologist who Nickie had contacted through the internet, had met us at the door. He showed us in to our first interviewee, a short, middle-aged man in glasses and a sharp suit. Sean asked his first question the instant Nickie had set up the camera.

"The idea to establish these services came out of the perceived huge demand of the Palestinian population in the West Bank, as our realization that the available services in the public sector, NGO, and private sector could not gratify such needs."

He continued speaking, without pause. While I thought it would be a normal interview, with pauses where we would have the chance to ask questions, apparently the director had everything prepared. He knew exactly what he wanted to say, and in English.

"First of all, we noticed that forty percent of those who are tortured in Israeli prisons suffer from Post Traumatic Stress Disorder. According to Israeli and Palestinian human rights organizations, more than eighty-five percent of Palestinians are tortured in Israeli prisons.

"The ex-detainees, victims of torture, are reluctant to seek help from the public sector, and these services are very primitive and cannot deal with the victims of torture. You know, forty percent of Palestinian males are detained or jailed once or more. The majority of these people are youth. In the private sector, psychiatrists are very few, and victims of torture cannot afford to pay the fees."

He explained how the center, which was a non-profit organization, mainly involved itself with treatment and rehabilitation. Their patients suffered anything from acute psychosis to depression. Patients were assessed first by general practitioners and then by psychiatrists. They were given medication if necessary, and finally, once they began to improve, they were seen be a social worker who helped them to find a new place in society. Since patients often did not come to them, they had to form an outreach program, where field workers would investigate who had recently been released from Israeli prisons, and contact them. They even made regular visits to Israeli jails.

"We also have training for mental health workers," Mahmoud said. "We train them in mental health and human rights; we consider human rights to be strongly linked to mental health."

The director concluded and thanked us, having said his piece. Then he shook our hands, thanked us for coming, and left in a rush. It was December 23rd and everyone, including Muslims it seemed, was preparing for the Christmas holiday.

Amjad led us into another room, while we waited for the patients themselves to prepare for the interviews.

"Over 28,000 Palestinians have been arrested since the beginning of the Second Intifada," he explained to us. "We have two main types of victim: direct, and indirect. The direct victims suffered torture personally, while the indirect victims are those who experience mental health problems when a family member or a loved one suffers from torture."

He took us into a room filled with children's artwork. Nickie, with her filmmaker's eye, bade me to take some still photos of the colourful murals, pottery, and posters decorated with sparkles and glued pasta.

"You have children here?" I asked in surprise.

"Yes, we have a children's program. We treat many children at the TRC. We feel it is an important part of treatment: family rehabilitation."

"Can we film the children doing this?" asked Nickie.

"Sure, why not?" said Amjad. "We will arrange it."

"So with children, we are always talking about indirect victims, right?" I asked Amjad. I thought it was a stupid question, but decided to ask it anyways. "Surely, children are never direct victims of torture, are they?"

Amjad smiled weakly.

"Actually, you'd be surprised."

"I am from the village of Bet Rima, and I am currently attending college."

The man facing us was twenty-five, dressed in a long black overcoat. He did not give his name, but allowed us to show his face on the camera. Because of the extreme political sensitivity of the topic, we offered every patient the chance to hide their face, and not to answer any questions with which they felt uncomfortable.

"I want to expose to the world what I underwent in Israeli prisons. I want to show the world the true Israel, the Israel that does not comply with human rights, international law, or the Geneva convention."

"Would you care to describe what you went through?" I asked warily, through Amjad the translator.

"There are a lot of hardships. Like when they admit dogs into the prison cells; or when they throw gas canisters into the prison cells. Basically, there is inhuman treatment in Israeli prisons."

I looked at his hands; they were shaking violently. Even this little information he was giving us seemed very difficult to say. He was terrified, or enraged, or both. He looked away from the camera; his downcast eyes and dark frown dominated the room. Everyone was silent. Sean, Kristen and I all felt we had to treat such a situation with extreme gravity and respect. It was the first time we had actually seen, with our own eyes, the human consequences of the Israeli occupation.

The Israelis had approved the use of what they called 'moderate physical pressure' to their Palestinian captives since 1988. 'Moderate physical pressure' could mean long sleep deprivation, violent shaking, forcing people into painful positions for long periods, or covering their heads with urine-soaked hoods. In 1999, the Israeli High Court ruled such practices illegal, but it was widely known that the IDF still used them. Western journalists had already gathered hundreds of sworn affidavits from Palestinian prisoners describing their torture.

To Sean and I, the fact that the Israelis made use of torture came as no surprise. We read it on the news years ago. What did come as a surprise was how many of their prisoners they tortured, and how often. It suggested far more than a simple method to gather information on possible acts of terrorism; it was far too systematic and impersonal for that. It seemed they wanted to inflict the greatest psychological pain possible on the people they captured.

Nickie shot me a glance. We had to wrap up this interview, since the camera had limited battery life and we had many more interviews to conduct. But there was one more question I just had to ask.

"What year were you arrested? When did this treatment take place?"

"It was December 2005."

Nickie stopped the camera, and the red light on top of the eyepiece blinked off. I thanked the man, and a wave of relief passed over his face. He got up to leave.

"Kieran, let's try to focus the questions on the TRC," Nickie said. "Ask them how the center helped them solve their problems and get back to a normal life."

I nodded. Nickie had a good mind for the end result: she knew we were not here to crucify the Israeli prison system, but rather make a decent short film about the TRC. I prepared myself for the next interview.

Amjad opened the door for another psychiatrist, a man with round glasses and flecks of grey in his beard. I realized the importance of having these people in the room: they were familiar faces, people whose presence would help to reassure our interviewees. He sat down beside us, and the next patient walked in.

This man was younger than the last. . .he looked barely twenty. He had clear eyes, and a small scar on his nose. The look he carried on his face was so pregnant with hatred that it almost made me gasp. His eyes were fixed forward—beyond Nickie, beyond the wall of the room—in a stare that could have burned a hole through paper. We offered to hide his face if he so wished. He violently refused.

"My name is Ali, from the village of Bet Rima."

Amjad explained that he was currently unemployed. "He has only been out of prison for three weeks, so he is a fresh 'graduate,' if you like, of Israeli prisons."

"Would you describe what happened to you?"

His voice was calm, despite the rage boiling behind his eyes. He took a deep breath, and began.

"It happened on the night I visited my mother in the hospital. I got home at one or two in the morning, and tried to get some sleep. Suddenly I heard heavy knocking on my door, and canisters thrown all around the house. There was the sound of a bullhorn, saying that all people should get out of the house.

"I was handcuffed and blindfolded, and taken to Hanish facility, where I was severely beaten, and they released dogs at me. I want to emphasize that they beat me *severely*. Eventually, they began to move me to a prison in Jerusalem. While they moved me, they beat me again, and cursed at me. My handcuffs were incredibly tight. I asked them to loosen my handcuffs just a little, but I received no response.

"When I reached the prison, they finally took the handcuffs off my hands, which were bleeding and swollen. For two months I stayed in solitary confinement where there were no baths and no haircuts. Many times they tied me up to a chair for three-day intervals, and whenever they saw I was about to go to sleep they would beat me so I would wake up. As for the food, I would not consider it food—no human being would eat the food that they gave me."

My mother once taught me that one of the chief symptoms of post-traumatic shock is a tendency to describe everything that happened in long and precise detail. I recognized it immediately. The man needed no prompting or prodding. His litany spilled out of him like a waterfall. His eyes remained fixed somewhere behind us, simmering with hatred. But he did not grow angry. His voice was forceful, but calm.

"After the solitary confinement, they took me to Hasharom prison for one and a half months. The conditions were the same: no food, no mattress, no sleeping covers, severe limitations on family visits. My father and brother were in Beer-shivah prison; I requested to be moved so I could be with them.

"I was moved. After a while, my father was set free. My brother was taken to court to decide what to do with him. My mother was denied visitation rights; she had not seen my brother for two years. When my brother asked if she could have more visitation rights, he was severely beaten on his head. They put him in handcuffs, put shackles on his legs, and from the severity of the beatings, he lost sight in one of his eyes.

"My brother had terrible head pain after this—it was so bad that he would beat his head against the wall to relieve some of the pain. They took him away for fourteen days, without being treated—and during most of these fourteen days he was unconscious. Once he came back, he could not even stand on his own legs. Since he had no treatment, I requested that I remain in his cell, to help him move if he needed to. But then they transferred me to another cell so that he had no help at all."

Ali paused and looked downwards, letting his words sink in. His sister later told us that the family had been told that one of their brothers was going to be let out of prison. They were overjoyed, because they would be able to take their sick, beaten brother into their home and help him heal. Instead, they freed Ali, and kept his brother in confinement.

"They take any chance they can get to beat the prisoners. If they are transferring them, they beat them; if they come inside the prison cell, they beat them; they take any occasion to meet with the inmates so that they can beat them. One of the techniques they used, which happened while I was in Negev prison, is that at one or two in the morning a huge force of Israeli soldiers will suddenly come into the prison cells and start shackling them and beating them. Then they take food, and they smear it into people's clothing. Finally, they would throw us outside in the rain. It is one of their techniques—to use violence on us without a reason. At one or two o'clock, when everyone is sleeping, there is no reason for this.

"I wanted to reach the world media to expose exactly what is being conducted in Israeli prisons— inhumane treatment. Israel says it accords with human rights, but it doesn't. What it does on the ground is not being reported."

He sat there, still staring violently past us. The whole time, I was conscious that Nickie wanted us to focus the questions on the Treatment and Rehabilitation Center itself, and that our camera was running out of time.

"Can you describe the process, when he first got to TRC, of some of the therapies he went through, and which ones assisted him?"

"I was released three weeks ago," he answered. "Someone at my sister's house received a call from the TRC saying that they wished to assist me. This is my first visit to the TRC; because of the holidays I have been unable to come until now."

"This is his first visit," said Amjad, with a smile. "You've probably met him before our therapist has had a chance to. In fact, perhaps this is even part of the therapy."

"Yes," nodded the psychiatrist who was in the room watching the interviews. "It's called 'testimony.'"

From that moment onwards, I understood the real purpose we served in sitting there and training that camera on our subjects. I dropped all pretense of trying to make the film fit our agenda, and of creating a perfect piece on the TRC. We were not here for that. These victims were not here for that. They were here to get off their chest the nightmares that they had experienced; they were there to retaliate against their torturers by telling all to a Western audience. And we were here to let them do just that.

From that moment onwards, we were no longer there to make a film. We were there to help these people with their mental health.

We had one more case that day.

This man had been there at the beginning, and fled during the first few interviews. They called him back and convinced him to come. He fled yet again while he waited. Finally, after calling him a third time, he came back to tell his story.

He shrunk before us when he walked in the room. He was a heavy-set man of thirty-six. His hands moved involuntarily at times, in violent, nervous jerks. He was adamant that we hide his face. We turned him around so that the camera was focused on the back of his head. The whole time, he looked around himself, perhaps out of habit, searching to see that everyone around him was safe.

This man was a 'graduate' of two and a half years. His story was nothing compared to his body language. I had never seen someone twitch or flinch so much. He was nearly paralyzed with fear. He had never again been recaptured, and he stayed entirely away from politics after his imprisonment. He said he came to the TRC because of violent shaking fits which he began to experience inside prison and once he came out. And because of fear. He sought the help of the TRC to help him to get rid of this. I asked him how the clinic had helped him integrate himself back into normal life—but I winced to even ask the question. I doubt he had integrated himself into normal life at all. He could barely even function; he had clearly gotten worse with time.

As he left, he barked a command to disguise his voice. He walked away, twitching and terrified. He was a shattered wreck; unable even to sit in front of a camera and deliver an interview. I dearly hoped that Ali, our 'fresh graduate', would not later regret having risked himself so openly on camera. I hoped it would not keep him up nights; that he would not spend the rest of his life looking over his shoulder.

As we packed up our things to leave, and thanked Amjad for his help, he told us one last thing.

"We do not only offer services to victims of torture. We also offer our services to people who have worked with the victims, to deal with any difficulties they may be experiencing. A year ago, there was a team who came from Europe to work with some of our patients in the field for a number of months, and when they were about to leave, they came here for counseling about the trauma they had experienced. So I just wanted to let you know, if you experience any difficulties at all, or any trauma, we also offer our services to you."

"What's wrong with Sean?" Nickie asked me.

"I don't know," I replied.

We had just left the TRC, and Sean walked ahead of us. He was wearing a hardened expression, and he kept his eyes straight ahead, saying nothing. We walked around the corner and up the street to the tomb of Yasser Arafat, something he had been really excited to come to Palestine to see. It didn't have any effect. He stood there, staring blankly at the green flag draped across Arafat's coffin, and said nothing.

I knew better than to try to talk to him when he was in this mood.

Instead, on our way back to the bus stop, he went on ahead in front of us, staring bitterly at the ground in front of him, lost in his thoughts.

18

CHRISTMAS IN BETHLEHEM

Sean acted strangely that evening and for the whole following day. I wasn't sure what the problem was, but there was absolutely nothing we could do.

Upon returning from Ramallah, we sat in Osama's common room, eating his free rice and vegetables, and conspired about what we would do the following day—Christmas Eve.

"So we are meeting Sami and his family at twelve," I explained. "We called them yesterday and they said Christmas lunch would be ready at about that time. Before then, we should go see the Church of the Nativity and downtown Bethlehem, and afterwards I think we should just wait around near Manger Square to see what is going on."

Kristen and Nickie nodded their approval.

"I think I'll skip meeting the family," Sean said.

There was a long and difficult pause. The silence was acid.

"Why?" I asked eventually.

"I just—really don't want to meet them."

We studied our half-eaten bowls of food. I breathed. Nickie and Kristen sat with blank looks on their faces. By our silence we acquiesced, and Sean retreated into his room to read.

The next day, he barely said a single word. On the bus to Bethlehem, he had a permanent frown furrowed into his brow, and his eyes stung us if we looked at him. Most of the time, we didn't.

Eventually the bus slowed to a stop. We were told to get out: the bus would go no further. We had arrived at the Wall.

Erected by the Israelis in 2003, the 'security barrier' is a massive wall built throughout the West Bank, with the stated objective to reduce the number of terrorist attacks in Israel. But one glance at a map of the snakelike barrier reveals that it is built for far more than that. It has fenced Palestinians out of forty-six percent of what was the West Bank, and cut off access to the river Jordan. It curls around every Israeli settlement and slices off Palestinian villages from their cultivated land. It also cuts the West Bank in two: there is now a North West Bank, and a South West Bank, which are both successfully segregated from East Jerusalem, which lies between them. In one stroke, the Israelis legitimized the existence of their settlements, all but captured Jerusalem, and left the Arabs nothing more than a moth-eaten Palestine.

Bethlehem, only a few kilometers south of Jerusalem, has suffered immensely since the construction of the wall. Tourism, the backbone of the city's economy, has dropped by ninety percent. The fact that violence within the city dropped dramatically during the same time was irrelevant. Tourists, especially Americans, simply wouldn't venture beyond the wall.

The barrier was four times the height of a human, and made of thick, reinforced concrete slabs. At intervals stood menacing circular guard towers with bulletproof windows. The top of the wall was strung with rolls of with razor wire. In the nearly empty checkpoint, we handed our passports to the Israeli soldiers. They checked them quickly and we walked through a maze of fences and metal turnstiles towards the barrier itself.

Immediately after exiting the chain-link labyrinth that separated Israel and Palestine, we began to see paintings on the wall. One of the chief reasons we had come was to see this guerrilla art. To protest its construction, artists had used the Palestinian side of the wall as a canvas, sometimes for simple graffiti, sometimes for large murals. We passed a scrawl in blue spray paint which read: "Jesus wept for Jerusalem, we weep for Palestine."

Another one, which looked like it had been sprayed on with a template, was the outline of an Arab woman's face with a shawl around her hair. Beneath the image were the words: "I am not a terrorist."

A lot of this graffiti was scrawled by members of the local population. But others were done by a British guerrilla artist known as 'Bansky.' His trademark is to paint something by the cover of night, and have it appear in the morning for everyone to see.

We passed one of his pieces, a small girl in a little pink dress frisking an Israeli soldier. Another one was of an Israeli soldier stopping a donkey and asking for an ID card. There was also a large drawing of a forest of cut stumps, and beside them, a decorated Christmas tree surrounded by a wall of concrete slabs.

Some of the images were harder to understand. There was one of them of two boxers slugging it out, one of them Sonny Liston. There was another of a silhouette of children riding an escalator out over the wall, while an insect below topples a line of dominoes which look like pieces of the barrier itself. In another, a small girl holds a bunch of balloons which are lifting her upwards.

But the most jaw-dropping picture of all is painted on the side of a store on the road into Bethlehem. I leaned out the window of our cab and managed to snap a photo of it while we slowed in traffic. It was a white dove wearing a flak jacket, with an olive branch in its mouth, spreading its wings. Over its heart was painted the red crosshair of a gun sight.

Eventually, we reached a point where the taxi could go no further. Two gates blocked vehicles from going any further into the city, guarded by smiley Palestinians with Kalashnikovs and bullet-proof vests. After we had gotten out of the cab, they waved and beckoned us up the hill behind them. Welcome to Bethlehem.

At the top of the hill, the street opened up into Manger Square. The giant Church of the Nativity stood at one end, and the rest of the square was lined with shops, and a large new-looking building hung with the letters "Bethlehem Peace Association." On one of the balconies of the building stood one guy with a giant camera, and two other men looking bored. Below them was hung a large banner, with a picture of Yasser Arafat waving his hand. In English, French, and Arabic, the sign read: *The Fatah movement in Bethlehem wishes you a Merry Christmas.*

The square was buzzing with people. Behind a portable fence, Palestinian Authority police, with guns and bulletproof vests, stood keeping the crowd back from the Church of the Nativity. Tourists of every age and nationality bunched around the fence, while the smiling guards gently held them back. Other Palestinians flitted about the square, which was adorned with a giant Christmas tree and strung across with lights. It was Christmas Eve, and the party of the year was being prepared. Above the square, a mosque was barking some rough Arabic prayers. Unlike the usual prayer which occurred at sunrise and then in the afternoon, this time the scratchy voice was belting out prayers in the middle of the morning. And unlike the usual prayer, this one didn't seem to stop.

Across the valley to the north, on the top of the opposing hill, I could see a white cluster of buildings built strategically in a circle. It could only have been an Israeli settlement: the buildings were planned and uniform, not crooked, multicoloured, and chaotic like the Arabs city blocks which stood nearby. And it was built right on the crown of the hill, commanding a strategic position over the surrounding land. The Israelis always built their settlements with defense in mind.

As I looked at it, I was struck by an immediate sense of how small and crowded the holy land was. It had not taken us an hour to drive from central Jerusalem to central Bethlehem, and yet in between, there was a strategic barrier, and numerous Israeli settlements. Even from Manger Square, the very heart of Bethlehem, I could see Israeli communities encroaching just a few kilometers away. During the Cold War, the Berlin Wall was actually two walls: two large concrete barriers, with a wide no-man's-land in between. But here in Palestine, where Arabs and Jews lived so close together, no such wall was possible. There simply wasn't the space.

The Church of the Nativity was packed with tourists on Christmas Eve Day. It didn't help that the only entrance to the church was a door too low for even a child to walk through erect. This was the Door of Humility, designed to make people bow as they enter the church, in reverence to the birthplace of Christ.

The church was almost as ancient as Christianity itself. It was built by a Byzantine emperor in 565 AD, before the birth of Islam. And time had taken its toll. Most of the mosaics had crumbled off the walls, though there were still portions that showed archangels and flowering plants, all surrounded in flecks of gold. The old floor of the church was done in the same style, but had been covered over save for a small trapdoor. Shafts of sunlight caught the dust that floated between the high Corinthian columns that flanked the main hall of the church.

In April 2002, only five years before, this building was the center of a siege. During the Second Intifada, the Israelis invaded and occupied most Palestinian cities. A group of militants, knowing full well Israel had a policy against the destruction of holy sites, took refuge inside the Church. With them were at least seventeen civilian hostages, as well as a group of Italian journalists. The siege lasted for 38 days, and Israeli snipers managed to kill nine insurgents by sniper fire. By this time, food within the church had been exhausted, and they had begun to eat the plants that grew in the courtyard. Eventually, a deal was brokered that guaranteed the safety of the insurgents, and allowed them to go to exile in Europe. Finally, the Palestinians surrendered.

We walked through the main hall towards the tabernacle, and its wide wall of faded icons. Elaborate candelabras hung from the ceiling on long silver chains. Amongst the crowd walked Orthodox priests, wearing black robes and square black beards, silver crosses swinging from their chests. I raised my camera to try to get a photo of one of these holy men, and he stared at me with such icy contempt that my hand lowered of its own accord.

I wandered around back to the Grotto of the Nativity, the tiny shrine underneath the church where it was believed Christ was actually born. A great line of people filled the grotto, waiting to kneel down and pray over the location of Christ's birth. I waited with them, in order to get my chance. A small star marked the exact location; around the grotto was hung a silk cloth laced with gold. I clutched my St. Christopher pendant as I knelt and prayed, drinking in the silent gravity of the holy place.

Mark Twain, during his travels to the same sites, had waxed sarcastic more than once about whether this was *actually* the cave in which Christ was born, or whether it wasn't fifty yards down the road. I did notice that the Christ's birthplace happened to be on a lovely hill which had a commanding view of the whole valley around it; a beautiful place to build a church. But eventually, I came to realize that it was far beyond the point, whether the church was *actually* built on the right spot; whether Christ was *actually* buried in that white stone quarry in Jerusalem; whether he was *actually* dressed for burial on that precise piece of stone. The authenticity of these monuments was long faded from the pages of history, and what's more, it didn't really matter. The symbol counted for all.

I reunited with Kristen and Nickie. Sean had long since vanished. We walked together back towards the Door of Humility, taking a quick glance along the way at the Armenian enclave on the side of the church. The church was shared by many denominations: the Armenian Orthodox priests had an enclave, as did as the Catholics. The main part of the church was Greek Orthodox.

Two weeks later, while performing the big cleaning before the celebration of Orthodox Christmas, a bitter fight broke out between the Greek and the Armenian sides. Over a hundred priests attacked each other ferociously with brooms. Luckily, all that was injured was pride. What event sparked the fight is unknown, but it invoked the bitter hostility that the Greek and Armenian priests of the church have felt for each other for centuries.

Why this hostility existed, I did not know. All I knew was the recognized fact that when people of different religions—no matter how similar—are forced to share the same sacred space, eventually their tolerance evaporates. Eventually their patience and goodwill run out, and hatred boils up like a fountain.

"Israel likes to use Old Jerusalem as an example of its tolerant multiculturalism. There is the Jewish Quarter, the Muslim Quarter, the Armenian Quarter, and the Christian Quarter. But this is a lie. All of the sides hate each other. Have you heard them play the *muezzin* in Jerusalem? They play it at a very high pitch—higher than in the rest of the country. They do this to annoy the Christians and the Jews. Everyone in the Old City is afraid of the day when the hatred will boil over, and there will be violence."

Sami was a red-haired Palestinian in his forties. His sister Samia worked in a blood bank in Canada with my mother. We had arranged to visit them before we even left for the Middle East. He picked up Kristen, Nickie, and I on the road down the hill from Manger Square, and drove us to his house nearby. We arrived at a dwelling which might easily have been a house in North America. There was a carport, and the living compartment downstairs was spacious and pleasant. Sami's wife came out to meet us; she shyly shook our hands and retreated to the kitchen to prepare food. His two youngest children, a girl and a boy, fled at the first sight of these strange foreigners. His eldest, a dark-haired young lady, waited until he had ordered the youngsters back into the room to shake our hands. They stood together in a row and greeted us with good manners before retreating away to join their mother.

We had come here for no other reason than to spend Christmas with friends of the family, since our own families were far away. Our cameras were back at the hostel and our microphones packed away. We hadn't asked Sami how life was in Palestine. It was something he volunteered.

"The Christians here feel trapped between two larger enemies," he explained. "Because we are Christian, the Muslims do not trust us. Because we are Arabs, the Jews keep us quarantined here in the West Bank.

"It's hard to explain just how frustrating it is to have to wait two and a half hours at a checkpoint just to be able to move through your own country. And this is what we must do, since the Second

Intifada. Since the Wall. Now we need permits to go to Jerusalem, and each time we try to cross, they make us wait for an impossible amount of time. I used to work in Jerusalem. I used to work at a tourism firm, alongside many Jews. I had many Jewish friends! We worked side by side, you see, before the Intifada. But all of that has changed now."

His eyes were downcast. In his voice, there was no anger. Just simple regret. And disappointment.

"I used to travel to Jerusalem every day from Bethlehem. Now I can't get a permit."

The word 'intifada' means 'uprising.' The Intifadas refer to two incidents of unrest in the West Bank, Jerusalem, and Gaza, when the Palestinians resisted Israeli rule with violence. The First Intifada began in 1987, when an Israeli transport truck rolled over a group of Palestinians, killing four of them. It was thought that this was a deliberate response to a stabbing murder of a Jewish businessman in a Gaza market just a few days before. Word spread amongst the Palestinians, and a riot began: they burned tires and attacked IDF outposts. Across the territories, there were general strikes and demonstrations, usually composed of rock-throwing youth. The Israelis put the uprising down with force—the IDF were given truncheons and were told to go out and "break their bones."

The Second Intifada began in the year 2000. Surrounded by riot police, the Israeli president

Ariel Sharon made a visit to the Temple Mount, in the shadow of the Dome of the Rock and Al-Aqsa, two of the holiest mosques in Islam. He did this largely to assert the right of Jews to visit the site, as it was under Israeli control. The next day, after Friday prayers, riots broke out across Old Jerusalem. Rocks were thrown from the Temple Mount down onto crowds of Jews visiting the Western Wall. The IDF responded by storming the Temple Mount and spraying rubber bullets into the Arab crowds. Four were killed, and three more in similar incidents in other locations around Jerusalem. The next day, demonstrations broke out across the Palestinian territories.

This time, the resistance was far more organized on the Palestinian side. They adopted the techniques of car bombing, suicide bombing, and shooting homemade rockets into Israeli settlements. It was during this period of violence when Israel constructed the Wall.

"The IDF entered my house once," Sami told us. "It was in 2002. They came at two o'clock in the morning. But they were very quiet, so as not to wake the children. I was very thankful for this. They knew I spoke good English, and they wanted me to translate for them. I did what they wanted; to other families they were not so nice. During that time, there was a permanent curfew, and it was technically illegal to leave the house to go buy food or go to work. But I did anyways, and it wasn't much of a problem. But the children didn't leave the house in those days—it was too dangerous on the street."

The Second Intifada continued until 2006, just a year before we arrived. It chilled me to think of how recent the violence had been in this country. In 2000, when I was just finishing high school, Palestine was peaceful and integrated into the Israeli economy. And within a few short years, a wall had sprung up, Jerusalem had been sectioned off, and the Palestinians had been quarantined within their own, destitute little territory, unable to do a single thing in response.

Eventually, Sami's wife emerged from the kitchen with the Christmas meal. After saying grace, in English and in Arabic, we tucked into an excellent feast. We spooned chicken stew upon steaming portions of yellow rice, and helped ourselves to plates of succulent tomatoes, cucumbers, and olives. The three children smiled at us and ate in silence. We traded Christmas stories with Sami and his wife, and for a brief moment, it truly felt like home. I thought wistfully of my brother and my parents; of my cousins, uncles, and aunts, celebrating on the other side of the world. And I was grateful that in Palestine, we had friends who would welcome us into their home, and celebrate with us the most special day of the year.

We made our way back to Manger Square after night fell. Lights glowed on strings atop the plaza, and a massive crowd of foreigners and Palestinians mingled below. In front of the Church of the Nativity, an American choir was singing "O Holy Night." I left the girls to run to a nearby store and purchase a bottle of wine; I returned just as the conductor puffed up his singers for the triumphant blasts of Handel's Hallelujah Chorus.

I poured out three portions of red wine into plastic cups. We laughed and embraced, wished each other a Merry Christmas, and for a brief moment, all of the stress of the journey fell away. Weeks of anxiety and looking over our shoulders, the seething, omnipresent tension of the Middle East, and the culture shock of being strangers in a strange land all melted into nothing during that one beautiful minute. And in the cold night air, surrounded by Palestinians who were eyeing my female companions and snickering at our consumption of wine, we raised our plastic glasses, and drank a toast to one of the most special Christmases of our lives.

When the night grew cold, and the choir had finished its performance, we wandered away from Manger Square. As we made our way down the hill, towards the taxi-accessible part of town, I saw painted on a wall one of the best pieces of graffiti I'd ever seen. It was a red warning sign of a tow truck pulling away a tank. The girls laughed out loud when they saw it, and I took a picture for posterity.

And as we walked back down the hill, I thought of the graffiti artist and his lightheartedness. As I reflected on it more, it became painful, even sad. For whoever painted that on the wall must have lived through the Second Intifada, if not the First. He must have seen the tanks rolling in the streets of Bethlehem, and heard the wails of neighbours and friends who had lost ones they loved. And yet, despite it all, he could summon the mirth to paint a "no tank parking" sign on the wall.

As we sat in the taxi for our trip back to the wall, I thought of our last few moments at Sami's house. After Christmas lunch, he had taken us upstairs to see his father, to show him the visiting foreigners who were friends of his daughter in Canada. We entered into a room with a bedridden man, in the later stages of old age. It was a hospital bed, propped up at an angle so that he talk to us; a saline drip bag hung from a metal stand next to him. He whispered a hello to us, and we all shook his hand, and wished him a Merry Christmas.

He didn't say too much. Although Sami told us that at one point knew English, he spoke through his son. During certain moments, in the middle of his speech, he winced in pain, and wailed softly as though he was crying. We stood through these moments with stoicism, trying to keep the moment happy. Sami sat patiently, with a look of loving sympathy for his elder, and translated our words for us.

As I gazed about his room, I noticed a photo on the wall. It was an old black and white shot of a fresh young man, about twenty-three, with a short moustache and dressed in a black tuxedo. Standing next to him, in a flowing white wedding dress, was his gorgeous bride. Sami noticed me regarding it.

"When was this picture taken?" I asked him softly.

"1949."

I nodded. 1949. One year after the war.

Before we left Canada, my sister had spoken to Samia, the old man's daughter, about the family story. Her father had lived with his family on a farm in Palestine, in what is now Israel proper. When the war came they fled, and the Israelis took their land. They settled in Bethlehem, where his father married and had two children. Samia was raised in exile, and was only a child in 1967 when the Israelis occupied the West Bank. As soon as she could, she emigrated to Canada, to get away from war and insecurity. Sami, her brother, remained.

We took a final look at Sami's father, who had married his bride in exile, a member of the last generation that had known life in the Palestine that was. And now, in 2007, he was ill and bedridden, and would pass away without ever seeing his beloved family farm again.

I thought of him as we taxied back to the outskirts of Bethlehem; as we approached the wall a second time. In the darkness of night, the guerrilla artwork had all but faded from view. Instead, we saw only the pale glow of the concrete against the white floodlights, and saw the tangles of fence which led back through the barrier to Jerusalem.

On the opposite side, I saw a banner on the Israeli side of the wall. It was brightly coloured, with three stick figures in dresses carrying a palm tree, a camera, and other festive ornaments. Whoever put it up must have gone to great lengths to tuck it under the rolls of razor wire, and the wide stretches of chain link fence which adorned the top of the barrier. Beside the banner stood the pillbox guard tower, standing tall and unforgiving against the night sky.

As I looked at it, a wave of cold passed over my skin. Leaving Manger Square, I had seen the lighthearted humour of the oppressed; now I was staring at the dark humour of the oppressor.

Upon the banner, in Arabic, Hebrew, and finally in English, was written: 'Peace be with you.'

19

YAD VASHEM

Christmas morning, for the other two religions of Jerusalem, was much like any other morning. People drew up their metal curtains, fired up the deep fryers and the kebab grills, and business went on as usual. Usually, I spent Christmas in total relaxation with my family, enjoying a day or two of doing absolutely nothing, and perhaps going for a brief walk. But Kristen and Nickie were flying for Canada on the 28th, and we realized we had a lot left to see.

And so it came to pass that on Christmas Day, 2007, we decided to visit two non-Christian sacred and holy sites: two places which were the symbolic epicenters of the two ideologies which struggle for dominance in the land between the Jordan and the sea.

The first was the Temple Mount.

We lined up at a walkway near the Western Wall, a ramp that was especially designed to let non-Muslim tourists in to visit the Temple Mount during special visiting hours. Earlier, we had weaved our way through the labyrinth of Old Jerusalem to a massive green door, where we had been turned away by the guard for not being Muslim. If we ever wanted to see the Dome of the Rock and the Al-Aqsa Mosque, we had to line up here.

A long line of tourists gathered behind us, awaiting the ten o'clock opening. Behind me in the crowd, I heard some people speaking in French-Canadian French about Montreal, a place home to one of the largest Jewish communities outside of Israel. Behind them, I heard thick New York accents. Most of these tourists, I realized, were Jews who were keeping their skullcaps at home. A sign on the wall beside us read: "According to Torah Law, entering the Temple Mount area is strictly forbidden, due to the holiness of the site." Below it read "The Chief Rabbinate of Israel."

The Temple Mount itself was a wide, flat expanse; an anomaly in the crowded landscape of Old Jerusalem. The Western Wall, all that remained of the Jewish Temple for which the site was named, was built into the construction of this wide expanse on which today stands the majestic Dome of the Rock: its walls covered with patterns on aqua blue tiles; its great domed rooftop bathed in gold. It is said that the Temple Mount was built on the very site where, in days far more ancient, the patriarch Abraham was asked by God to sacrifice his only son. . .and obeyed.

In the story, Abraham and his son climbed a hill, and solemnly prepared an altar on which to make a sacrifice, where at the last minute the old man bound his son, placed him on the altar, and through his great despair, prepared to offer him up. At the last moment, God offered Abraham a ram to sacrifice instead, and spared Isaac, Abraham's son, who was to become the father of all the peoples of Israel. The Lord made a covenant with Abraham, and told him that in return for his ultimate show of loyalty, his descendants would number the stars.

Abraham's other son, Ishmael, was cast into exile with his mother, since she was only Abraham's concubine and not his true wife. And though it is Isaac that is looked upon as the father of the Jews; Ishmael is looked upon as the father of the Muslims. According to Islamic tradition, when the Prophet Mohammed reached the mount where Abraham had prepared his son for sacrifice, he ascended to heaven on a winged steed and conversed personally with God. And thus it came to be that this one mount, the very heart of Old Jerusalem, became holy ground to two of the most ancient and powerful faiths of humankind.

The Romans expelled the Jews from the holy land not seven decades after the birth of Christ; the Muslims conquered it from the Romans six centuries later. And within three generations of the Prophet himself, the Dome of the Rock was constructed. Rising over twenty meters into the air, its dome is covered in eighty kilograms of gold. And the symmetrical, endlessly intricate crosshatch patterns which covered the walls upon tiles of delicate blue, green, white, and yellow, were a gift to Jerusalem by Suleiman the Magnificent, the same Ottoman Sultan who built the pale walls of the Old City. The building was a wonder of the ancient world—a deep and ancient symbol of a people and their faith; a testament to fourteen flourishing centuries of Islamic rule.

"You know what this building says?" Kristen asked me, with a wide, sarcastic grin. *"TAKE THAT!"*

I chuckled as we skirted the building together, snapping pictures of each other in front of this ancient marvel. Indeed, no Jew could ever visit this site without remembering that the Western Wall is but a fragment of the Temple that once stood in its place; without feeling that this sublime and ancient Dome, for all its beauty, is an intrusion onto their sacred space.

In the heat of the Six-Day War, when the Israelis first captured the Temple Mount, Chief Rabbi Schlomo Goren approached members of the Israeli

High Command. He put before them a plan to dynamite the Dome of the Rock, and clear the Temple Mount once and for all for the rebuilding of the Jewish Temple. He argued forcefully: now, when the Arab countries were already at war with them, when the eyes of the world were upon them—now, would be the only time they could ever perform such a deed. If they ever wanted to see Solomon's Temple rise again in Jerusalem, they had to act immediately.

Yet the Dome of the Rock stands today. By what logic it was saved, I could not say. Perhaps they Israelis were too afraid of the international outcry; perhaps they were afraid of provoking the other Arab countries who had not already gone to war. But I like to think that such beautiful feats of architecture, such immortal monuments of the human world, inspire awe and wonder in all men, no matter what their faith. I suspect the mosque stands today for the same reason that Lenin did not tear down the greatest cathedrals of Russia; for the same reason that Hitler's generals at the last moment refused to blow up the monuments of Paris. In the end, despite their beliefs, they just could not bear to destroy works of such timeless majesty.

At the Temple Mount we ran into Clayton, a friend who Sean knew him from Beirut. Sean remarked at a half-circle scar on his forehead, dressed with about a dozen stitches.

"Yeah, I got hit in the head by a tear-gas canister at the Friday Protest," Clayton replied.

"The Friday Protest?"

"Yeah. It happens every Friday in a town called Bilin near Ramallah. The Palestinians have been holding a protest there for three years now against the erection of the wall. Lots of foreigners go every week. . .they are allowed to stay for free in Abdullah's house."

"How was it?" asked Sean, intrigued.

Clayton laughed. "I don't remember much of it. They had a small rally and then when the IDF fired the first shots, I got hit in the head and I was completely out of it. I woke up later in the hospital." He smiled his big, broad smile. "But I'm going again next week for sure!"

Sean looked at me, excitement in his eyes.

"We may have to go to this Kieran," he said.

I nodded in agreement. But as I contemplated the stitches holding closed Clayton's moon-shaped scar, I wasn't so sure.

The other site we visited, that Christmas Day, was a Holocaust Museum.

It's name was Yad Vashem. We taxied into West Jerusalem, the Jewish side of the city. When we first laid eyes upon it, I felt uneasy. It's construction was postmodern, and unsettling: a long triangular corridor of steel set into the side of a hill.

The pale, square arches of stone at the entrance looked foreboding against the grey, spitting sky. A chill feeling of solemnity washed over us before we even entered the building.

Photos were forbidden. Admission was free.

At the entrance, mounted on strands of barbed wire, were half-burnt photographs pulled from the pockets of the dead by Russian soldiers, when they liberated the first of the death camps in Eastern Europe. They were photographs of families, of lovers, of children, yellowed and blackened by fire and time. From that vantage point, I could see that railings led us in a crisscross pattern through the tremendous triangular prism which was the museum.

The architecture bothered me, since I knew it was designed to mean something: in Germany, for instance, a museum about the plight of Europe's Jews was a dark, formless visual scar on the outside, and inside contained many entirely empty rooms, creating a feeling of uncertainty for the visitor. I wondered what the massive triangle, which was split at the top to let the daylight illuminate the center, was supposed to mean. Perhaps we crisscrossed through the corridor to show the twisted manner in which Jews were slowly and craftily led into their resettlement camps; perhaps there was a reason why the corridor itself was lit by daylight, while the exhibits at the sides were shrouded in darkness. As I looked at it, I could not tell.

The first exhibit was about anti-Semitism in Europe and the rise of the Nazis. It showed objects from the nineteenth century depicting Jews in gross caricature, there were ceramic mugs in the shape of a distended Jewish nose; there were propaganda posters of fanged, bearded Jews holding bags of money, or clutching the globe in their hands. There were tiny dolls of black-robed, bearded Jews in wide-brimmed hats, clutching coins. This collection was assembled from all over Europe, not just Germany. The objects dated from many years before the rise of the Nazis, to show that for ages and ages, Europe has always distrusted its Jewish population.

Next, behind the glass lay a perfectly preserved blood-red banner with a white and black swastika emblazoned on the center. Deutschemarks from the late 1930s were set on display, as well as photos of Hitler and of Nazi political rallies. These were on display alongside lesser-known Third Reich artifacts: board games for the education of children. One of them was a variation on snakes-and-ladders, where the players moved their tokens along the stages from the creation of the National Socialist Party to its victory in controlling a majority of the Reichstag. Another board game finished with the victor finally gathering up all of the Jews of Europe and shipping them away.

On a screen above, I saw a great procession of torches marching in a circle, and swirling in to form a rotating swastika of flame. It was a silent film. After a few seconds, the video cut to scenes of students burning hundreds of Jewish books in a bonfire. This combination of images—first, the torch procession, a semi-demonic symbol of the power of obeisance and disciplined coordination; and second, books going up in flame—made a chill creep across my skin. What certitude of mind, I wondered, would a man have to conjure, in order to set alight works of human knowledge? How fanatical a conviction would he have to have, that his ideology—his faith—was the true and final end of history, in order to burn forever the ability of future generations to learn from the works of the past?

And what would have to happen, to a society such as Germany, for millions and millions of citizens to embrace that same belief?

The next hall showed the occupation of Europe. A thematic photograph stood on the wall, of Hitler and a cadre of Nazi generals in long, brown coats, walking with the Eiffel Tower rising tall in the background. A plaque explained how the Nazis' policies differed from Eastern Europe to Western Europe. In the West, where Jews were more or less accepted into mainstream society, they were carefully monitored; and information on them was quietly collected. Plans to resettle them proceeded slowly, so that no massive public outcry would result. However, in Eastern Europe, where Jews were far more hated and segregated, they were herded into ghettoes immediately.

Maps and figures showed the movement of Jews from every occupied territory; from every enclave of Jewish population in Europe and beyond. From Libya, from Algeria, from Hungary, from Bulgaria, from Italy, from Germany, from France: I was taken aback by the painstaking detail. There was so much precise information about where each prisoner came from; even communities as small as a few hundred people were counted.

"This is such overkill," I said to Sean. "I'll bet you they did it because they didn't want any visiting Jew to be offended that their particular family was not remembered."

"I'll bet that's exactly why they did it," said Sean, studying the walls. He seemed to be in better humour today. As he toured the exhibits with us, there was little trace of yesterday's bitter mood. Whatever he had done in Bethlehem the day before, apparently it had helped.

The four of us walked together through rooms displaying endless personal effects of the people who had been taken off to concentration camps. A wall showed a portrait of Anne Frank, and her diary. There were countless photographs, countless tracts of text recounting individual stories. In

one room, we opened drawer after drawer showing thousands of personal items under glass: eye-
glasses, children's dolls, photographs of loved ones,
locks of hair.

As I wandered, in a kind of daze, through this
macabre forest of personal belongings, I began to
realize why this was set up in such minute, individual detail. Stalin had once said "when you kill
one, it is a tragedy; when you kill ten million, it is
a statistic." Much has been made of the impersonal-
ity of the Holocaust: that six million dead in a mass
murder in a bizarre and abstract concept to the human individual, divorced from anything meaning-
ful and tangible. All of this—the flecks of clothing,
the letters to mother, the family photographs, the
names, the personal accounts—all of it was designed to remove the abstractness of this demonic
act, and make it personal, tangible, and at the same
time, vastly more horrific. And yet to me, it had the
opposite effect. These personal trinkets, in their
numberless thousands, made the Holocaust seem
more boundless, more abstract than ever.

While I walked from exhibit to exhibit in this
endless, frightening mausoleum, I found it strange
to think that consciousness of the Holocaust was a
fairly new phenomenon in Israeli history. Contrary
to what one might expect, the vast amount of sur-
vivors of this act, which the Jews call "the Shoah,"
did not leave the concentration camps crying out

and protesting about what had happened. The vast majority came straight to Palestine in order to live in the holy land, and battle for their own country. But they were so ashamed of the disgraceful, degrading treatment they experienced at the hands of the Germans, that many kept an icy silence. It was only when the younger generation grew up during the sixties and seventies, and learned how their parents had been treated, and of the great gaps missing in their extended families, that the righteous indignation began, and that places like Yad Vashem were created.

This new generation of youth resented their fathers and grandfathers for their self-imposed silence. They had a derogatory slang name for those who were ashamed to look their own past in the face and identify with it. It is by far the most appalling term I have ever heard being applied to anyone; it goes far beyond any racist or anti-Semitic term ever invented.

They called them "soap."

It was in the Lodz ghetto in Poland, in the early 1940s, that Rabbi Chaim Mordecai Rumkowski stood on a platform above his people, and with a broken countenance and wavering voice, asked them to give up their children.

It was a community of about fifty or sixty thousand Jews, all who had been fenced into a few city blocks by the Nazis. The ghetto leadership had been informed, earlier that day, that the Nazis would be exacting a quota of ten thousand people from the Lodz ghetto to be sent to the concentration camps. Rumkowski and the rest of the ghetto leadership begged the Nazis to only take the old and infirm. . .not simply to choose at random from among them. After hours of argument and pleading, the Nazis budged. . .they would not select randomly from among the Jews. The ghetto itself would have the privilege of choosing.

But they would have ten thousand. Absolutely no less.

Rumkowski and his partners did some quick calculations. The aged population of the Lodz ghetto was nowhere near enough to make the quota. The sick, the wounded. . .those who would probably not survive anyways in the trials to come. . .these were only a few hundred. And so they decided that in order for the greater community to survive, every family would have to give up their children aged ten and under.

He gave his reasons. The community had a choice, he said. . .they could do this by their own hands, or suffer the brutal harm and senseless killing of having the Nazis do it. Chaim repeated his arguments, through his despair and courage, to help placate the crowd of crying and distraught families. "I am not proud to be a human being today" he said. "I am not proud to be a Jew." But he insisted, through his grief, that he was thinking for the good of the whole. That without this horrific sacrifice, god forbid, the entire community might perish. That if they were to inflict this one great tragedy upon themselves, perhaps, by the grace of God, some of them would survive the ordeal to come.

Rumkowski stood above his flock a broken man. And despite all their pain, the Lodz ghetto listened to him. In every family, parents bent down to their youngest children with strong faces, hugged them hard and tried to console them, and then watched the infants that they had nursed since birth walk off into the mouth of the lion.

As I stood, riveted to the spot, watching the words of Rumkowski's speech crawl slowly up a video screen, I couldn't quite pinpoint what exactly it was about this which made stomach turn over in my gut. For what, could be more disgusting, more revoltingly inhuman, than giving up one's children? What possible end could justify such means? Would it not have been better, to resist with all their might, no matter how futile such an attempt would be? Would it not have been better to wait inside their doorways clutching butter knives, and to give their lives in exchange for dignity and honour? Or, after the final end of such an ordeal, if even a few members of the ghetto survived, would it, by some Machiavellian logic, actually be worth such a monstrous sacrifice?

As I stood and contemplated the actions of the Lodz ghetto that day, it made me think of something I had previously read. Eric Hoffer, an amateur, proletarian philosopher of the twentieth century, wrote that hope was the single difference between the despairing, downtrodden Jews in Hitler's concentration camps, and the fighting race that stood their ground in Palestine a few years later.

Give people hope, Hoffer wrote, and they will draw endless courage from it, and fight until the end. Make hope impossible, and they will walk obediently to their deaths.

Later in the museum, I learned what eventually happened to the prisoners of the Lodz ghetto. In the end, they followed their children. They were deported to concentration camps and all but obliterated.

A mere handful, liberated from Auschwitz by the Russians, were all that was left to show for their horrific sacrifice.

The museum continued. It showed exhibits about the Jews who fought in the partisan resistance movements across Europe. It showed an exhibit called "the Righteous Among the Nations," about the non-Jews across Europe who showed compassion to their neighbours and shielded them from the Nazis. It gave particular praise to Denmark, whose people not only did all they could to shelter Jews in their homes, but who also placed Jews on boats and shipped them to neutral Sweden. It saved special praise for Schindler, the German factory boss who persuaded the Nazi leadership to give him some Jews to use for labour, thereby saving them from the camps. Today Schindler's body is buried in Israel.

And finally, near the very end, it showed the full brutal horror of the concentration camps. Auschwitz. Dachau. Treblinka. Bergen-Belsen. And on and on, in excruciating detail, they showed maps of every camp, no matter how tiny. They went through camp after camp, location after location, until the magnitude of it all made me want to vomit.

And then, we saw one of the concluding exhibits. The Allies liberated the camps. Russian tanks stormed through Poland and liberated Auschwitz. American and British forces thundered through Western Europe and liberated the camps there. When they saw the handiwork of the SS officers, they forced them to clean it up themselves. And the most gruesome footage of all played on a television screen on a wall above: a bulldozer pushing a rolling mass of bodies into a giant, common grave. There were far too many slain, and far too little labour, to bury them all individually.

When I saw what came next, I raised my camera and broke the museum's ban on photos.

It was a photo of seven Jews in concentration camp clothing, standing stalwart and courageous and looking into the distance, the flag of Israel flapping in their hands. In that moment, I realized just how much this country was born of the Holocaust. It was made up of Jews who saw no future for themselves in Europe after what they had experienced. And it was no accident that the blue and white stripes on Israel's flag resembled the blue and white stripes of their prison uniforms.

Below this photo, a black-and-white film clip was playing repeatedly. It was old and grainy footage of a small group of children singing the Israeli national anthem. The song was created by the Zionist movement long before Israel became a nation. And the words, ringing out in Hebrew by a chorus of children's voices, gave the degraded and crestfallen Jews of Israel the single thing they could never have in a Europe dominated by Nazi fanatics. Indeed, it is also the title of the anthem. One simple word.

Hope.

"This is. . .pornography," Sean said, once he had finished looking at the museum.

"Honestly, the only thing I thought while I was walking through it is what sort of museum the Palestinians would create to the victims of the occupation if they only had the money."

Nickie pointed to a group of IDF soldiers that were clustered in the Hall of Names. "They are the only ones ruining my experience of this place. They see everything that happened to their ancestors. . .and yet they themselves are helping to do this to somebody else."

I nodded. "I wonder how many of them realize the contradiction. I mean, I know that their education teaches them not to see it—that there is no similarity between what they experienced in Europe and what they accomplish in Palestine. And most of them probably buy it. But still, I wonder how many of them privately have doubts."

Glass doors before us led out onto a balcony, where I saw the great metal beams which formed the corridor split out in either direction. I finally understood the true meaning of the building's architecture. Directly in front of us, placed as perfectly as though in a painting, was a white Israeli city on a bare landscape of rolling hills. The light sheets of rain dimmed our view of it, and dark grey clouds loomed ominously above. But the message was sparklingly clear.

The building had taken us through the misery and pain of the Holocaust, only to display the wide land, the land of Israel, a land the Jews could finally call their own. A land, where such persecutions could never, ever happen again.

Or at least, not to Jews.

I left Yad Vashem that day with very mixed feelings. I couldn't help thinking that it was very easy to blame the Israelis without ever stepping into their shoes. If the Canadian people had gone through such a trial, and if Canadian society was under threat, it would look precisely like the society of the Israelis. There would be constant surveillance, military everywhere, universal conscription, passport controls, checkpoints, and maybe even walls. And what's more: there would be very few voices within Canadian society demanding that those walls be torn down. If it was our own homes, our own families, and our own existence at stake, it would somehow be a lot more difficult to criticize.

But without a doubt, the Palestinians could easily fill a museum with stories about their treatment at the hands of the Israelis. And although harsh measures to defend one's own society can perhaps be justified, that justification does not extend to taking land and forcing out its inhabitants for reasons of religious destiny. The Israelis want all of Jerusalem, and they want all of the West Bank, because it is part of the ancient Israel described in the Bible. And to this end, the current occupation is trying to make it so impossible for the Palestinians to live their daily lives that they decide to leave of their own accord.

We walked through the wisps of rain towards the parking lot at the entrance to the site. We waited patiently for our taxi to arrive as the museum shut down and the sky grew dim. And in the fading light, I looked to an inscription carved on the great white arches that spanned the road leading back to Jerusalem. It was a quote from Ezekiel.

"And I shall put my breath into you and you shall live again, and I shall set you upon your own soil."[8]

[8] Ezekiel 37:14

20

A WALK IN THE GARDENS

After Yad Vashem, we taxied back to East Jerusalem. As we neared the Damascus Gate, the taxi slowed and demanded twenty shekels above the price shown on his meter. We had already physically exited the vehicle before paying, a practice that we had developed since Egypt to deal with Middle Eastern cab drivers. In every country we visited, taxi drivers had always tried to draw every possible drop of blood out of the visiting foreigners. Israel, we found, was no different.

"He's not getting his extra twenty shekels," said Sean. "We'll give him what the meter says, and if he doesn't like it, he can follow us across the Green Line."

The cabbie shook his fist at us out the window and honked loudly as we departed. "Shalom!" Sean shouted back with a wave, as we walked twenty meters forward and crossed the imaginary line that separated Israel from Palestine.

I had certainly never seen a phenomenon like the Green Line before. Palestinians would not pass West of the line; Israelis would not pass East of it. But we, as foreigners, could trample all over either side with impunity; welcomed by Jews on the Israeli side, and welcomed even more warmly by Arabs on the Palestinian side.

And I found to my delight that whenever I felt like sidestepping some particular cultural inconvenience, I simply walked three blocks across the Green Line. When I got tired of garbage in the streets sticking to my shoes, or oil splatter on the walls of restaurants, I crossed to the Israeli side. When I became annoyed at high prices, or having to wait at crosswalks when no cars were coming, I crossed to the Palestinian side. When I wanted to buy some alcohol, I crossed to the Israeli side. When the stores were closed on Saturday, I crossed to the Palestinian side. When stores were closed on Friday, I crossed to the Israeli side.

Jerusalem really was one of the most unique cities in the world. It was not like Beirut, with its patchwork of many warring tribes, where one's personal security could alter so radically from block to block. Here, there were but two tribes, who had divided the city into two clean-cut halves, with walled Old Jerusalem as the nucleus. And although each side was eternally suspicious of the other, the people of Jerusalem lived out each day in a tenable peace. And perhaps, in a way, that did make it one of the world's great multicultural cities.

I awoke to a sharp, business-like knock which rattled my loose hotel room door. I sprang out of bed, rubbing my head groggily, my eyes bleary from beer and sheesha in the Faisal hotel common room the night before. I opened it to see a girl soldier in military fatigues bulging with equipment: a taser on her right side, a radio and a gun on her left. She looked at my half-naked body while I gaped at her, dumbfounded. Finally it occurred to me to reach for a shirt. Sean looked up from his bed and frowned in confusion.

"Passport."

I handed it over and just stared at her, wondering what right this woman had to enter the very room I was sleeping in and demand my documentation. She made a point of paying no attention, and keeping a calm, bored look to her.

"You were in Egypt, Lebanon, Syria, and Jordan?"

"Yes."

I'm glad she didn't ask me what I was doing there. One more question from her and I would have seized my passport and slammed the door in her face. This, needless to say, would have ended badly. I would have been hauled out and rudely interrogated as to the full extent of my activities in the Middle East, regardless of whether or not it was any of their business. My comrades would have been dragged into it to, and the film project would have been put in jeopardy.

Then, once they had left, and everything had calmed down, Nickie would have ripped my face off.

"They come by once in a while to check everybody's passports. The checks are totally random."

I was talking to Ali, Osama's cousin. My head was spinning: I thought they might have come because of the freckle-faced American girl who was snapping photos when we first arrived, or perhaps— God forbid—because of us! But apparently the checks were regular.

"In Israel, every hotel has to register a person's passport online immediately after they check in. That way the security services always know where people are. But in Palestine, we don't give them this information. So the only way they can keep track is to show up here themselves."

"Where's Osama?" I asked him.

"He always leaves whenever they come. They don't like him because of all the films he makes."

"How does he know when they are coming?"

Ali smiled. "Someone calls him. We are all friends here in Palestine. We look out for one another."

I remarked on this to Osama when he came back. He seemed amused at my indignation at the fact that the Israelis regularly invaded his hostel. He seemed almost proud of it.

"This place is well-known to the security services. Many journalists and foreign activists choose to stay here. Even the Lonely Planet says 'come for the politics.' You know, Rachel Corrie stayed here for a couple of weeks."

"Really?" I exclaimed. "You knew her?"

Osama nodded.

Rachel Corrie was an American who came here to protest the Israeli occupation. She died in 2003, when she stood up in front of an Israeli bulldozer that was there to demolish a Palestinian house in Gaza. She refused to move, just like the famous video of Tiananmen square, when a democratic protester held out his hand and forced a whole line of tanks to stop.

Only sometimes, the tanks don't stop. The bulldozer crushed Rachel and flattened the house she was trying to defend. She was 23 years old.

Osama was helping to film a documentary about the incident. There is a memorial website up for Rachel, and a play has been put into production entitled "My Name is Rachel Corrie." She was one of the few foreign casualties of the Israeli-Palestinian conflict. If she had been alive today, she would have been around our age.

As I watched my sister pack her bags along with my two best friends, and prepare to stash them in a room, I thought of the frightened email my father had sent us, warning us to stay away from Lebanon. I thought of the way Nickie's boyfriend must have read the news of the Beirut car bombing with his heart in his mouth. I thought of my interrogation in Shatila; of our interview with Ali Abdullah, thankfully unnoticed by the Syrian Mukhabarat. We didn't know at the time that only a few months later, another group of Western youths would try to film something similar in Syria—*and get caught*. They were not simply dumped out of the country, as we had expected to be. They were thrown into a Syrian prison.

Our original intent during this trip was to meet and film some of the participants in the conflicts of the Middle East, and bring their stories to the world. Whatever righteousness there had been in our purpose had died in Lebanon, after we filmed Mahmoud Homsi. And although we continued filming, perhaps we had not considered the scale of danger we had put ourselves through. Rachel Corrie was a Western girl, much like ourselves, had probably traveled here on a similar odyssey of investigation and activism. And she had, wittingly or unwittingly, become a casualty in another people's war—a martyr for a cause that did not concern her. Here in the Middle East, they played for keeps.

And one thing was clear to me—whatever we stood for, and however terribly people here were being oppressed—this was not really our fight.

"Ready to go?" asked Nickie.

"Yeah," I said. "Let's get out of here."

Osama allowed us to store all of our bags in one room while we traveled. It was only three days before Nickie and Kristen had to fly back to Canada. And in the little time we had remaining, we decided to see some of Israel proper: the city of Tel Aviv, and the city of Haifa.

"This is. . .like Vancouver," Kristen said.

When we stepped off the bus, we immediately noticed a change. The winter weather had all but evaporated; there was sunlight and warmth in the air. The streets of Tel Aviv were clean and straight, the traffic governed by lights and crosswalk signals, the buildings tall, symmetrical, and orderly. Trees were planted in neat rows alongside the cobblestone roads, and little public parks with benches and flowerbeds offered places of relaxation.

We had entered a different world.

As we walked to the hostel, we passed streets with names like 'HaHarash', 'Allenby', or 'Rothschild.' In the alleyways, we saw blue Shields of David scrawled upon the walls, and swastikas with cancel signs running through them. We checked in at a hostel to drop our bags before going to look around. We gulped as the lady quoted us the price. This far away from Jerusalem, prices had risen—by half. On the beach, we lounged in red lawn chairs and each ordered a Maccabee beer. Up and down the deserted shore, we saw rows of empty chairs and high-rise hotels. Not too far away, three girls in bikinis were walked through the surf. The smell of ocean salt floated on the breeze.

"What a cultural oddity," Sean said. "A little Vancouver by the sea, smack dab in the center of the Middle East. Unbelievable."

As if summoned, a chopping sound filled the sky. Three black helicopters buzzed into view, long and sleek, laden with weaponry. They flew out over the water, and made off south until their sound faded into the distance. As they passed, all of us let out a laugh.

It was impossible to forget this was Israel.

Tel Aviv was built around the old Arab port of Jaffa in the early days of the twentieth century. Boatloads of Jewish immigrants came from Europe and settled here, inspired by the nascent Zionist movement and its founder Theodore Herzl, whose dream was to build a homeland where Jews could be free from persecution. The city's ranks swelled during the rise of the Nazis in Germany, as more and more Jews left Europe for what was then British Palestine. When the 1948 war came, the population of Tel Aviv dwarfed that of Jaffa, and the Arabs fled eastwards after a brief skirmish. Tel Aviv has since become the main point of entry for the thousands of immigrants Israel has welcomed since the foundation of their state.

"I don't care *what* religion they are, if you take a couple million white-skinned Europeans and stick them in the center of the Arab Middle East, you are going to have problems. It has nothing to do with religion, and *everything* to do with culture!"

Back in Lebanon, my father's friend Andrew had given us a beer-inspired lecture at the local Irish pub.

"So they're Jews? Who cares? Other religions have been living in this place for thousands of years. It doesn't matter that they're Jews—it matters that they are Europeans: they have a different way of using land, and a different way of planning cities. And what would you expect from the Arabs if a bunch of foreigners show up and start living in their space, and using their resources? Really, what did they *think* was going to happen?"

We walked around the city till dusk, admiring the new age architecture, and enjoying the entirely Western feel. Here, we felt psychologically at home. Here was where most of the secular Jews lived: the very religious confined themselves to Jerusalem or elected to live in settlements and help occupy the West Bank. And Tel Aviv also showed the cultural diversity of the Israelis far more than Jerusalem did: here, the streets were lined with Ethiopian and Moroccan restaurants, and dozens of languages could be heard spoken on the streets: from Hebrew, to English, to Russian.

But after one day, we could already feel the downside to being in a Western-style city: it was downright boring. There was nothing interesting to see. We had come out of Jerusalem to see a different side of Israeli culture, and now that we had seen it, we realized that it felt just like home, and it was draining our wallets every minute we stayed. That evening at the hotel, we inquired about how to catch the train north to Haifa. That city, as far as we knew, was just the same: except for one key sight. Tomorrow, we were off to see the Terraces of the Baha'i, also known as the Hanging Gardens of Haifa.

I first saw the gardens as our taxi rounded the bend from the train station. They were built up the side of a massive hill, which was a brilliant architectural decision: they were a dominant feature of Haifa's landscape. They were surrounded by pristine walls of shining white, and they extended upwards on eighteen different levels, all the way up the mountain. On the center terrace was a massive white shrine with sharp, toothy features, capped by a glowing copper dome.

I couldn't wait. Nothing fascinated me quite like the architecture of the world's religions.

The gardens were built by the Baha'i, a relatively new addition to the world's pantheon of faiths. The Baha'i came from Persia in the middle of the nineteenth century. The religion officially began with a man known as the *'Bab'*, which is Persian for 'Gate'. He claimed to be the awaited Messiah of Islam; that he was one in a long line of prophets which God had sent to earth. He also proclaimed that another would come after him, who was much greater than he himself—a prophet on the level of Elijah, Jesus, or Mohammed. While his movement began to spread swiftly throughout Persia, it was swiftly condemned and persecuted by the Islamic religious authorities. Six years after he began his teachings, the Bab was executed for his declarations, and his disciples were scattered.

In the two decades after the death of the Bab, not less than twenty-five people declared themselves to be the chosen prophet whose coming he foretold. The most influential among them was Baha'u'llah.

Baha'u'llah, whose original name was Mizra Husayn Ali-Nuri, was a disciple of the Bab, who was thrown into prison in Tehran shortly after the Bab's death. There, in an infamous dungeon known as the Black Pit, he began to have visions: he was visited by a maiden, who told him that God had chosen him to be the great prophet that the Bab had foretold. When he was let out, Mizra changed his name to Baha'u'llah, which means 'the Glory of God,' and began a life of exile in Baghdad, Kurdistan, and Anatolia, until he finally ended up imprisoned in the city of Acre, just a few miles north of where Haifa now stands.

Baha'u'llah's followers, known as the Baha'i, believe that the prophets of every religion in the past are messengers of the same God, and that Baha'u'llah is the latest messenger in that line. They believe that he came to earth to deliver the message of the unity of all world religions and of all humankind. They believe in the elimination of prejudice, equality between the sexes, the cooperation of all religions, and the harmony of religion and science. And, most curiously, they believe in the political unity of the whole planet in a universal world federation.

On our right side, as we descended the terraces, we saw an ivory-white building that looked like a small version of the US Capitol: white columns surrounded the outside, and a white dome stood upon its roof. This, we learned, was the Universal House of Justice, the governing body of the Baha'i faith. I started to realize, however, as the tour group moved straight on down the simple terrace steps, that we were not going to be led past it. Though the garden extended over thousands of square meters, and though every inch of it boasted splendid violet flowers and tailored bushes, we were allowed to walk through very little of it.

And to the annoyance of Sean and I, we were forced to walk through it with a group of tourists, led by a guide who spoke to us in pure Hebrew.

Eventually, we slowed and let the tour walk a few terraces down in front of us. This gave us some room to enjoy the gardens for ourselves. The whole point of a garden, so I thought, was to create a beautiful, silent space for people to walk through, relax, and contemplate.

The gardens were alive with colour. Each terrace was paved with red brick, and had bands of white gravel enclosing planted trees and attentively arranged beds of flowers. Palm trees stretched their fronds above us, and shielding the fierce heat of the winter suns. As we walked the hundreds of stairs leading down through the terraces, we noticed a white marble sluice, itself cut into many marble stairs, to either side of us. A small stream flowed in each of them. Every couple of seconds, a small rush in the water would cascade down each step in turn, creating a sound of successive splashes. The bright city of Haifa with its white roofs, and the brilliant sparkle of the Mediterranean stretched out before us. Away from the bustle of the group, the Hanging Gardens of Haifa became truly tranquil.

There were eighteen terraces in all—nine above, and nine below the copper-domed shrine. It was the Shrine of the Bab, and it contained the remains of the original self-proclaimed prophet.

The eighteen terraces represented the eighteen disciples of the Bab, and they were arranged so that they each formed part of a concentric circle emanating out from the Shrine. When we finally arrived at the center platform, and caught up with our tour, we finally got to see this majestic building up close—its white toothy trim, its polished copper dome. The Baha'i tour guide drawled on in Hebrew for a bit, and then gave a nod. Some of the visitors walked forward to go visit the Shrine. But when others tried to follow, they were held back.

Of course, I realized. Only those who had little nametags pinned to their chests saying 'Pilgrim' were allowed to enter. Just as we had experienced at the Al-Aqsa Mosque, and the Dome of the Rock, only the faithful were allowed to enter.

"What do you think, Sean?" I asked my friend. "Is that sort of thing good for a religion? To block off access to everyone who doesn't believe?"

Sean looked thoughtful for a moment.

"I suppose it is," he said. "It shuts out the rest of the world, but it is probably really good for making their own followers feel like an exclusive group. There has to be *some* kind of privilege for the flock. Still, it makes me wonder why the Catholics don't do it. They will let anyone in to see the Vatican."

After the tour, we exited by a stairway onto the streets of Haifa, and began to weave our way down from Mount Carmel towards the rest of the city. Kristen, Sean, and Nickie stopped to eat at a Chinese restaurant, while I continued down the hill until I found a small shop near the sea, where I ordered a simple meal of hummus and bean soup.

As I reclined outside, I looked back at the Gardens on the slopes of the mountain, far above the city. Another religion, this one only a hundred and fifty years old, had come to make its home in the holy land—in this hallowed strip of earth between the Jordan and the sea. It had come to unite the faiths of the world and declare all men equal, and yet it had only succeeded in creating another division. How unsurprising, I thought. Perhaps it was just the nature of religion to set up boundaries dividing the holy from the many—no matter how universal it professed to be.

At least, I thought, it had added one more rich and unique doctrine to the thousand philosophies of the human race. And at least it had graced the world with yet another magnificent form of religious architecture.

Sean and I bade goodbye to Nickie and Kristen the following evening. We packed their bags into a taxi and sent them shuttling off to Tel Aviv airport. We had gotten almost all of the footage necessary to make some decent short films. Sean and I needed to do a little bit more work with the Torture Rehabilitation Center in Ramallah, but for the most part, we had accomplished what we came to do. When they left, I breathed a great sigh of relief. Although I would later look back on this whirlwind tour as one of the most profound experiences of my life, I was incredibly relieved that these lightning-paced five weeks were over. Now, for a brief time, I could relax. I walked back up to the Faisal hostel, ordered some peach sheesha from Ali, and sipped a beer.

For Nickie, however, the stress was not over. She was interrogated for a full four hours at Tel Aviv airport. They went through her computer and film equipment in excruciating detail; they scanned the film tapes with equipment that damaged the sound. She almost missed her plane. But eventually, once they realized she was not a threat to Israeli national security, they gave her back her footage and film equipment, and she boarded the flight to Canada.

21
NOVY GOD

I first got to know Dasha through couchsurfing. com, a website where young travelers from different countries could contact each other and possibly meet. Back in Egypt, I had sent her an email about our journey and what we wanted to film, and she told me she would be delighted to meet me. Sean and I were debating what sort of things we wanted to film on the Israeli side of things.

"We should do something on immigrants if we can," Sean said. "Perhaps we should do something on the Russian Israelis. Most of them come over because the economic situation in Russia is terrible and they have more opportunities in Israeli society. There are some who aren't even Jewish."

"What?" I asked, surprised.

"Yeah. They're Orthodox Christian. But they have a Jewish grandparent, so they are allowed to come to Israel."

"So you don't even need to be Jewish? All you need is a Jewish grandparent?"

Sean looked at me slyly. "Having a Jewish grandparent was the requirement to be considered Jewish by the Nazis. It's no accident that it's the same requirement to be considered Jewish by the Israelis."

Dasha was our best Israeli contact. I met her on a street corner in West Jerusalem, just twenty minutes walk from the Green Line. She was a tall girl, with dirty blonde hair in braids, brown eyes, and a wide smile. Like everyone who knew what winter in the Middle East actually felt like, she was dressed in a long coat and a toque. I, conversely, looked the part of the ignorant foreigner, with socks under my closed-toed sandals, lacking a proper jacket, huffing through my bunched hands to keep warm. We found a dimly-lit pub and settled inside to take refuge from the chill.

"So how long have you been in Israel?" I asked her, after the waitress had served us each a frothing pint.

"I came over with my mother when I was eight. I guess that makes it fifteen years ago."

"Wow. That must have been about. . .1992. Right after the Soviet Union fell."

She nodded, grinning at my obvious fascination with the subject.

"And where did you live again?"

"Leningrad. Of course, it's St. Petersburg now."

The Soviet Union was one of the great exceptions to the Israeli experience of immigration. After the Second World War, millions of Jews living in places where they felt unwanted, persecuted, or uncomfortable immigrated to Israel. And most of their host countries let them go, for they were eager to get rid of them. But the Soviet Union refused.

The first reason was directly political: Israel was a new ally of the West during the nascent Cold War, and the Soviet Union was not going to send its citizens to help fight for the other side. But there were deeper reasons as well. The Soviets had always preached a philosophy of total ethnic inclusion: that the USSR was a new type of society, one in which race and religion no longer mattered—a classless society where everyone lived in harmony under socialism. For the USSR to let the Jews go would be to admit two things to the world: first, that some people were eager to leave the drab society and defunct economy that communism had created; and second, that beneath its Soviet skin, Russia was the same xenophobic, Jew-hating culture that it had always been.

Soviet Russia treated Jews far more poorly than did most other countries after the Holocaust.

In 1953, Josepf Stalin, who had hated Jews since the early revolutionary days, accused a number of doctors of trying to poison the Kremlin leaders. In what became known as the Doctor's Plot, Stalin had nine prominent doctors arrested, six of them Jewish. It was widely expected that this was the prelude to another great purge—fanatical episodes when Stalin cleansed the general population of 'enemies of the people.' The victims were often selected at random, kidnapped by the KGB under the cover of darkness, and never seen again. Thankfully, Stalin died before this all took place, and the doctors were set free.

In the late 1980s, when Gorbachev became General Secretary and the Soviet system began to open up, a new wave of anti-Semitism swept the country. In Jewish neighbourhoods, hooligans broke into houses, destroyed furniture and painted swastikas on the walls. Jewish cultural organizations were padlocked by the KGB, and racist pamphlets were stapled to the door. KGB stalked the synagogues, spying on the occupants. An organization known as Pamyat wrote articles blaming Jews for Russia's social problems, and posted handbills signed: "Russia for Russians: The Organization of Death to Yids."

At the same time, the Soviet Union was reforming, and the traditional strictures were being relaxed. The first trickle of Soviet Jews were allowed to immigrate to Israel. And when the whole system came down, in late 1991, Jews began to leave Russia in droves. It was in this atmosphere that Dasha had left St. Petersburg for Israel. She became part of the most recent great wave of Israeli immigration. In a population of seven million people, one million Israelis are Russians. Russia has become the third most spoken language in the country, after Hebrew and English. And Israeli society has received them uncomfortably: much like the black Jews of Ethiopia, the Russians are discriminated against amongst Israelis.

"Have you ever been back to Russia?" I asked her.

"Yes, once. I went back to St. Petersburg a few years ago. But it's different there now. I don't really feel safe."

"I hear the Israelis don't really like Russians that much. Would you ever want to move back?"

She laughed and took a sip of beer. "Yes, we are discriminated against here. But it's nothing like how Jews are treated back home. I would much rather be a Russian in Israel than a Jew in Russia."

Dasha had grown up in Jerusalem and learned Hebrew and English. Like all young Israelis, she had been drafted into military service at age eighteen.

"Those were two of the best years of my life," she told me. "I had so much fun in the army. And

I met so many great people—friends I will have forever."

After her service in the military, she told me, Israel had given her a free ten-day trip around the country, on a program known as 'Taglit,' or 'Birthright.' The program took Jews from around the world—South America, North America, Africa, Europe—and gave them a free ten-day journey around Israel. It was a program designed to encourage Israeli immigration.

"So, why did they put you on the trip? Was it for protection?"

"No. They regularly send three people from the military on each Taglit tour. They are there to show the other participants that being in the army isn't actually all that bad."

I asked her what her duties were during her two years in the army.

"I was stationed in Jerusalem. We worked at an intelligence center, monitoring possible threats to the city. I translated intelligence reports, and helped to coordinate prevention of terrorist attacks. This is when the wall was going up. Since the wall, attacks on Jerusalem have decreased by ninety-five percent."

"Ninety-five percent?" I exclaimed.

"Yes," she nodded. "Ninety-five percent."

"You know," I said to her quietly, "I'm beginning to see another side to this place. In Canada, everyone criticizes Israel for the occupation. But I'm starting to realize how one might think if they actually lived here. It is really easy to think of Israel as cruel and oppressive when you come from Canada or America, societies where there really is no danger."

"You don't have to be from Canada to think that!" Dasha said, chuckling. "You can be from Tel Aviv and think that. But really, you are right. On the surface, everything here looks peaceful. But you have no idea just how many dozens of threats a city like Jerusalem faces every day. By being in the security forces, I can tell you that if there weren't hundreds of people working all the time to keep it safe, the place would be a war zone."

I shuddered. We had been very lucky to choose this time to travel to the Middle East. We had watched the news closely, and Israel had not had experience a single attack in a very long time. I did not know until that moment, that one of the things largely responsible for this. . .was the wall.

"We're having a celebration for New Years in a couple of days," she told me. "I'm having lots of Russian friends over for a party. If you want to meet some of them, perhaps for your film, you should come."

"Absolutely!" I replied, delighted. "Where's it going to be?"

"It's at my house. It's a bit far—you'll have to take a bus to get there. It's in Ma'ale Adumim."

I nodded. Ma'ale Adumim was east of East Jerusalem, a suburb built in the West Bank to curb the growth of the Palestinian part of the city.

I was going to celebrate the New Year in an Israeli settlement.

"Make sure you come back to the hostel later," Osama told me. "We're having a wild party here. It's going to be great!"

I told him I'd be back when I could. I had spoken to Dasha, and I would be unable to sleep over at Ma'ale Adumim. So it was either catch the last bus home, or go through the impossible madness of trying to find a taxi home at three am on New Years Eve. This, I have found, is impossible to do in Vancouver—I didn't want to try it in Israel. Especially not when I was sure to be in my cups.

I bought a bottle of vodka at a local shop across the Green Line before setting out. The bus climbed far north of Jerusalem's city limits—from the window I could see its flickering lights below. They must have built this special highway to connect West Jerusalem to the settlement, I reasoned. No Israeli bus could safely pass through East Jerusalem.

Dasha picked me up from the bus stop. As I got in the car, she introduced me to her friend Ivan, who was driving. When we got to her flat, I was introduced to a host of other Russian women and men, most of whom shook my hand and said 'hello' with those brave smiles that told me they didn't know much English at all, and conversation that night would be fairly limited. One girl was dressed like a Goth, with heavy eyeliner and red streaks in her hair.

"Hello, I'm Kieran" I said, offering my hand.

"You have very beautiful eyes" was all she said back, in limited English. I laughed and turned a shade of scarlet, and retreated to another part of the flat.

Dasha introduced me to Galit, a small, dark-haired young girl who looked very relieved to see me.

"I'm from America," she said.

"Really? Do you speak any Russian?"

She laughed. "I'm learning. These are my good friends from university—I like to practice with them. But I'm really happy to see another English-speaker here."

"Are they all from around here?" I asked Dasha. "From Ma'ale Adumim?"

Sean had told me that settlements were usually populated by two types of people: by ultra-zealous Jews eager to help claim back the land of the Bible, or by immigrants. Life in the settlements could be dangerous, and so ordinary Israelis born in Jerusalem or Tel Aviv did not want to live there.

"They are all from here," said Dasha. "There are thousands of Russians in Ma'ale Adumim. They make up a large percentage of the population."

I nodded. "I heard that most immigrants get put in places like this."

Dasha grinned. "We moved here because it was cheap. We used to have a flat in Jerusalem— but my parents found a much better place in the settlement for less money. In Israel, you will find Russians anywhere it is cheap."

There was a commotion in the flat as it neared eleven o'clock. The TV was switched on, and everyone fought for a space on the couch to watch it. On some outdoor stage, two men dressed like old ladies squawked at each other in Russian, while everybody in the room except Galit and I shook with laughter. Then, the anointed hour came. The TV focused on the massive Kremlin clock tower, which was striking midnight in Moscow. Finally, the camera panned out, to reveal the austere figure of Russian president Vladimir Putin.

He began a speech in Russian, and everyone squeezed in to watch. After a few minutes, he finished, and the TV began to flap the Russian tricolour and play the glorious bars of the Russian national anthem. While I adored this song, my Russian Israeli comrades were already bored, and they flipped off the TV and cranked the speakers, and Russian rock music once again shook the walls.

"What was the speech about?" I asked Dasha.

She looked uninterested. "The Russian President makes a speech every year at the stroke of midnight," she told me.

"So do you all. . .like Putin then?" I asked.

She shrugged. It was Russia, I realized—not really her country. The people at the party didn't seem to care about President Putin much at all. I got the vibe that they only switched on the TV because it was tradition—because *Novy God*, the Russian New Years, would never be complete without the President's speech.

Everyone dropped back shot after shot of warm vodka. My gut clenched at the first few, but after the alcohol began to hit my veins, I didn't mind it so much. They had stretched out a wonderful meal on the table before us: salad, bread with caviar, potatoes, fried chicken, and a dish of a brilliant purple colour known as 'shuba'. It looked strange when I first spooned some onto my plate, but it turned out to be a mixed salad of red beets, eggs, onions, and herring—it was delicious. We threw back more vodka and stuffed ourselves with food.

The moment of the New Year came, and we all shouted out the countdown. When it was over, I knew that even though I hadn't stayed all that long, I soon had to go. Everyone in the flat moved out the screen door to have a cigarette on the balcony. I joined them.

Dasha's house was on a hill, and I could see a landscape view of the cul-de-sacs of the Israeli settlement. The streets were perfectly planned, and each house had a yard and looked just like the house beside it. Pale yellow lamps lit the streets, trees sprouted along the sidewalk, and each house had a car in the driveway. I thought I was looking out onto one of those fancy model communities from home, named something like 'Nicowynd Acres' or 'Amblegreen Boulevard.' It was entirely different from the crooked houses and winding streets of the Palestinian districts that lay just a few kilometers east.

The crowd bantered and moved back inside. Dasha looked at me from the screen door, as if to ask if I was coming. I told her I would stay a little bit longer. I turned and leaned my arms on the balcony railing, nursing the wet, ragged end of a cigarette, and one haunting thought.

The Israelis, I realized, were just like us.

Israel represented Western culture when pushed to the wall. I knew in my blood that if I lived on a postage stamp of land surrounded by enemies, that I would don my olive-green fatigues just as my brother, sister, and cousins would alongside me. If buses full of my countrymen exploded on the streets, my people would erect a high wall around the community of the offenders, and my friends and family would man the checkpoints.

Except perhaps for the continued appropriation of Palestinian land, all the fascistic trappings of Israeli society, no matter how evil they seemed, were aimed at only one thing. Survival.

And I realized that it was very easy to preach democracy and human rights if one came from a peaceful society such as Canada. But it was a different thing entirely to step into Israeli sandals and try to walk a mile.

When I returned to the Faisal hostel, I found the place nearly dead. Half a dozen drunk people tried to dance in the corner as though the crazy celebration Osama had promised was still raging, but the lights were on in the rest of the common room, and most people lounged around on the cushions, dazed and tired. The crowd still dancing consisted of four men trying to dance as closely as they could to two women, who were looking uncomfortable in their revelry. I ordered a beer from Osama and sat down to relax.

I soon fell into a conversation with a German man named Paul. Paul was twenty-seven years old, and he wore a black, red, and orange scarf that three of his friends were also wearing to signify their membership in the German army. He had been to Israel and Palestine three times, he explained. He was a combat medic, and he was here mainly to see Palestine and attend the Friday Protest in Bilin.

"Really? My friend Sean and I were thinking of going this Friday. But I don't know—I've never experienced tear gas before."

"Tear gas is. . .not fun," he told me. "But it's not really that bad. Rubber bullets are worse. They are little pellets of metal wrapped around with rubber. They are designed to cause intense pain and immobilize a person. But they can be fatal if they hit you in the head. Just whenever they shoot, remember not to duck. They will probably be aiming at your legs, and you don't want to put your head in the way."

"Are there a lot of internationals there?"

"Absolutely. There are tons. I've been to the protest seven or eight times. It has changed my entire view on the Israeli-Palestinian conflict. The way they treat those people, just for having a protest. . ."

His voice trailed off. Resentment burn behind his eyes.

"In fact," he continued, "I actually taught a few of them what to do. I gave them a bit of training on how to deal with tear gas. And basic first aid."

"Really?"

"Yeah, but I had to hold back. Because—I don't want it to be known that a guy from the German army trained some Palestinian protestors in how to be combat medics. I have my career to think of, after all.

"But go to the protest. It is a little bit dangerous, but most people get through it just fine. And
as a foreigner, you're not really taking such a risk—
just think of the people who live there and who do
it every week. We are all taking a taxi from here together on Friday. Honestly, come with us. I swear
to you, it's unforgettable."

22

THE THIRD TRIBE

From the car, we watched a man in a grey suit come out of the blue-windowed Bank of Palestine building in Ramallah. Sean and I got out to greet him. He shook our hands vigorously, without a smile.

"I am Abdullah" he told us. "Come. We will take my car."

Sean followed him up the road while I helped the two Palestinian women behind us get out of our vehicle. One of them was almost forty and wore a sweeping blue veil; the other was twenty-six and was dressed like a Westerner. She was a stunningly beautiful, dark-eyed girl, whose bulging stomach showed that she would soon be a mother. These two were psychologists that from the TRC.

Sean and I were traveling north into the West Bank to collect the final bit of footage for the TRC short film. We were off to film some of the people who could not make the trip to Ramallah the day before Christmas. Amjad had sent two psychologists from the center along with us so that the patients would not be afraid to talk. He had asked us to find a translator.

"I will find you one. No problem. I will find you someone, or I will go myself and translate. I promise you."

We had taken Osama up on his 'anything you need, anything at all' proposal. I was kind of hoping that he would come with us personally, since we knew him well. Instead, he had summoned his brother Abdullah to the task.

Abdullah, in his sharp-looking grey business suit, wore a surly face as he drove us north. He pushed the car within inches of its limits, flying along the potholed highway at breakneck speed. He had three cell phones spread out along the dash. One of them rang, and he grabbed it and barked into it severely. Then, during the same conversation, another one would ring, and he would ask the other person to excuse him while he picked up the second one.

"Oh! He is so angry!" said the women, looking shocked, when Abdullah stepped out of the car to go deposit a cheque at a bank we passed. I realized with chagrin that Abdullah was doing his brother a favour because it was his brother, and he considered us a waste of his precious time. We probably were.

"Wow, you have three telephones!" I exclaimed to him, trying to loosen him up.

"Four" he said back, with a smile.

During our first interview, with a wiry gas station owner who had lost his brother in an Israeli firefight, one of them rang to life. As the camera was rolling, Abdullah got up and started barking into it, and moved to the back of the room instead of listening to our interviewee. Eventually, he shut the phone and came back, translating only the very last of the guy's long-winded speech. I cringed and tried to sit by patiently.

"It's a bit of a pity" he said, when we got back in the car. "You know the former Al-Aqsa Martyrs' Brigades? The leader is a friend of mine. I could have gotten an interview with him. What we are filming now is nothing."

We went to the house of another family. Inside, we saw three little children bouncing off the walls, and three women in headscarves. One, the old grandmother, was in the kitchen doing the dishes. The others—the mother of the kids and her sister—sat down and talked with the psychologists, preparing for an interview.

"Who's that?" Sean asked me. He pointed to a photo of a man's face surrounded by a drawing of the Dome of the Rock, mounted into a gilt picture frame. Golden Arabic letters were scribed under his portrait.

"I think that's Dad," I said.

Three years ago, the woman told us, the unfortunate father had heard a protest down the street. He went out to close the windows and doors of his shop, to protect his merchandise from damage. He was shot by IDF soldiers, though he wasn't even taking part in the protest. He bled to death in the street. The Israelis didn't even stop to apologize.

The woman looked crestfallen as she looked at our camera and answered our questions. She held a photo of her fallen husband, while her three children sat beside her. We asked her how she made ends meet today. Her extended family helped her, as well as her husband's family.

"These two young ones will be ok," she said, pointing to the two smallest kids. "They were too young to really understand what was happening at the time. But my eldest," she paused and drew a breath, "he's got a bigger problem. He still hasn't quite gotten over it. He knows he will grow up without a father."

The Torture Rehabilitation Centre was helping her cope, as well as her children. The two youngest sang a song for our camera, a song they had been taught to help them deal with the pain of loss. When we left that day, I felt again what I had felt on many occasions before during our interviews—guilty. I had come into these people's lives and invoked these painful memories, and pointed a camera at their faces while I did so. But at the same time, I reflected, they gave me their stories for a reason. They wanted people in the outside world to know what happens in occupied Palestine.

Back in the car, we headed south to Ramallah. The sun was sinking; the working day was done. Finally, Abdullah's cell phones stopped torturing him. Finally, Abdullah began to relax.

"Do you have any children?" I asked him, thinking of the three youngsters in the family we had just visited.

"Yes," he said with a smile.

"How many?"

"You guess how many I have."

"A man like you must have at least four children," I said.

He laughed. "You have named half of them!"

Abdullah had eight children: five boys and three girls. His eldest, a son, was just completing university. His youngest, a daughter, was born a couple of months ago.

"Eight children!" I exclaimed. "You are very lucky."

Abdullah beamed. I was surprised that he had so many. He had an excellent job at the bank, and was part of the Palestinian business class. For most places in the world, more money meant people would have fewer children, in order to maintain a high standard of living. But Abdullah outdid even the typical Arab family, which had between four and five children on average. After a while, it dawned on me why.

Population was a weapon in the Israeli-Palestinian conflict. Israeli families, like most families in the West, typically had one or two children. Palestinian families had far more. While the Israelis rely on mass immigration for their population growth, the Palestinians rely on their own capacity to reproduce. This one factor, above anything else, has recently frightened members of the Israeli government into pushing for a Palestinian state. The Israelis are afraid that if they continue to deny the Palestinians a state of their own, eventually they will be pressured into giving them a stake in the Israeli state—they will be forced to give them the vote. And then it would only be a matter of time before the Palestinians outnumbered the Israelis and voted Arab leaders into power, forever ending the Zionist dream of a state for Jews alone.

"It seems the strategy is to make life so miserable in Palestine that people will just leave," I said to Abdullah.

"That is the strategy," he said.

"We don't talk about having our own country anymore. It is like a joke to us now. Today, a Palestinian is only thinking of two things: how to feed himself and his family, and how to get the pass to go to Jerusalem. The Israelis have taken everything from us. We can't even go to Jerusalem anymore to bury our dead beside their grandfathers."

Abdullah spoke with the same heavy patience that Sami had in Bethlehem. There was no anger, no depression in his voice. Instead he seemed simply fatalistic. He accepted that things were the way they were; that there was little he could do.

"Osama is filming a documentary on the Wall," he said, "but what good will that do? It is like what that man today said."

At the gas station, I had asked our interviewee if he had a message to give to the world.

"No I don't," he said. "Because the world has already heard the message, hundreds of times. But no one seems to listen."

"It's alright," Abdullah said to me, as we rounded another hill. "We are patient. Nobody can stay here forever. The Turks were here for four hundred years, but then they left. Then the British came, and then they also left. One day, the Israelis, too, will leave. But nobody knows when."

It was Thursday evening when Abdullah let us out in front of the TRC in Ramallah. From there, we said goodbye to the psychologists who came with us and made our way to the bus station. We hopped on the bus to Bilin. Sean knew of a man, also named Abdullah, who made his house available to foreigners to come sleep in during the evening of the Friday protest. We arrived there after half an hour, and marched through his yard and knocked on his door.

"Hi, we're crackers," Sean called out. "We're here to die for Palestine!"

A Palestinian woman, leaning out of her window, welcomed us inside in pure Arabic. We found rooms laid out with mattresses in the downstairs of the house, as well as a common room with a fridge but no cooking facilities. There was no one else there. I laid my pack down beside one of the mattresses and sat down on it. Sean did the same. I had originally thought to go check out the town and perhaps find a restaurant, but now that I was here I felt an uncontrollable fatigue sweep over me. I lay down fully clothed, and lapsed into an afternoon sleep.

When I awoke it was dark. Sean was still deep in slumber, and I decided not to wake him. But as I looked around the room, I realized we were not alone. The backpacks of at least three other people were there, each laid out beside a mattress.

I walked around the common room and switched on a weak florescent light. Around the walls there were hanging yellow posters. One of showed four maps of Arab-inhabited Palestine: the full territory under the British Mandate in 1947, and how it had shrunk each year until the present day, when it was a few disconnected blotches of paint surrounded by Israeli settlements. Another poster showed an iconic photograph from the 1970s of a crying black South African child running with his dead brother in his arms. It set this aside a photo of a crying Palestinian man running with his dead son in his arms. Finally, the last poster was a black-and-white photo of Hendrik Verwoerd, the architect of South African apartheid. Beneath his photo ran a quote of his from 1961: "Israel, like South Africa, is an apartheid state."

Beside these posters was a wall of large, blown-up photographs. I saw scenes from countless Friday protests since the tradition began in 2003. I saw lines of white people in a line, face to face with Israeli troops with helmets and riot shields. I saw white kids, their faces covered in blood, lying on the ground and being helped up by Palestinians and other foreigners. I saw groups of people fleeing tear gas explosions. And the most chilling photograph of all was a line of seven body bags filled and zipped, all lying out in a circle around the fountain that I recognized was in Abdullah's front yard.

This was the Bilin Friday protest, the demonstration I would be participating in tomorrow.

"We are university students from Italy. I am doing my graduating thesis on an Israeli court decision made in 2005 about the Bilin protest."

I was seated face to face with a young man and a young woman, at Bilin's only ramshackle restaurant, where I was busy spooning up hummus out of a bowl with a piece of flatbread.

"What was the court decision?" I asked.

"The decision was that the barrier boundaries here were unjust, because they took away most of the farmland from the people of Bilin. The Israeli Supreme Court ruled that they had to rewrite the boundary, and give these people back most of their land. But of course, this is just something the court has said. It remains to be seen whether the government of Israel will actually listen."

I was surprised. In their incredibly asymmetric, uphill battle for control of their own land, the Palestinians had scored a marginal victory. And they had done it with the constant help of foreign activists: with the presence of foreigners every Friday since 2003, resisting the occupation of Palestinian farmland.

"I'm a film student from Austria," the other resident in Abdullah's house told me. "My name is Ferdinand. I'm here to do film work on the Israeli-Palestinian conflict."

He showed me the camera he had brought: it was a massive number that he had to mount on his shoulder in order to use.

"It's not mine," he told me. "It's from my university."

"And they let you take that *here?*" I asked, incredulously.

He grinned. "I didn't tell them exactly where I was going in the Middle East. I know they wouldn't be happy if they knew what I was doing with it."

"Have you been to this protest before?"

"Oh yes, many times."

As I looked at the protest photos on the wall a final time before retiring to bed, I realized that there was a third tribe engaging in the struggle for land between the Jordan and the sea. It was us.

The foreigners were not here in Israel as mere passive observers to the conflict. We were active participants. In the early days of Palestinian hijackings, it had been the Western media that began to bring news of the conflict to the world, to expose what the Israelis were trying to do. During the First Intifada, it had been the Western media which showed the iconic images of the Israeli occupation: tanks rolling into Palestinian villages, and lone Palestinian children throwing rocks at them in response. And now, after the Second Intifada it was Western activists who were painting protest murals on the wall; it was foreign university students who were resisting its construction in places like Bilin.

And it was the foreigners, above all, who held the most power. It was we who brought the story of the Palestinian struggle to the outside world. It was we who had the ability to convince our own governments of the injustice of the occupation. It was we, and we alone, who had the power to turn

Israel's supporters against it, and perhaps, one day, force the conflict to end.

"You probably want to buy an onion," Ferdinand told me. "Or some chewing gum. They're really good for the tear gas."

It was about ten in the morning, and people had started to gather around in the street in front of Abdullah's house. The town mosque stood nearby, draped with a giant banner of Yassir Arafat's face. Sean stood by, fiddling with his camera. I went into a local Palestinian shop and bought a couple of onions. The shopkeeper smiled at me proudly, with a look in his eye that told me he knew exactly what they were for.

The Friday prayers had started. The minaret was barking constantly, and a crowd of Palestinians from all over the village filed inside. Suddenly, a couple of buses arrived. Out jumped my German friend Paul and many of the Japanese and Koreans that were staying at the Faisal hostel. As they waited in the road, little Arab children wandered up and tried to sell them little wristbands of red, black, white, and green beads: the four colours of the Palestinian flag. The Japanese snapped photos of them, and fumbled in their handbags for some money. Sean and I looked at each other awkwardly as the realization hit us both at once. We were about to experience the tourist version of the Israeli-Palestinian conflict.

Eventually, the minaret stopped its tirade. Palestinians began to stream out of the mosque. A younger one, at the front of the line, brandished a flag and began to shout. All the rest of the Palestinians exiting the mosque formed a giant crowd and began to chant. This was how the protest started, every week, right after Friday prayers.

I snapped countless photos of the growing demonstration. I saw no women in the crowd, but it was certainly a family affair. The men had taken their smallest youngsters out: children as young as two and three wore the Palestinian colours and paraded out with their fathers and elder brothers. As the crowd swelled and headed down the street, I ran along with the other foreigners in front of the mass to get photos of it. Palestinian flags waved wildly in the air, along with yellow banners and other flags of the Palestinian cause. Protest songs rang out in unison as they marched.

Finally, at a certain point in the road, one of the men waved his hands back and forth in the air and hailed the crowd.

"Mish shabbab! Mish shabbab!" he shouted. No youth, it meant.

The road dipped downwards, and as we marched, I saw a roll of razor wire stretch across the bottom of the hill. And a little bit further up the other side of the road, in olive-green fatigues, and holding military rifles, stood Goliath.

There were twelve of them, standing in front of a black armored personal carrier. The Palestinians lined up along the line of razor wire, while I strafed to the side of them to get some photos of the front line. They shouted slogans at the Israelis, and held up their fists in defiance, challenging them. I was crouched down against a rock wall, snapping all of this on my camera, when it occurred to me to check behind me. Sure enough, hidden amongst the olive trees on the terraces up above me, were camouflaged soldiers holding guns.

So there were far more than a dozen of them. And my fat head was sticking right up above the rock wall, turned away from them. So much for my plan to remain behind good cover in case of fire. Those Israelis had drawn targets on me before I even knew they were there. In a real war, I'd already be finished.

The line of Palestinians would not step over the razor wire. A couple of Japanese came down beside me, and trained their cameras on the protest. The Palestinians still stood there, calling out to the troops. There was something about them, I noticed, that seemed rather docile. And there was something about the Israelis that seemed rather bored. This was another Friday protest, just like every week. And eventually, I thought, the shouting and demonstrating would simply fizzle. The Israelis weren't cracking down on this. There was nothing to crack down on! They would just stand there and wait till the Palestinians got tired of shouting, and eventually plodded home.

Just as I was thinking that, a shot cracked through the air. I jumped. The Palestinian leading the protest buckled and slumped to the ground, screaming. I retreated backward with the Asian tourists nearby. Shot after shot burst into the sky behind me. I was immediately possessed by the maddening combination of the urge to duck on the ground and the urge to stand upright, in case it was a rubber bullet aimed at my legs. I looked back at the line of Palestinians. It hadn't broken. Clouds of white smoke billowed up from canisters on the ground, and five men stooped to help the one who had fallen.

More gunshots. A canister of gas fell right beside the tree where I had been standing moments earlier. I grabbed out my camera to get a shot of the tear gas up close.

The sign on my display screen read: "low batteries."

I cursed. Just my luck. As I fumbled in my pocket for new batteries, my eyes began to sting. I drew in painful, raspy breaths. The white clouds were not even close to me, and even now my legs were propelled forward of their own accord, unable to stay with the tear gas so close. I summoned all my will and turned to snap a single photo, before I went into full retreat, coughing and sputtering.

The Palestinians and foreigners were scattering up the hill in front of me. I ran around the side of a wall and collapsed to the ground. The gas was torturing me. I fumbled in my pocket for an onion and tore it open. As I buried my nose in the pungent vegetable, I took a long, beautiful breath. The chewing gum had done nothing, but the onion totally neutralized whatever stinging agent was present in the gas. As more shots rang through the sky, I sat behind that concrete wall and coddled my beautiful onion.

Within five minutes, to my delight, my red eyes opened. My throat ceased to sting. I grinned. Tear gas—it was smothering to be near, but five minutes later, it wears off. I rose, ready for the second wave.

The Palestinians who had been carrying the wounded man set him down on a patch of road up the hill from the Israelis. But the soldiers had stomped over the razor wire and were advancing up the hill, firing tear gas canisters into their path. One young man held up his hands before them, pleading for ceasefire so he could evacuate his fallen friend. A soldier landed a gas canister right at his feet.

He sputtered and retreated, grabbing the shoulder of the wounded man as the group carried him further up the hill. A medic in a first aid vest, who was standing beside a tree handing out smelling salts for the tear gas, was ripped away by a frantic Palestinian, shouting that he was needed elsewhere. The wounded man was brought inside an unfinished concrete house, and laid down on a cot. I sprinted across the road and knelt down beside him, reviewing in my mind the steps of first aid that I had been certified for just months before. Ferdinand came in as well, and knelt down against the wall with his camera.

As one young man peeled back the man's pant leg, he wailed in despair and threw up his arms, running from the unfinished house. I looked down at the wound. It was a reddened and bruised area, surrounding a patch of broken skin the size of a coin. There was no blood.

Since there were too many people in the hut, I went out of it and stood by the stairs of another concrete structure, nose nestled in my onion. While there, I encountered a middle-aged Palestinian man, wiping his eyes from the gas. I gave him a piece of onion. When a chubby Korean came trotting back from the front line, bleary-eyed and dazed, I gave him a chunk of my onion as well. Then I saw a steaming canister of tear gas being fired right through the window of the house where the wounded Palestinian man lay with the people helping him. Ferdinand was still inside. While the billows of acrid smoke poured out the windows, rubber bullets splattered against the walls and entrances. No one escaped the hut while it was under fire.

Finally the clouds broke. The saving rain wisped down and dampened the streaming clouds of gas. Everyone evacuated the hut, including the wounded man who was limping and leaning on someone's shoulder by now. More gas canisters bounced up the road. This time, we were back by the lines where the children had been kept. Now they leapt into the fray, soccer-kicking the gas canisters right back down the hill. Some of them put rocks into slings and whirled them above their heads, casting their stones out with fury and abandon.

I approached one child, standing with two of his friends. My eyes widened when I got nearer. He was holding a grenade—it bulged like a melon in his eight-year-old hand.

I held out my hand, beckoning him to give it to me, parentally. He shook his head.

"Photo?" I asked. He shook his head again.

"That bodes ill," Sean told me, when I met up with him later and told him of the incident. "One day, that kid is going to use that thing. And the soldiers are going to retaliate."

The protest was winding down. The fire had died. The Palestinians were beginning to turn around in groups and plod homewards. The rain drizzled down lightly, washing our heads and cooling us off. On the road home, Sean and I passed a white girl pointing a camera and a microphone at a middle-aged Palestinian man, interviewing him about the protest. This jogged our memory.

Sean flicked on his camera and handed it to me. I brushed the rain off the lens with my coat sleeve before I pointed it at him.

"So. Any thoughts on today?"

"Yeah," he said. "That was the scariest amusement park ride I've ever been on."

He pointed the camera at me.

"Well, my first thought is: why don't they just let them protest? We have protests in Canada and America all the time, and it doesn't change a damn thing. I don't understand why they have to break it up with tear gas and rubber bullets.

"But anyways, now it's over. Another Friday protest complete. The soldiers are still there; the wall hasn't fallen. The world hasn't changed. And now the Palestinians are all going back to their homes, and we are going back to our hostel."

23

JERUSALEM

On our last day in Jerusalem, Sean and I did nothing in particular. It was a quiet morning, one in which the sun shone too brightly after a heavy rain. We walked from out hostel across the Green Line, into East Jerusalem, our morning breakfast ritual. We climbed the stairs of an oily Palestinian restaurant, where the smiling chef made us world-class hummus with falafels the size of ping-pong balls, which we washed down with a coke. After breakfast, we collected our clothing from the laundry man around the corner, who operated a shop about the size of a bedroom. Bags of clothing were stacked to the ceiling, and his washing and drying machines were operating at full tilt, even at nine in the morning. I was happy for him; at least business was good.

As we walked back, blinded by the shimmering puddles in the crooked East Jerusalem streets, we saw a money exchange shop. I went inside and waited as the clerk flipped through my Israeli shekels, and counted out a stack of Egyptian pounds to give back to me.

Egypt. After five whirlwind weeks in the Middle East, I was headed back across the Sinai to Cairo. Sean had decided he was going to stay and tour around Israel, since there was much he had left to see.

"I'll stay in Jerusalem for a few days more—not longer," he told me. "I've already spoken with Osama, and he said I can dump my bags here at the hostel. I'm going to take off north, see Nazareth and Dimona, maybe ride a bicycle around the Golan Heights."

We were seated in the hostel common room, poring over a game of chess, sipping on sugary tea and peach sheesha. Osama had long given up waiting on us; he left a large grill of burning charcoal beside us for us so that we could change the coals of our water pipe at our convenience. The warmth was heavenly on that cold January morning.

"What about the Friday protest? Are you going back to that?"

"Absolutely," he told me. "I'll be back for every Friday that I'm still in Israel."

He paused while he studied the board. Finally, he moved his white pawn forward.

"Well, I've seen what I need to see here," I told him. "I'll be happy to get back to Egypt where the prices are a bit cheaper. I think the only thing that I regret is that I didn't get to see the full range of wall art around Bethlehem."

"I did that a couple of days ago," Sean said. "I had to pay a taxi-driver twenty dollars to take me around to all the paintings. But I got to see and photograph all the ones that I missed. . ." he paused for a brief moment, "on Christmas."

His words hung in the air like a weight. I was still sore at him for ditching us on Christmas, and he knew it. I stared silently at the chessboard.

"When you and Kristen were downstairs at the hostel in Tel Aviv," he began, with a heaviness in his voice, "I had a chat with Nickie about Christmas. I told her that I truly regretted not hanging out with you guys that day, and not coming to sit with the family for Christmas lunch.

"Nickie guessed why I didn't. It didn't have anything to do with you, or the way the trip was going. I just had a lot to think about after the interviews at the torture clinic."

He paused for a moment. I sucked peach ash out of the water pipe.

"Kieran, I have studied the Middle East for all of my youth: during university, and for a good many years before that. For a long time, this has been my world. I was truly excited to come here, finally see the region up close, and get involved in the politics. But, now that I've spent a bit of time here—I think the place kind of spat me back out."

"How so?" I asked, after a silence.

He took a pull on the spent sheesha before he spoke. The water in the pipe bubbled furiously. The chess game sat neglected.

"When I was in Egypt, I spent a lot of time in the bookstore at the American University of Cairo. I wanted to see if I could find books on climate change, alternative energy, or on the greater need for international governmental institutions. I looked there because I wanted to see what people in this region of the world cared about.

"You know what I found? *Nothing.* There was not a *single book* on the environment or alternative energy. There were lots of books on the Israeli-Palestinian conflict, on terrorism, on the invasion of Iraq—but nothing on climate change, nothing on international cooperation. Pan-Arabism was the closest it got.

"And then I finally came here and got to see the tribes in action. Here you have your Friday protests, and your Rachel Corries, and your torture clinics, and your immigrant soldiers, and for *what?* Osama is a documentarian, doing work on the wall! I don't want to work on the *WALL*, man! What a waste of time!

"This part of the world is locked in struggles it should have outgrown decades ago. Not only the present, but the *future* of the debate in the Middle East, for the next ten years or more, is imprisoned in these petty tribal mentalities that should have been outmoded a hundred years ago. They don't care about climate change, they don't care about global integration, they don't care about anything that you and I know will be the future of political thought in the West, and the world.

"I got my first inkling of this when I was standing on top of a castle in Lebanon with some journalist friends from the Hotel Talal. It was in southern Lebanon—literally in the corner of the country, a castle that the Israelis occupied during the 2006 war. We saw our first Israeli settlement and cheered. And we could see Israel, we could see the Golan Heights, we could see Syria. And we pointed to them and marked them out, because we knew where the boundaries were. But there were no real boundaries—nothing physical at all to mark one country from the other. It was all just—one land.

"The other day, when I was going around to the paintings on the wall, I had the closest thing to a spiritual experience I've had in years. I saw a quote by Arundhati Roy, the Indian author, spray-painted on the wall. It made me think of so many things we've encountered on this trip. It made me think of a guy I chatted with in Lebanon, who wanted to spread an idea he called 'Pan-Terranism.'

It made me think of the Gardens of the Bah'ai—that silly little religion that believes in a world federation. It made me think about all the feckless infighting here: the dozen tribes of Lebanon, the Kurds and the Syrians, the Christians and Muslims, the Arabs and the Jews, and the Westerners running around among them trying to make sense of it all."

"What was the quote?" I asked him.

Sean drew up and stared into space, searching for the exact words.

"Another world is not only possible, she's on the way. Many of us won't be here to greet her, but on a quiet day, if you listen very carefully, you can almost hear her breathing."

On my last evening, I strolled up a hill to the east of the old city. I wanted to spend some time in my favorite place in Jerusalem to contemplate—the Mount of Olives. On the way, I passed on my right the high walls of an overblown Catholic sanctuary, the Garden of Gethsemane. Though it was said that this was the very place where Jesus went to pray on the night before his death, I wasn't so sure. And in any case, I knew that if Jesus were around today, he would never pick a place so busy and ostentatious. He would walk quietly to some forgotten, inauspicious glade, sit down, and know that in the next few hours he would not be disturbed.

I chose a small terrace, with a low granite wall that had been built by Catholics. By the wall behind me there stood a polished stone memorial to a French priest who had lived in Jerusalem, and was a good friend of the late Pope, John Paul the Second. A low bench stood nearby, the wood was soaking wet after the day's rain. I sat myself down on the cold granite of the low wall, and looked across at the last pink strip of open sky between the clouds and the rooftops of Jerusalem.

From here, I could see the pale walls of Old Jerusalem, built five hundred years ago by Suleiman the Magnificent. I could see the forest of headstones of the Muslim cemetery, and the equally numerous headstones of the Jewish cemetery close beside it. It was still light enough for me to see the many landmarks of the old city—the silver domes of the Church of the Holy Sepulchre, the white spire of the Lutheran Cathedral, the golden gleam of the Dome of the Rock.

I remembered our arrival to the city by bus. Sean and I had been watching the landscape of the West Bank out the window: the thirsty desert plains with the odd crooked branch of broom; the green-grey infertile fields dotted with countless rocks.

"Would you fight over this, Sean?" I asked, sarcastically.

"No!" he replied with a smirk. "I absolutely would *not* fight over this."

Two minutes later, we rounded a bend, and the bright stonework of Jerusalem came into view. The walled old city rose atop a great hill, with the dazzling gold of the Dome of the Rock standing in the center. I felt my heart pound, and a flush passed over my skin. Here it was, before me. Zion. *Al-Quds.* Yerushalaim, jewel of the Holy Land. Jerusalem, which both Israeli and Palestinian claim as their immortal capital. Jerusalem, where both sides resisted street by street and block by block, in a slow and silent battle for control.

One of the most famous psalms in Western literature is a lament by the Jews over the loss of the city, when they had been taken captive and forced into exile by the Babylonians.

> *By the rivers of Babylon, there we sat down, yea, we wept, when we remembered Zion.*
> *We hanged our harps upon the willows in the midst thereof.*
> *For there they that carried us away captive required of us a song; and they that wasted us required of us mirth, saying, Sing us one of the songs of Zion.*
> *How shall we sing the Lord's song in a strange land?*
> *If I forget thee, O Jerusalem, let my right hand forget her cunning.*
> *If I do not remember thee, let my tongue cleave to the roof of my mouth; if I prefer not Jerusalem above my chief joy.*[9]

[9] Psalm 137

Since their exile from the holy land two thousands years ago, the Jews have said a special prayer during the celebration of Passover. No matter where they went, be it the rainy isles of Britain, the cold steppes of Russia, or the arid deserts of North Africa, every Passover, the head of the family would raise a toast and say "next year, in Jerusalem." The Jews, during two thousand years of exile, kept the memory of their fair city in the heart of their culture, waiting for the day when they could finally return.

Then, in 1948, in the wake of the unspeakable horror of Hitler's concentration camps in Europe, that day finally came. And they fought three wars against the Arabs to establish their presence in the region, and emerged victorious every time. And when the Israeli army finally pushed into Old Jerusalem in 1967, when it finally reached the Western Wall, the last standing piece of the Temple of Solomon, the soldiers of Israel broke down and wept. They had reached the very heart of their ancient faith. After twenty long and painful centuries, the Jews were finally home.

In Rome, Sean and I had visited the Arch of Titus on the Palatine Hill, the victory monument of the emperor who sacked the Jerusalem after the Jewish tax revolts. The Arch was engraved with a distinctly Roman procession called a Triumph, a parade through the center of the capital in which the spoils of war, the captives, and often the vanquished heads of state were displayed to the Roman people. In this triumphal procession, the victors held aloft a nine-candled Menorah, a symbol of the fall of the Jews and the destruction of the Temple.

Strung across the arch was a thin iron chain. My Roman history teacher had taught me that to cross under the arch was a symbol of anti-Semitism and disrespect to the Jewish people. Sean and I, iconoclasts to the bone, made a point of crossing under it. We even took pictures of the act. We did it to show our contempt of Israeli hypocrisy, who used international sympathy for their people's suffering to ethnically cleanse another. The Jews, only years after being victims of one of history's most horrible acts of persecution, had persecuted victims of their own.

But now that I was here, scanning the skyline of Jerusalem with my own eyes, I realized that things were not quite so simple. For what were the Jews to do? I thought of Rabbi Chaim Rumkowski, who asked his people to give up their children. I thought of the despairing inhabitants of the Lodz Ghetto, who followed his command. I thought of Dasha, who would rather be a Russian in Israel than a Jew in Russia. I thought of the thousands of years these people had been persecuted, landless, and oppressed—how they had preserved the story of their exile deep in their cultural memory. I thought of the daily security threats against the Jewish population of Jerusalem, and the immense effort the IDF had to expend just to keep their citizens safe. And I realized that the Jews truly did need a homeland—a place to raise their children in peace and safety, a place to call their own.

And yet, for that simple right to exist, did they have to drive the Palestinians—the innocent descendants of conquerors past—into their own exile, to the shores of the rivers of strange lands where they could do nothing but weep and remember Jerusalem? Did they have to trample upon the likes of Sami and his family, on his father who married his bride in exile, and would never again see the land of his birth? Did they have to torture young people in military prisons? Did they have to shoot at the Bilin protestors whose only crime was to peacefully resist the theft of their own farms?

One thing, I knew, was certain. As the Jews kept the longing for their homeland in their cultural memory for two thousand years, surely the Palestinians would keep the memory of their own persecution in their culture for just as long. And the brutal resentment the Israelis have stirred amongst the Arabs, who coexisted peacefully with Jews for centuries, will be the bitter and enduring legacy of Israel's triumph.

For there is a darker side to the psalm sung by the rivers of Babylon. At the end, there is a deep and violent vow to revenge, to repay the conquerors by atrocities even more horrible than those they committed.

> O Daughter of Babylon, doomed to destruction,
> happy is he who repays you
> for what you have done to us
> he who seizes your infants
> and dashes them against the rocks[10]

Many find it strange and unfitting that such appalling acts should be mentioned in one of the most beautiful psalms in the Bible. On the contrary, I believe they fit perfectly. For such is hatred of those who have been uprooted from their homes and villages and cast into exile to suffer. Such is the unbearable pain of persecution; of raising children in a land that cannot be called home; of the bitter memory of prosperity that once existed, and then was ripped away.

And unless such enmity can somehow be ended, unless, one day, terms of peace can finally be found, then forever the lands of Israel and Palestine will be locked in bitter conflict; forever there will be constant hostility, constant violence, and the constant threat of war.

[10] Psalm 137

Above me, somewhere on the hill, a minaret wailed the call to prayer. In the distance, a lone dog began to bark. And as the forest around me dimmed beneath the darkening sky, I heard the rolling prayer echo from the many minarets of East Jerusalem, until at last it sounded from the Dome of the Rock itself. I closed my eyes and listened to the lolling Arabic chanting, strange and beautiful in the advancing dusk, until at long last it expired into silence.

And in my last look at the city in the dying glow of the day, I put on my headphones and found a special song. It was 'Jerusalem' by Steve Earle, a song about the conflict in the holy land—a prayer, beautiful in its simplicity, for a day that never seems to come—a day when peace and amnesty will finally settle upon the warring tribes of the Middle East.

> *There'll be no barricades then*
> *There'll be no wire walls*
> *And we can wash all this blood from our hands*
> *And all this hatred from our souls*
>
> *Oh, I believe that on that day*
> *All the children of Abraham*
> *Will lay down their swords forever*
> *In Jerusalem . . .*[11]

---

[11] Steve Earl, *Jerusalem*, 2002

24

MY HOUSE IS YOUR HOUSE

Eilat was the southern border town of Israel. Nestled between Aqaba, Jordan and Taba, Egypt, Eilat had a very strategic purpose: it allowed Israel a presence on the Red Sea. It was also Israel's outpost south of the Negev desert: like most border towns, it was living and breathing proof that Israel owned the land. And finally, Eilat had an important purpose for destitute backpackers such as myself. Since Gaza was closed, Eilat was the place one needed to go to catch a bus to Cairo; the only overland gateway from Israel to Egypt.

I got off the bus to Eilat and breathed a thankful sigh of relief. Halfway through the Negev desert, a bum had stepped on the bus and begged the driver for a ride. He was wearing oily army pants, a dirt-covered sweatshirt, and had a beard and hair like the mane of an unwashed lion. And after the driver let him on the bus, he went back and occupied the only seat available—the one next to me. He smelled like a barn. For three hours, I crushed my face against the window next to mine, closed my eyes, and tried to block out the man's reeking odour. It didn't work.

Finally, I hauled my pack out of the belly of the bus, and plopped it on the concrete, and stepped back to breathe in the cool night air. The bum wandered off; every other passenger slowly dissipated, including many Israelis who hugged relatives and clambered into their cars. After ten minutes, the only people left on the sidewalk were me and three other young people, two guys and one girl, all sporting backpacks and chattering in American English.

"So where are you guys going?" I asked them eventually.

"We're going to Jordan for a day and then Egypt," they told me.

"I'm headed to Egypt too," I told them. "I have a flat rented in Cairo. I'm going to try to find a taxi and see if I can head across the border tonight."

They looked at me with raised eyebrows.

"Don't you know about the Sinai visa?"

"What?" I asked.

They explained to me that even if the Israeli border was open at this hour of the night, I would only receive a special visa which allowed me to visit the Sinai. I wouldn't be able to cross the Suez Canal and make it to Cairo.

"We're heading to the Egyptian embassy to get a proper visa," they told me. "But tonight, we're just going to hit a hostel."

I accompanied them. The tallest introduced himself as Paul, the second tallest as Nate. The girl's name was Brenda. They were college students from Wisconsin, all a few years younger than I, and they were traveling during their Christmas holidays. They had just come off the Birthright program, and had postponed their flight to spend some time in Jordan and Egypt.

"So what was it like?" I asked them, once we had checked in at the hostel and the sullen, angry cokehead who worked there had shown us to our room. We wandered outside and sat on a picnic table, while Nate fired up a water pipe he had bought in Old Jerusalem.

"The Birthright program? It was a lot of fun," Paul answered. "We were in a group with so many different people. There were Jews from everywhere."

Nate chuckled. "Hey Paul, now that we're off that program I think we should go find some meat and cheese and put them together."

Paul laughed. He told me about some line from the Bible that says "you should not cook a lamb in its mother's milk," and how that had been interpreted into a law forbidding Jews to eat any dairy product and meat together: a killjoy for pizza lovers.

"It gets ridiculous," Paul explained. "As Birthright participants, we all spent the night in the house of an Orthodox Jewish family. It was interesting, but I could never live like that myself."

There are basically three types of Judaism: Orthodox, Conservative, and Reform. The Orthodox follow a very strict reading of the Torah laws that have been handed down for thousands of years. The men wear skullcaps, and a have long curl of hair that hangs down from around their ears. They wear a prayer shawls with white tassels that hang down from their clothing as a symbol to remind them what the Hebrews wore while they were following Moses through the Sinai. They follow strict Kosher dietary laws, and do no work on the Sabbath, which extends from sundown on Friday to sundown on Saturday. During this time, some of them often keep a non-Jew in their house to open doors for them and turn on light switches, as both of these actions are forbidden by a strict reading of the laws. Conservative Jews still practice Kosher dietary laws, but generally do not wear special clothing such as skullcaps in public: they recognize the need to assimilate into whatever culture they have joined. Reform Jews are even more radical: they eat bacon.

"Yeah, basically we don't really practice at home," Nate told me, as he took a sip of sheesha from the water pipe.

We chatted about the fact that they were Jewish in the way that I was Catholic, and in the way most North Americans were religious: non-practicing, basically agnostic, but still in touch with their faith as a part of their heritage. Although Orthodox Judaism was the only variant of the religion officially recognized by the state of Israel, the greater number of Israelis were like my American friends: secular Jews.

"So," I asked, grinning, "now that you've seen it, are you going to immigrate?"

Paul scoffed. "Are you kidding me? I'm not joining the army! And why would I leave America? America is home."

I told them how in the Israeli school curriculum, students study Jewish diaspora communities in all different places: Germany, France, Russia, England, etc. But the one diaspora community that is never studied is that of America. Why? Because American Jews have never experienced serious persecution. And thus, when the American example is considered, there is no clear reason to show why Jews must have a state of their own. They are all perfectly happy in America.

"You guys should really come to my flat when you arrive in Cairo," I told them, before we packed up the water pipe and headed off to bed. "It would be way nicer than a hostel. And I can take you to some really cool places in the city."

"Absolutely," they said, delighted. We exchanged contacts, and they said they would call me when they arrived.

"Oh my God," Brenda said, "this flat is so wonderful!"

It wasn't. But she had just been to Luxor and Aswan, and had slummed in hostels with common bunks and bathrooms, frigid showers, and leering Egyptian doormen. She was now faced with the prospect of her own room and bed, a large living room to relax in, a kitchen to cook in, and a place to wash her clothes. My flat may not have been much, but to them, it was heaven. The three of them laid down their packs, had a hot shower, and began to relax.

"I invited my friend Tamer over tonight to meet you guys," I told them. "I hope you guys don't mind. He's an Egyptian and he speaks almost no English, but he really wants to meet you."

Tamer showed up an hour later, and shambled inside, walking awkwardly on his fake leg. He carried a bag full of beers and a sheesha pipe, which he proceeded to plop on my floor and set up while I brought the coals to the gas stove in the kitchen.

He greeted the Americans with glee, and seemed perfectly comfortable understanding none of what they said, and always asking me to translate.

"Are they Christian?" he asked, almost immediately.

"Of course they are," I slapped him on the shoulder. That was Tamer for you—before he even got to know someone, he had to know what to which tribe they belonged.

"He is a Christian, Kieran," Paul said, once we had fired up the coals and the air began to fill with smoke. "Maybe he wouldn't care that we are Jews."

Paul had an interesting point. Tamer was quite prejudiced against Muslims; perhaps he would get along with people who were also known not to like Muslims. As the old saying goes, the enemy of my enemy is my friend.

"Jews? NO! I don't like Jews. Jews are no good."

Tamer waved his finger and smacked his lips in disapproval. He curled his face into a frown, the expression I saw him pull whenever I mentioned a people that he didn't like. He took another pull of the sheesha, while I turned to my friends, shrugged, and laughed.

I couldn't imagine Tamer, or any Egyptian for that matter, would be too fond of Jews. Wherever they happened to come from, Jews have a bad name in Egypt, because of Israel. Egypt's last major war with Israel was 1973, called the Yom Kippur war by most of the world, and the Third War or the Sixth of October War by Egypt. In 1967, during the Six-Day War, the Israelis had taken the Sinai peninsula from Egypt and marched their troops to the Suez Canal. Egypt wanted it back. It conspired with Syria and other Arab nations to coordinate an attack on Israel on the same day. This time, the Arab nations were able to keep their plans secret; Israeli intelligence had no idea it was going to happen. On the Jewish festival of Yom Kippur, when the Israeli Army was manned only by a skeleton crew, they attacked.

There is a special memorial built in Cairo in honour of the war, known as the "Sixth of October Panorama." It was a large circular building, surrounded by gates. The grounds were reserved as a display area for some of the military equipment: there were jets and mounted rockets; there were pieces of fuselage from Israeli planes shot down by Egyptian forces. There were tanks and gun batteries from both sides; there were sand-coloured Soviet-built Egyptian tanks, there were smaller green British model tanks, and American anti-tank guns captured from Israel. All the Egyptian tanks had their guns pointed upwards in victory; all the gun-barrels on captured Israeli machinery were lowered in defeat.

The Panorama itself was a circular room of red marble, with six white stone reliefs hung on the walls. The reliefs showed scenes from every war in Egypt's history which could possibly be ideologically analogous to the Sixth of October War. There was one showing the ancient war of the Pharaoh Narmer, who conquered Upper Egypt from Lower Egypt and thus unified the country. There was another relief of the Egyptians expelling the Hyskos: foreign invaders who had occupied Egypt for a few centuries. The next one was of Arab armies expelling Christian crusaders. Another showed modern Egyptian troops liberating the Suez Canal in 1956, and Israeli soldiers looking on helpless.

Finally, there was a plaque called 'The Great Crossing'—a memorial to the day when Egyptian troops stormed across the Suez Canal and pushed the Israeli troops back. The depiction of it was jaw-dropping. Strong, glorious-looking Egyptian soldiers marched boldly, carrying the flag of Egypt. It showed Zodiac landing boats filled with soldiers, and rows of tanks and rocket-mounted trucks advancing in line. The sculptures were a combination of Soviet pomposity and ancient Egyptian art: each marching figure, and each driving tank, had numerous identical outlines carved right beside them, giving the appearance of a whole line advancing as one. It was precisely the same manner in which I had seen Pharaoh's warriors depicted on ancient Egyptian temples. And the mighty centerpiece of The

Great Crossing was a handful of defeated Israeli soldiers, carved in the same ancient Egyptian style, on their knees with their eyes closed and heads bowed in surrender, their helmets lying on the ground beside them, bearing the six-pointed Shield of David.

The final relief was called 'The Return of the Land.' It showed president Anwar Sadat, who led the war, standing with a flag of Egypt in his hands. A large public celebration was going on in front of him; devout old Muslims clutched their prayer beads, men danced with joy, small girls offered bunches of flowers to lines of soldiers who stood at attention.

The Great Crossing, and the Return of the Land. I took a picture of the archway between the two. The war memorial had missed a relief. They forgot the one where the Israeli army retaliated and smashed the Egyptians back to the gates of Cairo.

The Egyptian army was crushed, as it always was, by the superior firepower, technology, and organization of the IDF. But the Yom Kippur War nevertheless was a victory for Egypt; all historians agree. Egypt was the small kid in school that always got his lunch money taken away by the big Israeli bully. One day the small kid fought back, kicked the bully in the shins, and bit him. The bully then beat the tar out of the kid in retaliation.

But the bully won't take the lunch money away again, because he is wary of provoking such a response.

Sinai was returned to Egypt during the Camp David Accords. Under the conditions of peace, Egypt would sign a treaty recognizing Israel's existence as a nation, and would permit Israelis Sinai-only visas to travel to resort towns on the Red Sea. And through some loophole, the local Bedouins inhabiting the Sinai would be legally allowed to grow marijuana.

Paul sprinkled a dash of Egyptian hashish onto the sheesha tobacco, and replaced the coal on top of it; Tamer took a long pull before passing it on. He didn't care for Jews at all; none of his countrymen did. Twenty percent of the army was Christian; they had all suffered equally at the hands of the Israelis. For Tamer this was just one more knee-jerk xenophobic prejudice that I somehow found childishly charming.

"What are they reading?" Tamer asked.

As the room slowly filled with smoky haze, my American friends had become engrossed in some of the literature I had picked up from Cairo's mosques. There was one in particular which encouraged non-believers to convert; which began with scientific 'proof' of the rightness of the Qu'ran and the existence of Allah. I handed the book to Tamer, who couldn't understand a single word of

English. But within seconds he saw the cover photo: a massive crowd in white robes, assembled around the Qa'baah in Mecca. . .

He grunted, pitched the book across the room, and folded his arms like a stubborn child. I burst into a laughter, and rushed to my bookshelf for other books to see what reactions they would provoke. I found one called *Saint Saul* about the apostle who had changed his name to Paul and changed the history of early Christianity. I handed it to Tamer. His hands brushed gently over the face of the icon on the cover, and he put his three fingers together and crossed himself, and put his hands together, raising his eyes in reverence to heaven. I chuckled and brought him *The Portable Nietzsche*, with a photo of the German philosopher and his long mustaches on the cover. He sat there puzzled, while my American friends watched and giggled, as he tried to figure out what this could possibly mean. I brought over a history book, *The Islamic World on the Eve of Europe's Expansion*, with the outline of a mosque and two minarets on the cover. Tamer grunted violently and hurled the book at the floor.

When my friends had stopped laughing and drying their eyes, Paul said "Kieran, after we leave, I think you should tell him that we're Jews."

"Yeah," I told him smiling, "I think I will."

The night wound down when we ran out of beer. The Americans wanted to get to sleep for another good day in Cairo, and Tamer needed to get back to his house. While Paul, Nate, and Brenda retired to their rooms, there was a knock at the door. It was Asharaf, Tamer's taxi driver, and I invited him in. He and Tamer smoked the last of the sheesha together, laughing and slapping each other on the knee.

"Bush. . .is a donkey!" they said, using one of the more pointed Egyptian insults.

"And president Mubarak. . .is a donkey!"

"Yes, Mubarak is a big, big donkey. When is he going to die?"

I recalled earlier in my journey, when Tamer and I had a discussion about Muslims in Egypt. At the time, I had tried to challenge his hypocrisy, and ask him whether he did really like Asharaf the taxi driver.

"No," said Tamer. "He's a Muslim. Muslims are no good!"

But after so long in Egypt, I began to wonder if this duplicity was even genuine. Did they really mistrust Muslims so much? Or was this just something Tamer had to say around his Christian buddies? As I watched the two of them sitting across from each other, trading jokes about prostitutes, and laughing deeply, I couldn't help but think: was

Tamer really pretending to be this man's friend? Or was he pretending not to be?

When I approached Tamer's fruit shop a few days later, he pulled up an extra chair and bellowed at his cousin in the coffee shop for tea with lemon, my favorite drink.

"Where are Paul and Nathan and Brenda?"

"They had to leave for America."

Tamer looked insulted. "They didn't even say goodbye? Why didn't you bring them to say goodbye!"

"Sorry my friend," I told him with a smile. "They didn't really have time."

"Why does Paul keep hanging up on me? I call him every day and he just hangs up."

I started to laugh. "He doesn't speak any Arabic!"

"I know, but I can still say 'hello.'"

"What time to do you call him? During the day?"

"Yes."

"Tamer!" I punched him in the shoulder. "That's the middle of the night in America! Don't call up these guys in America and speak Arabic to them at 3:00 in the morning!"

He looked sheepish.

"Ok, I won't. No problem."

"Did you like them?" I asked as I started in on my tea.

"Yes they were great. I really liked them."

I nodded.

"You know something? They were Jews."

He paused, and regarded me with surprise.

"Really? Jews?"

"All of them. Paul, Brenda, and Nathan."

"Huh" he said, and looked thoughtfully into the distance. After a brief moment, he spoke.

"Well. They were great."

25

THE ISLAMIC BERLIN WALL

In February 2008, Saudi Arabia cracked down on Valentine's Day. A religious governing body known as the Authority for Enjoining Good and Preventing Evil gave store owners a strict time limit on when all Valentine's Day paraphernalia had to be off the shelves. There were raids by the police to seize greeting cards, bundles of red roses, and other Valentine-like material. Restaurant owners were told to remove pink and red hearts from their walls, and teachers warned children not to wear the colour red to school on February 14th.

Valentine's Day is banned in the Kingdom because it is un-Islamic. In addition, religious authorities say that it encourages sex outside of marriage, which is strictly punishable by law in Saudi Arabia. But most of all, the holiday is a Western holiday, derived from the Christian feast of St. Valentine—not a Muslim one. And so the citizens of Saudi Arabia ordered black-market bouquets to be delivered in the middle of the night, they crossed the border into neighbouring Oman or Jordan where the holiday is not illegal, or they simply attended 'very distinguished dinners' in restaurants and swore that the special soirees with their wives and fiancées had nothing to do with Valentine's Day.

In the Middle East, only Saudi Arabia and Iran are actually governed under religious law. The governments of Egypt, Sudan, Syria, and many other Islamic nations are entirely secular. But what is practiced in the courts of Saudi Arabia and Iran is echoed in the culture of every Islamic nation in the Middle East. Islam is in the midst of a backlash against Western influence, and the strictest interpretations of its values are currently being reasserted amongst its people.

As I walk around the streets of Cairo, I cannot help but to wonder whether any of the countless youths I see feel Islam's rigid moral code to be a bit of a burden. Religion exerts more control over daily life in Egypt than in any other society I had ever visited. There are prayers to say for entering the bathroom; prayers for waking up; prayers for putting on new clothes; prayer to perform before intercourse. People speak prayers while they are waiting for the train doors to open, *while they are sitting in traffic, while business is slow at their shops. There are copies of the Qu'ran on sale everywhere; pocket Qu'rans pulled out and read on the metro; Qu'ranic verse being chanted in every marketplace, in every second shop, in every second taxi. Many keep a prayer mat with them at all times. Here in Egypt, Islam dictates the food that people eat, the drinks they drink, how they dress and how they shave, what time they get up in the morning, the names of their children, whom they marry, and how they interact with the opposite sex.*

In Egypt, the commandment to remain chaste before marriage is heavily enforced. This religious phobia of pre-marital sex dictates strict rules about social mixing; young women and men rarely spend time together in public, and spending time in private places is strictly forbidden. In traditional families, the first date between a man and a woman anticipating a marriage happens under the supervision of both sets of parents; social intercourse barely takes place before an engagement is contracted.

I had always thought a taboo on pre-marital sex was an excellent value for an ancient society. It cut down on disease and prevented unwanted pregnancies. In ancient societies, the general age for beginning working life was seventeen or eighteen, thus, at that age, a young couple could marry and economically afford to begin a life together. For the societies around when these religions were created, the rule against pre-marital sex had immediate advantages.

But in the twenty-first century, conditions are different. Today we have contraceptives that prevent not only unwanted pregnancies, but also the spread of disease. Our industrial and information economy requires intense specialization, meaning that young people have to work for years to build their careers before they are in an economic position to think about marriage. Marriage, in Egypt, requires the bachelor to be in possession of some fairly serious property. The cost of the celebration itself, paid for entirely by the groom, often runs into the tens of thousands of dollars. These traditions, in the economic realities of today's world, pushes the average age of marriage toward thirty. Young people are asked to master their sexual desires for around fifteen years, which apart from being frustrating, is biologically unrealistic.

In the case of marriage laws, as in the case of so many other social customs, the cultures of the Islamic world are trying to resist change. But any religious authority that wishes to determine the character of a culture must contend with one of the strongest forces of the human world—economics. In a thousand ways, economic conditions put stress on a culture, pressuring the most outmoded values to reform. Eventually, the pressure builds to a point, and there is an eruption. It can be as violent as the French Revolution, or as peaceful as the hippie movements of the sixties. But the lesson of history is that any moral code that is too strict for the economic pressures of its time will eventually yield.

Already, foreign influence and technology is beginning to undermine the Muslim world's most unforgiving customs. Instant messaging on internet and cell phones is giving Arab youth a chance to meet; young lovers can have social contact, and get to know each other before they become engaged. Many Egyptian men are working abroad and marrying foreigners, to escape the hideous cost of a traditional Egyptian marriage. And Western women, ever more interested in the Middle East, are spending time in the Arab world, and having relationships with Arab men.

While my friend Nermine was studying the Qu'ran before taking the veil, she gave up listening to Western music. She studied the scriptures for months and months, knowing that the decision she was making was quite serious. I admire her devotion to her religion, just as I admire the devotion of all Egyptians, and their constant prayer: five times a day, in the direction of Mecca. Nermine told me that the reason she didn't want to hear Western songs was that she didn't want anything external to influence her decision.

At that moment, it occurred to me that Western music and movies, which flood the markets of the Muslim world, are actually effective forms of cultural preaching. Many of them display sex, drinking, and even drug use as desirable or normal, as well as other trappings of Western culture forbidden by the laws of the Prophet. To this end, countries like Iran and Saudi Arabia have banned them, considering their influence to be impure and un-Islamic.

But although these governments rightly view such media such as this as a threat to their ancient traditions, their actions may backfire. The communist government of East Germany, at the height of the Cold War, also banned Western music and literature. This only served to increase its popularity on the black market: young people who might never normally have cared suddenly became curious as to what their mighty government had to fear from something as small as a Beatles album, or a book by Orwell. Closer contact with the West, which eventually ended the hostility and brought about the reunification of Germany, became unavoidable largely through the government's energy and effort spent trying to make Western culture unavailable. And it is happening in the Middle East today: the more governments censor the internet and ban satellite tele-vision, the more people will begin to see their govern-ments as weak, petty, and unnecessarily strict, and the greater will be the threat to the survival of the national culture in its present form.

As the years go by, my prediction is that the pressure will continue to build. Frustrated youth will lie awake at night, wondering why listening to Britney Spears is so taboo; wondering why sex before marriage is so harmful in a world teeming with contraceptives; won-dering why giving roses to their sweethearts on Valen-tine's Day is so damaging to their faith.

One day, I predict the youth will tire of this draco-nian strictness. One day there will be a revolt against this cultural rigidity—a revolution: political, social, or sexual—and on that day, Middle Eastern culture will open of its own accord, and the Islamic Berlin Wall will come crashing to the ground.

I tossed a dozen times in my bed that night, trying to get to sleep. Nothing worked. Ever since I had begun to type, I felt a doubt growing in my mind. I was leaving the Middle East in a matter of weeks—it was time for me to sum up what I had observed, and deliver a pronouncement on Islamic culture. This was to be posted on my blog, and sent in a mass travel email to hundreds of people.

Initially the doubt was small and nagging; I ignored it. But as I continued to write it grew until nausea spread over my body. I sat staring blankly at the text in front of me, physically ill. I had never shunned the controversial in any of my writings, and now, it was time to be honest about the cultural straight-jacket I saw forced on so many millions of young Arabs. But the more I wrote, the more I wondered whether or not the ugly presence of my own culture was appearing in the text.

Wasn't that the soul of prejudice, to see things in one's own terms? Was I simply looking at the Middle East through Western lenses? Through Western history, and Western examples? Well, no. . .just because I was born in a liberal society didn't make Islamic culture any less strict. Or would the people of this society consider it to be that strict? Were there actually youths in Egypt who felt as smothered as I might feel in their place?

I roused and flicked on my laptop while my bleary eyes adjusted to the florescent light of my room. I read over the piece again, and again. The nausea returned. *'The Islamic Berlin Wall'*. . .did I really just write those words?

26

DEVOTION

As I walked the white granite sea wall, I watched the waves slowly wash and break against the concrete base below. Gulls wheeled in the blue sky, and countless coloured boats rocked softly in the ocean in front of me. To my left, passersby and traffic moved along in a constant stream. But along the very top of the wall of Alexandria's Corniche, where no one was meant to walk, nothing barred my path—nothing but the odd young Egyptian couple, touching shoulders, holding hands, looking dreamily at the sea.

I loved this city—its glittering ocean, its delicious air. I had come here to write for twelve days at the end of my trip to Egypt: to live simply in a bare hotel room; to eat light meals of cucumber and tomato sandwiches, and the occasional tub of *kushari*. I had come here to escape the buzz of Cairo—to relax my mind, breathe the air, and walk along the walls each day.

I snapped photos of the coloured boats in the harbour, of the little Egyptian children running about the beach, of the city lights of the Alexandria skyline flaring to life in the oncoming dusk. As I walked back towards my hotel, I saw the last light of the day fall on a mosque built near the sea. Its pale walls glowed orange in the sunset; its tall, thin minaret struck upwards into the sky. . .towering above the Egyptian palms which stood planted alongside it.

My eyes drifted to the patterns above the door, woven and intricate, cut with care into a solid canvas of stone. These designs formed every window, and were excelled only by the elegant carved stonework on the pinnacle of the minaret itself. The mosque stood alone against the sky and the ocean, with no buildings near to cramp it, its door hanging open to welcome the faithful for the final prayer of the day.

"Beautiful isn't it?" she asked.

"It's gorgeous."

"Yeah. It was actually designed by an Italian."

At a cafe along the darkened beach, I sipped an over-sugared cappuccino. Nermine sat across from me, tasting some drink that came with a chocolate spoon. It was in the evening, after work and after evening prayers, that she came to meet me at precisely the same ice-cream stand where we had met the first time. She took me to a cafe she knew on the beach, where we sat at a table surrounded by a wall of driftwood, our shoes resting on the sand the sand. The wind was light.

"Those Islamic designs in the walls of the mosque. . .I like them," I told her. "I think I'm starting to appreciate the style. I mean. . .I had initially thought that symbols were so powerful—how could one religious art do without them? But now I'm starting to see that it can be done."

Nermine nodded. "You know why we don't make images?" she asked.

I shook my head.

"Because God is too awesome to be represented by a mere image. Imagine—you could look at it and say: 'I am taller than God. I am stronger than God. My eyes are clearer than God's.'"

"Well," I said, "I can understand why there are no images of God. But why no images at all? Why couldn't you paint the figures of history?"

"No images of anything living. That's the rule. Sometimes they cheat and depict plants and floral designs. But no humans or animals."

"Why?"

"It makes the artist arrogant," she said. "The artist gets all sorts of ideas of fame and self-love when he creates a painting that is that beautiful."

"I wonder if the designer of the Taj Mahal was arrogant," I said.

She chuckled. "Who is to know? Didn't he design it for his wife?"

Nermine wore a blood-red veil today, a brilliant splash of crimson which ran around face and her neck before disappearing into her black sweater. She had a soft smile. Sean's father, who had lived in Saudi Arabia, had told us on the day before leaving to Egypt not to talk to anyone about their religion. 'So f——sensitive!' were the words he used. But Nermine, patient yet confident way, was more than delighted to talk to me about Islam. I barely knew her, but already, the silence was comfortable.

"You know Nermine, I have to admit I have been inspired by the Muslims since I came here."

"Have you?" she said.

"Yes. And I can sum it up in one word. Devotion. Devotion to one woman. Devotion to one's family. Devotion to the Islamic faith. I finally understand the five times a day, Nermine. If you pray five times a day, you can't hide from your morality. It's not like sinning for seven days and then praying for an hour on Sunday. You do this all day, every day. . .and if you do something wrong, you see the contradiction right away."

Nermine looked at me intently. Pride was in her eyes.

"You see it," she said.

"Yes, I see it," I told her. "I finally understand. And since I've been back from Israel, I have prayed once a day. It's nothing too formal—I just think of everything I'm grateful for. I do it right after exercise. I don't know if I have the strength to pray five times a day. . .that would take true dedication."

"It's like. . .yoga," she said. "You move your body, you bend, you kneel down. You stretch your limbs. And you clear your mind. And it only takes what. . .four minutes? When I am at work and I've been sitting in a chair all day and I am uncomfortable and my work is difficult. . .I go down to pray. It refreshes my body and refreshes my mind.

"I once knew a friend from the West who went to live in a Muslim family. . .he converted. Once they were having an argument around the table about something. . .something cultural, I don't remember what. It was very heated. Then they heard the call to prayer. They didn't want to stop arguing, but eventually the mother convinced them to go pray. After the prayer, they all came back to the table, and there was no more argument. All the anger was gone."

I stared at my coffee cup. Frothed milk hung on the rim.

"You know," I said, "I don't think we have enough devotion in the West. It's something we've almost forgotten—it's no longer a virtue anymore. Since January I have started to exercise more, waste less time, eat better. . .to do all of those things I always wished I could do but never had the strength. Prayer helps me do it, no joke. It's kind of like. . ."

"Jihad."

We both said it at the same time.

She looked at me with admiration; a Westerner who knew the other meaning of the word. 'Jihad' simply meant 'struggle.' It could mean a violent struggle against a conqueror, but it in its most common use it meant a personal struggle—a struggle to make oneself a Believer: a struggle to overcome bodily urges and selfish feelings, and surrender oneself to the higher morality.

"Mohammed said, after the Arab tribes had conquered Mecca, that the wars are now finished, that we do not have anyone to fight," said Nermine. "Now we must fight ourselves, against our own weakness. That's what 'jihad' really means."

"Nermine," I said quietly. "I might just ask you. . .to teach me to pray. Just so that I know how to do it."

She beamed. "I will send you some links and videos online. There are some good directions and diagrams."

"But. . .*you* couldn't teach me?" I asked hesitantly.

The question lingered for a moment. Then I slapped myself in the face.

"Of *course*," I said. "Men and women can't pray together."

"It's for modesty" said Nermine. "It's just the idea that men and women should never have sexual thoughts when they are praying to God."

I nodded.

"Yeah, males and females seem to be a lot more segregated here," I said. "I mean. . .girls and guys don't really seem to hang out together that much."

She looked at me quizzically.

"Well, tell me, is it normal for girls and guys to, say, sit in coffee shops together?"

"Are you *kidding?*" she said. She looked at me like I had spent all my time in Egypt living under a rock.

"Kieran, *of course we do!* How do you think we meet? I have lots of guy friends! Honestly, let's go out tomorrow to a great coffee shop I know with a group of Egyptian young people. I even know ones that speak perfect English."

I stared at her, mouth agape.

"Really!" she said, rolling her eyes. "I wasn't kidding when I said we were just like you."

I sat staring at my plate on the table, somewhere between sheepish and amazed. Another prejudice fell to the floor like broken glass. Was I really that. . .blind? Was my culture shock so profound, my assumptions so ignorant. . .that I had missed this? And suddenly, my lips loosened. I threw any last vestige of plastic political correctness to the wind. Everything I was uncomfortable with about Egyptian society poured out. In no particular order.

"And prayer scars? Really, do you think it's beautiful to mark someone's face?"

"Hah. They only come from men who pray in mosques with very crude mats. They're hard and they irritate the skin. I have a friend who puts a silk cloth down every time she prays, so she will never get something like this."

"And would you ever want one?" I asked.

Nermine winced.

"No, Kieran," she said. "And not for my husband either."

We talked about naming children 'Mohammed,' about men shaving their beards like the prophet, about women taking the veil. We talked about religious study, about Christians and Jews, about the revelations of the Prophet. We talked about Muslims in Europe, about Islamophobia, about the Danish cartoons, about recitations of the Qu'ran. We talked about little programs you could get for your cell phone that would sound an alarm, five times a day, at each interval measures by the light of the sun. We talked about how the prayers of Muslims across the world encircle the earth in concentric circles— with the Qa'bah in Mecca at the center. We talked about Djinns—half-human, half-angelic creatures which inhabit the world and listen to the prayers of ordinary people.

"Yes! Tell me about Djinns!" I said. "I am truly interested in Djinns!"

"Oh you know about them?" Nermine asked me.

"I read about them in the Arabian Nights. I am truly interested to learn about them because. . .well. . .in Egypt sometimes it seems like Islam is. . .pretending to be the only thing in this culture. It just seems so total. . .there are so few things I can actually discern in Arab culture which predate Islam. So I'm always happy to hear about them."

Nermine smiled at me faintly.

"It's. . .not really like that, Kieran."

My face fell.

"The idea is this. . .it's not just a religion. . .it's our life. That's the point of Islam. . .it's not just something you leave in the mosque. It's in every part of our day."

I sat stunned, reflecting on the paper-thin commitment to Christianity in the West.

"Have you ever heard of the book 'Fortress of the Muslim?'"

"No. What is it?"

She pulled out a book from her purse. It was dog-eared and tattered, and had long since lost both its front and back covers.

"It's a book of prayers to say at every moment of the day. These prayers are for everyday things. . .before a meal, putting on clothes. Sometimes when I

have free time, instead of just sitting, or daydream-
ing, I say a few of them. It's calming. . .its doing a
small amount of good, like building up good karma.
If something good happens, you praise God; if something bad happens, you ask God's help to accept it.
It's kind of like. . .hypnotizing yourself, to help you
deal with life."

"Really?" I said. "So what do you say when
something bad happens to you?"

"Well, I like to think that God does things like
that so he can avoid doing something worse to me.
Once I left my work and I found a huge, huge dent
in my car. . .the whole door had been smashed.
And there was no one there that said they did
it. . .someone crashed into my car and drove off.
And I didn't even have the money to have it fixed,
so I sold the parts, and now I walk or take the tram.
And what I thought to myself was. . .well, perhaps
that happened to me so that I wouldn't have been
in the car while it crashed. And walking is better
exercise. I try to be thankful for everything."

I had long reflected on how much it profited
an individual be to grateful for everything in life,
and to look at the good side of every situation. It
led the mind away from such moods as frustration
or despair, and kept it always positive, always looking forward. And I could see that Islam gave this to
Nermine, and to every devout Egyptian. . .it took
all the fortunes and misfortunes of life as gifts from

God, and it led every one of them to receive them, to live through them, to accept them.

And if the Muslims did believe in a higher power to accomplish this. . .so what? Islam did for millions of Arabs what armies of psychologists could not do for the people of the West. . .it gave them a sense of purpose, a stable mind, a centered soul—to deal with all the problems they encountered.

The prayers they said at every instant of the day were not suffocating. They were not oppressive. They were the poetic mantras of the devout and the faithful. Where I first saw an overpowering ideology, I now saw the beauty, the release, and the *joy*— that comes with the discipline of faith. The joyful surrender, the joyful sacrifice to an ancient code of truth. The refusal, five times a day, to commit sins and give into selfish thoughts. The acceptance, five times a day, to walk the path of discipline, purity, and light. Devotion. Submission. *Islam.*

"You see, this is why I think there are less suicides and broken families in Muslim countries," said Nermine. "Even with the most horrible things in life, you learn to   cope. You always have family; you always have community.

"I remember visiting my father in the hospital while he was dying. And in the moments when the pain was the worst, when he could have shouted, when he could have cursed, he said only 'Allah'."

Nermine voice did not waver. She cast her eyes gently into her lap.

"It was. . .beautiful to hear. That he had the strength to turn even the agonies of death into a prayer."

"I can't tell this to most Westerners," she told me. "Some people don't get as far as you do. There are some things I realize I just can't say to people until they've learned more about our culture. For instance. . .the polygamy thing. I mean, maybe there's s a war—maybe there are lots of children and orphans. Maybe having four wives is a way to integrate them back into society and the community. But most Western people don't want to understand things like that.

"I can't tell my friend from Germany that 'Islam' means 'submission,' and that 'Muslim' literally means 'slave.' It means 'one who submits.' I cannot tell this to him because he simply doesn't understand."

I sat back. Wind rustled the palms behind us.

"He and I disagree upon things," she said. "He believes that the Danish cartoons must be allowed to be published because of freedom of speech. But really, there is nothing sacred in a democratic society. Nothing that people hold back and always have the respect not to insult."

"Yeah," I said blankly. "We really allow people to insult anything."

A news article I had read came to my mind—about a statue of the virgin Mary that someone had constructed out of cow dung.

"When I was in Germany, Kieran, I remember it was bad to talk about religion socially. You were expected to keep that to yourself, and never speak about it in public. And I don't know why that is the case in the West. In our society, you are allowed to say you are religious! You can say you are a Christian, or a Muslim, or that you don't believe in God! In the West, you aren't free to. I mean, what is this, the Middle Ages?"

Nermine spoke with passion, without accusation. Her words stunned me. She had just criticized the West for it's lack of religious freedom. . .in precisely the way a Westerner might criticize Egyptian society. . .for exactly the same thing. And. . .the strangest thing of all was. . .she was making absolutely perfect sense.

"I think you were sent Kieran, to teach me hope. To teach me to be patient with my friend from Germany. . .that he might one day understand."

The night was winding down. The air grew slightly colder, and we paid the cheque and made to leave.

"So. . .please send me those videos, Nermine. Of prayer. I really want to see them, and learn."

She held my gaze for a moment longer.

"You know they say that on the Day of Judgment, you will know the Muslims by the light. By the light that shines from our knees, our arms, and our foreheads—for all the thousand times we've prayed."

I shivered. Her words were music.

"When you pray, picture God at your front, and the angel of death at your back. Picture the gardens of heaven to your right, and a lake of fire to your left. And bend down, so straight you could balance a glass of water on your back. And say, *'God is the most high. . .'*"

And in that one glowing moment, the vase melted away, and the crisp and elegant outline of two female faces surfaced from the painting before me.

I jumped in a taxi, my skin tingling, my mind overflowing. As I rested upon the faded leather, and breathed the destination to the driver, I was enveloped by the soft lull of Qu'ranic chanting. The taxista, with a prayer mat furled on the dashboard and prayer beads dangling from the rear-view mirror, was playing it at pitched volume.

I was amazed at the immediate effect of our conversation upon my sense of aesthetics. Instead of hearing the grating wail of another Muslim acolyte, I heard the deep, lolling call of the devout. Instead of seeing another brainwashed taxi driver,

I saw a believer—a man using his spare moments to fill his life with guidance.

Any time before tonight and I would have winced at this music. But now it gave me a strange sense of peace. I closed my eyes and fell into the poetry—the soft throbbing of the Arabic tongue, the rhythmic, rolling wail, beautiful in its ascetic pain, swallowing the world and all that was in it—until only the imam's mesmeric voice painted upon the blank and silent canvas of my mind.

The next day, I saw Nermine for the final time. Her parting gift was a small white book. Upon its cover, in blue letters, was written *Fortress of the Muslim.*

"It's the second book one should read, after the Qu'ran," she told me softly.

I flipped through its pages. It had a prayer for everything in life. There was a incantation for putting on new clothes. There was a prayer asking Allah for guidance before a major decision. There was an invocation to be said while washing before performing the prayer. There was an invocation to say before sleeping. There was an invocation for closing the eyes of the dead.

And there was an invocation for the traveler, setting out upon the journey.

"Enjoy Germany, Kieran. And enjoy Russia." said Nermine.

"I will."

"Go and find your Katrina."

"I will."

It was time to say farewell. We stood on the street, not looking one another in the eye. Her milk-white veil curled softly around her fading smile; her feet stood with grace and gravity on the torn-up pavement below. I wanted to embrace her in my arms, in true Western fashion, and thank her for existing.

I looked at her trying not to look at me, trying to find the words to say, words that, despite all our conversations in the past few days, were slow and hard in coming.

I realized that no Western hug would ever be appropriate in Egypt, in an Alexandrian street, and that I would have to say goodbye to her with a handshake.

"Take care Kieran" she said, grasping my hand in hers with the traditional Arab limpness.

"Take care," I replied

"I'm going to leave you now. . ." she said with a smile, "or I'm going to cry."

I nodded.

"Go," I said.

"And thank you."

It wasn't till I had left that I remembered that I had just shaken a woman's hand which, in Egypt, was also taboo—much less the Western hug I wished to give her. But that was Nermine. For all her devotion, she, for the affection of a friend that was not from her culture, could make a compromise.

I returned to Cairo only a few days before I had to leave. There was much to do: friends to say goodbye to, things to pack up.

"I love you lots, Kieran," said Tamer, when we shook hands for the final time after our last sheesha and beer night.

I went back to the flat and started to pack finally folding up my clothes, bundling together my books laying them in whatever fashion I could inside my massive bags.

I had been waiting for this day for a long time. I was flying to Germany, and I would slowly make my way across Eastern Europe to Belarus. I was finally going to meet my girlfriend, whom I had met on the internet, and leave Egypt and my culture shock behind.

But as I began to fold my clothes and place them in my baggage, a profound, inexplicable sadness came over me, as I contemplated that this was the last I would see of this society for a long time to come. Its crowded market streets. Its bustling sheesha shops. Its honking traffic jams. Its half-developed neighbourhoods teeming with its friendly, devoted, wonderfully hospitable people.

As I pulled my David Roberts prints off the walls—the classic, nineteenth-century lithographs of the Middle East; as I held the statues in my hand that I had bought at the Gran Bazaar, I was almost overcome. I made a special playlist of traveling songs and listened to them to try to feel good enough to keep packing.

I had spent so much time complaining to myself about the garbage in the streets, about the soot in the air, about the relentless blasting of car horns, about, the obsession with religion, that somehow I forgot to notice that deep within me, in some strange recess in my heart, I really loved this place.

And I would really miss it.

After a goodbye coffee with an Indonesian friend of mine, I found myself in central Cairo on a gorgeous March day—blue sky above, and clear, warm air. Across Midan Tahrir I spied an elaborate minaret of a mosque I had not yet entered. The door was hanging open. The noonday prayer was finished, and it was not a Friday. Almost no one was around.

I decided I should visit it. For when, I asked myself, will I be in central Cairo again? As I walked through the door, inside I could see it was no vaulted cathedral. As always, the floor was carpeted with hundreds of identical arches, each designed for a single person to stand at and pray, each pointing toward Mecca. The mosque was bathed in yellow light. The ceiling, with its myriad patterns, was made of some material thin enough to glow with the light of the sun.

There was not a soul inside; despite the rush of the cars only a few metres away, the mosque was tranquil and calm. I thought curiously, with no one about, why it would be standing there, with its door wide and open, as though it beckoned me inside to offer me a final private moment with this temple of the Muslims and the powerful God they adore.

I walked over to the bookshelf on the side wall and took from it the most beautiful Qu'ran I could find. I ran my fingers over the elegant patterns on the cover and turned the first few pages, holding them like delicate porcelain, and gazed upon the Arabic letters, dancing in such graceful design that I could not see where the illumination ended and the script began.

On the mosque's wall, beside me, there was a flowered enclave cut into stone. I stood before it, touching the cool marble, knowing that this sacred enclave directed the prayers of the servants of Allah, in concentric circles the breadth of the world, towards the holy city of Mecca; towards the great conquest of the Prophet and the beating heart of Islam.

And as I knelt on the mosque's floor, I leaned backwards and looked upon the ceiling, lit by the luminous glow of the heavens beyond. I studied the patterns on the surface: hypnotic in their intricacy, exact in their symmetry, countless winding paths of red, green, and blue which wove through one another endlessly. It was a paragon of complexity and simplicity, of chaos and order.

I hearkened back to my Greek philosophy, to the ancient Stoics, who believed that God and the universe were one and the same. They believed that through the fathomless complexity of the nature before our senses, all was moved by the same fire, all was created and destroyed by the same rhythmic pattern, all died and was reborn to the beat of the same cosmic drum.

And as I remembered the incantations of Allah which I saw playing on television where the verses were sung to images of the dawn coming over the mountains, with the waves crashing upon the beach, the wind whistling over the sands of the desert, suddenly I understood why this God had no face, why an image could never capture His nature, why Muslim sculptors could only resort to the pattern, humble yet intricate, to glorify His presence.

And as I knelt and stared at the ceiling, my limbs shivering, I finally saw before me a wonder built high to awe the faithful; a visual expression of the majesty of God. I closed my eyes and prayed a prayer of thanks, that today, for the first time, I had entered a mosque and was left absolutely breathless at its beauty.

"Hello?"

"Hello Nermine. It's Kieran."

"Kieran! How are you? You're still in Egypt?"

"I'm at the airport, I only have thirty minutes left, then I fly. Nermine," I breathed. "I called because I wanted to thank you, so very much. For everything."

"Kieran. . .if you keep going on like this, I'm going to cry."

"I have a story to tell you. You remember what we said about fate? When I arrived at the airport I realized I forgot the jacket I bought in Egypt. I had some time, so I took the cab back to my flat and back to the airport to get it. And when I picked it up, *Fortress of the Muslim* was sitting under it."

"Ok, Kieran, now I am crying."

"Alright, I'm sorry. I just wanted to call you to say see you later. Because this isn't goodbye. I never say goodbye. I'll see you again."